THE DEATH OF AN ADULT CHILD
A Book For and About Bereaved Parents

Jeanne Webster Blank

Death, Value and Meaning Series
Series Editor: John D. Morgan

Baywood Publishing Company, Inc.
AMITYVILLE, NEW YORK

Library of Congress Catalog Number: 97-9835
ISBN: 0-89503-178-7 (Cloth : alk. paper)

Library of Congress Cataloging-in-Publication Data

Blank, Jeanne Webster.
    The death of an adult child : a book for and about bereaved
parents / Jeanne Webster Blank.
        p.   cm. - - (Death, value, and meaning series)
    Includes index.
    ISBN 0-89503-178-7 (cloth : alk. paper)
    1. Bereavement- -Psychological aspects.   2. Grief.   3. Adult
children- -Death- -Psychological aspects.   4. Loss (Psychology)
I. Title   II. Series.
BF575.G7B53 1998
155.9'37- -dc21   97-9835
                                                                CIP

DEDICATION

In loving memory of my daughter,

Catherine Jane Blank, 1948-1987

Acknowledgments

I want to express my thanks to those who answered my questionnaire, the more than sixty bereaved parents of adult children who died. I know it was painful for them; it was also very generous. They have my gratitude for sharing their experiences with me.

To my husband, Bob, and to my surviving children, Laurel Andrew and Paul Blank, to my grandson Paul Inglis and my daughter-in-law, Annette Makino, I say "thank you" for many helpful suggestions and for their unflagging support.

I also want to thank my Compassionate Friends, near and far, my grief counselor, Eileen Leary, my editors, Dr. John D. Morgan and Pauline Bartel, Dr. H. William Batt, who helped with computer problems, and the many friends and relatives who encouraged me in this endeavor.

Special thanks are also due to Bobbi Olszewski, production manager at Baywood Publishing who was so kind and helpful during my illness.

Table of Contents

Introduction

"In the middle of the journey of this our life, I found myself in a dark wood, for I had lost my way. Ah, it is a hard thing to speak of what it was, that savage forest. Even recalling it renews my fears. So bitter it was, death is hardly more severe."

So wrote Dante Alighieri as he began the *Inferno,* the first book of his Italian masterpiece, *The Divine Comedy*. If he was describing himself in the early years of the fourteenth century, Dante was also accurately describing my own condition in July 1987, when one of my children died.

Like the narrator in Dante's *Inferno,* I found myself, a woman well along in years, lost in the midst of a dark savage wood. The serene and happy life my husband and I shared was suddenly shattered when Catherine, the second of our three adult children, died of breast cancer in July 1987 at the age of thirty-nine. Beautiful, talented, intelligent and a wonderful human being, she had everything to live for. And now, suddenly, she was dead.

Cathy had come to our home in Albany, New York, at the end of May 1987 to visit us for the Memorial Day weekend, taking the bus from Boston, where she worked as an architect's renderer. Unusually fatigued, she spent a good share of the weekend resting on the couch, although she felt well enough to walk the seven blocks to her sister's house one afternoon. She was being treated by a Boston physician for a food allergy and had lost a lot of weight.

Slightly more than a week after her return to Boston, early on the morning of June 9, Cathy phoned. She was too sick to care for herself. Would we come? My husband and I tossed some clothing into a suitcase and started out in our car, planning to bring her home with us. But when we arrived at her apartment, we realized she was too sick

1

for a long automobile ride. We stayed with her in Boston, driving her to appointments with doctors and specialists. Admission to the hospital followed a few days later. Tests revealed that she had breast cancer which had metastasized to the liver and bone. She died less than three weeks after the correct diagnosis—her parents, sister, and brother at her bedside.

This cataclysmic event was devastating to our family. It so devastated me, as her mother, that I lost nearly all vestiges of my personality for a long time. My ability to find words, to put sentences together, to think clearly, disappeared. I could not concentrate, could not carry out normal daily tasks and could not control my tears. My self-esteem disappeared. My memory failed. My energy was gone. I got sick. I fell and got hurt. I did not care whether I lived or died.

I had considerable trouble grappling with those terrible feelings after Catherine died. For a long time I floundered, slashing out at the threatening branches of my dark wood, trying to find some stability, if not a pathway back to my old, carefree, happy life.

In those early days of my bereavement, I knew nothing about grief except the conventional sadness attendant upon the death of my aged and sick parents. Because their deaths were expected and occurred in the normal order of things, I was not plunged into despair when they died.

Members of our modern society tend to avoid thinking about death. Most of us are unschooled in the phenomenon of grief. Those who are forced to deal with the death of a child come to the task as babes in the woods. I was totally unprepared for the effect my daughter's death would have on me.

I did not know that in order to find some stability, some reason to go on living, I had to go through a long and painful process which is sometimes referred to as grief work.

While grappling with my grief and long before I thought of writing about it, I sought solace and guidance from a bereavement self-help group called "The Compassionate Friends." I learned about the organization the day we selected Cathy's coffin. My son saw their brochure lying on a table at the entrance to the funeral home. "Mother," he said, "I want you to get in touch with these people right away."

I did get in touch with them, attending my first meeting less than a week after the funeral. I not only attended local meetings of *The Compassionate Friends*, my husband and I traveled considerable distances to regional and national conferences as well, once with our surviving daughter and grandson.

I also listened to everyone and anyone who proffered advice, both good and bad. I was desperate for help. I sought counseling, first from a destructive counselor, and then from a helpful one.

And I read voraciously, searching for experiences similar to mine, even though my powers of concentration were seriously diminished. Some of the books and articles I read dealt with the personal stories of grieving people. Others were written by and for trained psychologists and psychiatrists, some of whom were not themselves bereaved.

The former selections rang true to my own experience. The latter, particularly those written by non-bereaved professionals, seemed to cry out for consultation with those who had "been there"—the bereaved themselves. Those selections did not adequately describe my condition nor meet my needs.

Baywood Publishing Company, publishers of this book, produced a detailed research study of parents of Israeli soldiers killed in war. In addition, there are a few books which contain a chapter or two devoted to the death of an adult child. Isolated articles on the subject are available in magazines. I did not find any books that dealt in any detail with the way parents cope with the death of an adult child. Rather, the printed material I was able to find concentrated on the illness and death of a young child, the adult's loss of a parent or sibling, and spousal loss.

The scant availability of literature confirmed my opinion that there is a need to address the special problems I faced. Parents whose adult child died are a breed that is growing in numbers. As the life expectancy of the population increases, so will the proportion of adults who predecease their parents. Such demographic changes open up new areas of concern.

When my daughter Cathy died, our local chapter of bereaved parents had very few members who had lost an adult child; most had lost young children. This situation has changed dramatically since my first years. Most meetings of our local chapter today find a preponderance of parents who are grieving the death of adult children.

In those early years I felt great sympathy and affection for those very young parents. But I was beginning to sense that my situation as the bereaved parent of an adult child was in many ways unlike that of those who had lost a young child. Their problems, except for the sheer grief we all shared, were not the problems I was facing. I found myself longing for someone whose experience coincided with mine, with whom I could compare my feelings and responses—someone who was not a grieving mother a decade younger than my Cathy.

The pain and intensity of grieving for a dead child of any age is the same: ten on a scale of ten. I believe there is nothing worse in the world. It is not the pain of grief that is different. Parents who have lost an adult child are at another place in the journey through their lives. Having lived longer, their ways are set, their relations with their children are on a different level. That adult child was already formed, the "finished product" of all the parents' endeavors.

The involvement of other adult survivors (spouses and children, adult siblings), a condition not shared by bereaved parents of young children, complicates the lives of older parents. Often these other survivors have an agenda differing from that of the bereaved parents, which may provoke misunderstanding and estrangement.

Several years after my daughter died, I found myself in a situation not unlike a recurring dream I have had throughout my adult life. Suddenly thrust onto a stage, audience waiting in anticipation, I haven't a clue what is expected of me. I somehow sense that I am supposed to act or sing or recite, but haven't learned my part, haven't brought my music and haven't memorized my lines. Anxiety becomes so intense that I wake up, relieved to discover it was only a dream.

But if a similar episode happens when you are awake, in real life and not a dream, then the "dreamer" must seek a better solution than the traditional "and then I woke up. . . ."

More than six years after Cathy died, my grief counselor asked me to speak to her college class on Grief and Loss about the peculiar problems faced by the parent who has lost an adult child. "My class needs to know, and there's not much out there for them to read," she said. "It would be so helpful if you told them about your own experience; I know you can do it."

Well, she may have known I could do it, but I was not so sure. Emotionally wounded, beset by a host of physical ills, I felt completely inadequate to the task. My confidence in my ability to speak was no longer intact; my disorientation, my confusion in sorting out my own feelings and thoughts was so great that I did not even trust the validity of those feelings and thoughts. I found it nearly impossible to put together a coherent sentence even when talking one-on-one. How could I speak to a college class?

Nevertheless, because the date of my presentation was to be more than five months in the future, I agreed to do it. Perhaps, I reasoned, I could use the intervening time to contact others whose adult child had died so that I did not have to rely on my insights alone. If I could describe my painful experiences in a questionnaire, asking whether others shared any of those experiences, a pattern might emerge, thereby validating my own reactions. For I was ashamed of my responses to my grief, feeling weak and defective in character because of my inability to get on with my life, as many others had told me I should have done by now, six whole years and more after Cathy's death.

In those six years I had been in contact with no more than a dozen parents whose children were adults at the time of death, some at regional and national conferences of *The Compassionate Friends* and a few at our local chapter. But I sensed they were out there; I had to reach out and find them.

Not being a professional in the field of grief or social research, I had neither the ability nor the intention of doing an objective survey. I merely wrote down some of my feelings and experiences, added a few from my conversations at conferences, asked if they rang true, and sent them out to anyone who wanted to respond.

At the outset, the answers which came in made me realize that I had to have a cut-off age to differentiate between a young and an adult child who died. Arbitrarily, I decided that for the purpose of the questionnaire, an adult child was one who was old enough to vote, old enough to have been required to register for the military draft when the draft was compulsory: eighteen. I regret that I had to refuse several requests from parents whose children were younger. I did not accept any responses from parents whose children were under eighteen at the time of death. The oldest was forty-nine.

Because tragedy strikes without regard to circumstances, I did not seek any data on race, social or economic class, educational achievement or religious affiliation, though many answered my question about changes which had taken place during their bereavement in regard to their belief structure.

In the end, it became an open letter rather than a questionnaire, a letter which continues back and forth between the respondents and me even now.

The first eight questions of that questionnaire dealt with biographical data of the parents, the cause of their child's death and relationships between the parents and among the other survivors after the death. Question nine asked what is hardest to bear. The next several questions dealt with possible involvement of medical, legal, or military professions. In thirteen to eighteen I wondered if their attitudes toward life, religion, and friends had changed and if they had sought and found help. Number nineteen asked if they felt there was a difference between the loss of an adult and a young child. Twenty and twenty-one sought information about physical and emotional problems. Twenty-two and twenty-three asked if they had had any after-death contacts with their child. Last, I asked if they had any further insights to share.

Most important for me, was the opportunity to match their reactions to mine in order to determine whether my personal responses to my grief were aberrational or normal.

The questionnaire, which in its final form appears in Appendix I, was publicized with the aid of the national office of *The Compassionate Friends* (though not sponsored by them) and was distributed initially at their regional conference in Bethlehem, Pennsylvania, and later throughout the United States.

The Compassionate Friends tell us that a mere 20 percent of bereaved parents reach out for help during their grief. Out of that slim percentage, only a small segment read my ad and responded with a request for the questionnaire. Of those who requested the questionnaire, several found it too painful to fill out the answers and return them to me. ("Oh, Jeanne," said a mother whose adult daughter died some twenty years ago and who had asked for a copy of my questionnaire, "I have to give this back to you unanswered. To answer it would kill me.")

Thus the questionnaire represents only a minuscule sampling comprised of those bereaved parents who were willing to accept the difficult task of filling out the answers and sending them along to me. Most of them asked me to let them know the results so they too, would more clearly understand their own grief experience.

Their courage and generosity are very much appreciated. Each of them made the decision about whether to remain anonymous. Each has signed an official permission slip allowing me to use their stories in this book. Only one declined, and her story has been deleted. Those anonymous members of *The Compassionate Friends* whom I have quoted have granted me permission to use the quotes, for it is understood that whatever transpires at a meeting of that support group is confidential.

By the time I made my presentation to the Adirondack College class of my counselor, Eileen Leary, I had obtained thirty responses to my questionnaire; there would ultimately be more than sixty. Even with such a small sample in March 1994, a dramatic similarity of responses had emerged, and with this ammunition my confidence received a boost.

That confidence was not well placed, however. Even though I had been accustomed to public speaking over the years, my presentation to that class on Grief and Loss was poor. My voice was weak and wavering. I was often reduced to tears. I hadn't trusted myself to speak extemporaneously so I read the text, a practice which usually detracts from spontaneity and interest.

Nevertheless, the audience was sympathetic, aiming many questions in my direction, probing the special problems of the bereaved parent of an adult child which my talk had revealed.

I have spoken to Ms. Leary's classes twice annually since then, with better results. In the intervening years I have regained my ability to think on my feet, to talk loudly and clearly in sentences, with only an outline to guide me. When tears intervene, I accept their appearance without embarrassment and expect my listeners to do the same, assuring them I consider it OK to cry.

In the course of those few years since my first talk to the class, a change took place in my life. Using the metaphor of Dante's *Inferno* once again, that change might be described as my leaving that dark wood in which I had been lost for so long. The landscape into which I emerged was familiar in many ways; in other ways it was forever changed by my years of painful wandering. But in that new landscape, the sun is sometimes shining and I have regained my will to go on living.

Perhaps you are newly bereaved and do not believe that you can ever emerge from your own dark wood. In the early days after my daughter died, I did not believe it would ever happen to me.

I am reluctant to divulge the depths to which my despair took me and the length of time I spent in my dark wood. I do so only to assure other bereaved parents who are going through the same wretched experiences that they must persevere, must hang on at all cost, until they can find some stability in their lives.

A clergyman who is a childhood friend read one of my chapters and wrote advising me to "lighten up." His advice was well-intentioned, but I did not take it; I must be honest. As one of the fathers who responded to the questionnaire said, "If you are going to write about this, tell it like it is—it ROTS!"

Of great importance to me in my journey through grief has been acquiring an understanding of what I was experiencing. So many of the perplexing questions are now answered: Why did this happen? Why do the non-bereaved fail to understand? Why do other adult survivors behave as they do? Why do I feel guilty? Why did I lose my self-esteem, my will to live? Why did I get sick? What is it that sets me apart from bereaved parents who lost young children? Why do I continually search for my dead child? Why do birthdays and the anniversary of my child's death resurrect all the early pain of grief? . . . and many other questions.

The answers to those questions are hard-earned and complicated, but not one of them is "Because I am a bad/weak/crazy/stupid person."

This is not a "how-to" book. I am not a therapist; only one of the respondents who answered the questionnaire is, and she is still groping and searching too. You can read and perhaps identify with our stories, but none can tell you how to heal. I can only tell you what I and some others experienced and that I am healing. Some of them too are healing, though a few have died. I have been aided by a talented grief counselor (Eileen Leary), two understanding physicians (Dr. Paul Okosky and Dr. Jose David), a sympathetic clergyman (Reverend George Williams), a host of friends, both in and out of *The Compassionate Friends*, and a loving husband and family.

I hope this book will meet the criteria for which it was written: to be a comfort and a guide along the painful pathway of grief; to indicate, by sharing our experiences, that we parents are not alone in our responses to the death of our adult child; to assure us that we are not demented, weak, defective in character or otherwise inadequate because of the way we grieve; to spell out ways in which some of us have succeeded . . . or failed . . . in our attempts to dispel guilt and anger, overcome depression, come to terms with other survivors, memorialize our deceased children, and to take the first steps toward healing.

Some of the stories of those who answered the questionnaire can be found in Appendix II. Preceding their reports is a mini-table of contents which will tell you how each of the children died. You will not be burdened by reading details of their deaths. You can imagine the sadness attendant on those events without the wrenching pain a retelling might inflict. The emphasis in this book is on the aftermath of the child's death and how the parents reacted.

It may be a comfort to read about the parents of a child who had a death similar to your child's death. I recall how emotionally gratifying it was the first time I met and talked with the mother of a woman who had died of breast cancer. She really knew. She could say, "Yes, that's the way it was; that's the way it is." She sat across from me at the final dinner of a national conference of *The Compassionate Friends* in New Orleans.

This is a book without a plot. The first chapter attempts to place the contemporary bereaved parent in a continuum of generational bereavement, a phenomenon to which we may have been oblivious until our sensibilities were heightened by the death of our child. It is a chronicle of one family among my ancestors and how the death of an adult child affected them.

The second chapter lays out an overall picture of the stages of grief through which the bereaved, not just those who have lost an adult child, will probably pass as they try to restructure their broken lives.

The whole first section deals with aspects of grief the parent of an adult child who died may experience in a more or less chronological way: the funeral and subsequent condolence calls; the first faltering attempts to return to daily routines; then the various demons we must fight and the pitfalls we may encounter as we progress through the grief experience.

Although I write primarily from my own experience, in each chapter, portions of my respondents' stories will be woven in to make appropriate points. My own answers to the questionnaire can be found in The Last Word of Appendix II.

No matter how comforting it may be to touch the experiences of other bereaved parents of adult children, the way toward healing for each individual may still be long and hard. Accepting, recognizing, then finding explanations for the painful manifestations of grief, helps us understand that it is normal to feel and behave as we do. And when we try to cope with, rather than succumb to our grief, we show strength of character rather than weakness. With these assurances, let us consider *The Death of an Adult Child* as the surviving parents forge their way through the tangled branches of their dark savage wood of grief.

CHAPTER 1

When Joey Died

My grief experience as described in the introduction is intensely personal. Because the death of a child is almost akin to a physical assault—perhaps analogous to being struck by a car or lying on the operating table—it is difficult for the grieving person to think of anything or anybody else during the immediacy of the ordeal. As a result, his or her response is apt to be extremely egocentric. I heard another bereaved mother chastise herself for being so self-centered in the early days of her mourning, so I know I am not alone in having responded the way I did.

Although I was almost totally caught up in my own sorrow, I realized even on the day of my daughter Cathy's death that I was not alone in my grief, not grieving in a vacuum. She was surrounded on her deathbed by her family: father, brother, and sister as well as her mother. At that moment, each of us was set on a mutual yet separate pathway of grief.

When she died, it was as if a gigantic shock wave hit our close-knit family, fracturing it into a million pieces, sending us hurtling in different directions, unable to connect, unable to function as before, and unable to understand what was happening to us.

A Russian novelist tells us that all happy families are alike and all unhappy families are unhappy in their own way. Quoted so often that it has become a cliche, this generalization is, like most generalizations, much too inclusive.

Until the moment of Cathy's death perhaps we were indeed, like most happy families, for my husband and I had raised our three children to adulthood untouched by tragedy. Having overcome the trials of caring for our offspring, we were enjoying the fruits of our efforts. During their childhood and adolescence there were difficult as well as good times, but the parent/child relationship was sustained by mutual love. By the time they were adults, our children had put aside their youthful rebellion to become responsible citizens, spouses, parents, professionals—our friends.

Cathy's death transported us to an uncharted wretched place, transforming us from a happy to an unhappy family. But were we, in that dramatic and terrible transformation, unlike any other unhappy family who had lost a beloved member?

As I came into contact with increasing numbers of bereaved parents whose adult children had died, I began to discern a similarity which belied the novelists' statement. We were not all unhappy in our own way; we shared a whole host of responses and problems.

In fact, I sensed that our unhappiness was shared not only by others in our category, but we also shared that same unhappiness with other families in past generations. Knowing that bereaved families have a link to our predecessors in the way we feel, the way we react to our grief was a comfort to me. For one of the greatest problems I dealt with was a feeling that I was isolated and unworthy as I mourned for my dead daughter. Finding the commonality, the almost universality of those responses among bereaved families, gave me courage as well as comfort.

In telling the tale of this discovery, I must go back in time more than fifty years to 1942, and thence to the nineteenth and early twentieth centuries.

In August 1992, as our fiftieth wedding anniversary was approaching, my husband Bob and I went up to the attic searching for memorabilia, wondering if anything remained after all those years and after several moves to different dwellings. The search turned up some old photos, including our wedding picture, and a box containing the clothing we wore at the ceremony. For me, a cream-colored wedding dress and a faded, pressed corsage; for him, a U.S. Army corporal's uniform.

We also found a faded blue barracks bag bulging with letters and telegrams we had received during World War II in the first years of our marriage. We dragged the bag down the stairs and began to go through its contents.

During the War, telephone calls were only for emergencies; it was either letters or telegrams which kept us in touch with family and friends. And keeping in touch was extremely important, for every emotion was heightened by the stress of that conflict. Unlike subsequent wars, involvement of the populace was universal in World War II; hardly any American was untouched by the uncertainties of the times. Men and women were separated from those who were dear to them, shipped out to foreign service or dislocated by wartime duties on the domestic front, constantly threatened with death or injury, always lonely and homesick.

My husband was reared in New York City. I grew up in rural Wisconsin. We met at the University of Wisconsin in Madison where we were both students. Bob had to surrender his scholarship in philosophy when he was drafted into the army on December 2, 1941, and sent to Camp Croft, South Carolina, to begin basic training in the infantry.

Pearl Harbor was bombed by the Japanese just five days later and war was declared. During the first year of the war, on August 27, 1942, Bob and I were married in an army chapel at Camp Croft and took up residence in a tiny apartment in a private house in nearby Spartanburg. The early days of our marriage were filled with worry about the approach of the day when Bob would be shipped overseas, which came soon enough.

The South represented a different culture for us. Lonesome for our family and friends, we were hungry for contact with them, which came through the mails, with letters in abundance: parents, siblings, cousins, uncles, aunts, childhood friends, college friends, friends of friends or friends of our parents, all of them rallying to cheer us up during the disruption caused by the war.

Rereading those letters in the old barracks bag—there were hundreds—over the span of several evenings in 1992, was a precious nostalgia trip for us, especially letters from people we loved who are now dead.

In one of my mother's letters, dated just before Christmas 1942, she told about the Christmas celebrations of her childhood, which were strongly family-oriented.

Until the year after my birth, my parents lived in Montfort, Wisconsin, our ancestral village. Pioneers on both sides of my mother's family settled the town in the early years of the nineteenth century. My great-great-grandmother maintained a fort there during the Indian uprisings, the Black Hawk Wars.

My father's people were relative latecomers. They came from the Cornwall region of England to work the lead and zinc mines near Montfort in the mid-nineteenth century.

Montfort is a pretty town, its modest houses climbing two hills on either side of a tiny valley. At the base of the hills, where the earliest homes were built, there is a gushing spring. Early in its history, Montfort was a way stop for the soldiers patrolling a strip of highlands called the Military Ridge between Madison (which later became the state capital) and Prairie du Chien, at the confluence of the Wisconsin and Mississippi Rivers.

I was born in Montfort, as were my parents and grandparents. Its cemetery is filled with my ancestors. My memories of Montfort and my relatives there are steeped in tradition, warm and rosy, joyous and filled with love. Those memories, formed when I was a carefree child, contained no hint of sadness. I had to experience life more fully to understand that sorrow will always be present in the history of any family.

In August 1992, reading the letter my mother wrote on my first Christmas away from home, December 1942, I was brought up short by something I had not noticed when I read it the first time, so long ago. "We all used to go up to Grandma Susan's for Christmas, my parents and four brothers and I," she wrote, "until Aunt Jo died. We never went after that. After Aunt Jo's death, everything changed."

Grandma Susan was my great-grandmother—Susan Moore Parish. I remember her; a slight, bent old lady, sitting in a rocking chair smoking a clay pipe, her gray hair pulled back in a bun. I was six when she died.

Grandma Susan lived a long time and during her lifetime she buried three adult children: her son Henry was killed in an accident while working on the railroad when he was twenty-three; another son, my grandfather Frank, died of cancer at sixty-four the summer before I was born; and Aunt Jo, Grandma Susan's daughter, who lived just down the hill and ran the hotel with her husband, Jim Frankland.

About four years before Aunt Jo died, her nineteen-year-old daughter, Joey, had succumbed to tuberculosis. She was Aunt Jo and Uncle Jim's only surviving child, their first daughter, born in 1885. A second, Claire, died on Christmas Day 1892, a month after her birth. Jeanetta, their third child, died at the age of five.

Because they had already lost two children when Joey died, the fact that she had lived to young adulthood must have represented a miraculous triumph for her parents. The life of Aunt Jo and Uncle Jim revolved around their daughter and they were a loving and beautiful family. A picture of the parents, with Joey standing between them, her arms thrown over their shoulders, is in the tattered cloth-covered family album in my living room.

Aunt Jo appears in the photograph to be in her thirties, slender and beautiful, with a serious expression. She wears her dark hair up, as was proper for a married woman of that day. Her dress has a yoke of elaborate ruffling. A pearl brooch is at her throat and she wears matching pearl earrings.

Uncle Jim is thin, almost gaunt; his expression solemn; his hair neatly parted near the middle. A droopy moustache dominates his narrow, bony face. He is wearing a suit, white shirt, and a wide tie.

Neither of the parents looks directly at us, but Joey looks straight into our eyes with a direct gaze, a faint smile on her lips. A poised and self-assured young woman in her early teens, her long dark hair falls over her shoulders with a soft wave in the bangs across her forehead. She wears a pretty light-colored dress.

Another photo in that same album shows four generations of women: Joey with her mother (my Great-Aunt Jo), my Great-Grandma Susan and her mother, my Great-Great-Grandmother Anne Leadbetter, who maintained the fort during the Black Hawk War. A third photo shows Joey, now grown to young womanhood, tall and elegant, wearing a long gown and an elaborate plumed hat.

One of my mother's older brothers, born in 1890, was fourteen when Joey died. Immediately after Joey's funeral, my young uncle heard Joey's father, Uncle Jim, cursing God, shaking his fist at the sky as he stood on the front porch. "You God, you goddamn God!" he shouted.

My uncle never forgot the scene, telling and retelling it over the years.

If you have experienced the loss of a child, you can probably identify with what that family went through when Joey died. In fact, you might even be able to reconstruct their story fairly accurately. You have surely heard of bereaved parents who are angry at God.

Somebody else besides my fourteen-year-old uncle must have heard Uncle Jim cursing God. Because it was a terrible sin, the minister was probably informed that Jim Frankland was heard cursing God. The minister may or may not have had the stomach to confront Uncle Jim or even visit the family. Clergymen who behave quite adequately in conventional situations do not always get high marks in dealing with bereaved parents. But if he did visit the Franklands, chances are that Uncle Jim escorted him to the door soon after the minister said, "It was God's will that your Joey died." Perhaps Uncle Jim announced that he would never set foot in a church again. Anger like Uncle Jim's is hard to defuse. Raising his little girl to womanhood and then losing her, after having already lost two younger children, must have made him bitter toward life, the world, and the God he had trusted.

As the days went by after Joey's death, Aunt Jo couldn't seem to pull herself together, no matter how many friends insisted that it was already six months or a year since Joey died, and she had to get on with her life. Surely someone informed her that Joey was happier in Heaven, and besides, God needed another angel. Joey wouldn't want her mother to grieve this way. Aunt Jo would feel better if she did something for others, like visiting the sick or the poor, and she should stop going to the cemetery so often. You know God never gives you more than you can handle. And she should pray; yes, praying would help.

I don't know whether she prayed, but I am sure she cried a lot and got sick and didn't seem to care anymore whether she lived or died. Many bereaved parents are vulnerable to hopelessness and illness after the death of their child. Some of them, like Aunt Jo, do not survive.

I have no one to ask about Aunt Jo; everyone who could tell me is dead. Who knows what carried her off? I have to guess it was something like pneumonia, a common killer of that era, or cancer, which runs in my family. Or perhaps she died of a broken heart. When she died, a lot of other hearts broke, too, including Grandma Susan's.

When Joey died, a whole chain of events was set in motion, changing every aspect of life for that family. It precipitated her mother's death. For my great-grandmother, the loss of her granddaughter and then her daughter cast a pall of grief over Grandma Susan's life.

Christmas was never again celebrated in her house, with my own mother and her brothers and all Grandma Susan's other little grandchildren assembled around the Christmas tree on the morning of December 25th. It is not hard for those who are struggling with Christmas today to empathize with Grandma Susan's response to the death of her daughter and granddaughter. For many of us, trying to escape the pain of that holiday is a recurring challenge.

When I was a child, many of the relatives of my grandparents' generation had long since left Montfort. They were a restless lot, going West to homestead in the Dakotas or to California, Oregon, and Alaska. One went East to settle in Virginia.

When they got old, those great-aunts and great-uncles used to return to Wisconsin every few years, almost always arriving during the late spring or summer. When any of them returned to the ancestral village, great gatherings were arranged; picnics, parties, and Memorial Day reunions at the cemetery.

At those reunions, I used to hear my mother's aunts, uncles, cousins, and friends talking about Aunt Jo and her premature death. "Ah yes, everybody loved Aunt Jo. She lost that lovely young daughter, you know. The only one of her children who grew up to adulthood."

When a Russian novelist was quoted as having said that all happy families are alike but unhappy families are unhappy in their own way, he was not speaking of families who lose children to an untimely death.

How can he tell us that every unhappy family is unhappy in its own way? When we lose a child, we are all unhappy in more or less the same way, from generation to generation. And in our lives, everything changes, as it did in my great-grandmother's life when Joey, and then Aunt Jo, died.

If you are feeling alone in your grief, please reflect for a moment on what the story of their deaths revealed to you. Unless you are only a few weeks bereaved, you will have anticipated and automatically understood what that extended family was feeling. I strongly believe that it is helpful to us bereaved parents everywhere when we realize our reactions to our grief are more or less universal, outside of time, intense and yes, normal!

If there is, as I believe, a pattern which prevails across the generations in the way parents grieve the death of an adult child, it might be helpful to place that pattern in perspective, to distinguish it from the experience of bereaved parents of young children.

Except for the devastation of loss, which is surely the same for those whose children died at any age, the issues bereaved parents of adult children must deal with differ in many ways from those parents whose young child died.

Merely describing the distinctions between the ways the two categories of parents grieve would leave the bereaved parents of an adult child in exactly the same situation at the end as they were at the beginning; with no clear understanding of their grief experiences and no suggestions about how to cope with them.

Insights into the ways bereaved parents of a young child respond to their loss may be obtained by reading the many books which have been written on the subject. Libraries and bookstores abound with such literature. The ordeal they face will not be discussed in any detail here except to say that their pain is every bit as great as ours.

Nor is it helpful to place a value judgment on these differences. To concentrate on these differences, at the expense of finding a greater understanding of the parents' experiences, is not helpful either. Gaining this understanding is a principal goal of this book.

For those whose child was small and living at home, being cared for by his or her parents, there is a radical change in their daily lives: an empty bedroom, a closet filled with clothing, a chest full of toys and a physical void which constantly reminds them that their child is dead.

When parents lose a mature son or daughter, their lives may be outwardly the same: alone together in a house which used to be shared with children. The child who died may have established his or her own home, with spouse and children. Yet with the death of that adult child, everything about the parents' lives changed, even if they seem on the surface to be unaltered.

The parents' feelings, their attitudes toward life, toward their religion, and the society at large may be altered. Their friends and family may appear to be the same persons but are not. The parents' bodies and minds no longer function as before. The anchors which held them securely on course now pull loose, setting them adrift and threatening the continuity of life itself.

It is almost as though the mother and father have emigrated to another country whose landscape is identical to that which was left behind when their child died, yet everything else is unfamiliar. The inability to perceive any outward change in those parents' lives may indicate how subtle, how unexpected, are the hidden problems they now face.

These changes are not unique to those whose child was an adult; they are shared by most bereaved parents. The primary, overriding difference is this: the bereaved parents of an adult are at a different place in their journey through life. Most of their years of living and striving are behind them. The victory represented by their having raised their child to adulthood has turned into defeat with his or her death. Every response older parents make to their loss must rest upon this premise: it is late; life is winding down; they have less energy, flexibility, and resiliency to cope with the tragedy.

The chapters which follow will address in some detail the grief manifestations of these older parents. One category I have called pitfalls: dangers against which the parents must beware.

The dictionary defines a pitfall as a "hidden or not easily recognized danger, error, or source of injury or destruction into which one that is unsuspecting or incautious may fall."

Some of these pitfalls will be dealt with in separate chapters. They are: 1) The unexpectedness of such strong reactions, leaving the parent unprepared and unnerved; 2) Getting stuck in one or another of the early stages of grief; 3) A greater option for divorce or suicide; 4) The irrational urge to search for and replace the dead child; 5) Health problems; and 6) Conflicting agendas among other survivors.

Other aspects of grief specific to bereaved parents of an adult child, discussed more fully in subsequent chapters are: 1) Differing responses to different occasions, such as rites of passage and holidays; 2) Greater emotional and/or financial dependency of the parent on the adult child who died; 3) Loss of self-esteem, sometimes leading to a painful reexamination of the parents' lives to find clearer understanding; 4) Disallowed grief (discrimination because of age; deaths caused by murder, AIDS, suicide, military action); 5) Memories and memorials; and 6) Coming to terms with injustice and/or unfairness.

An essay at the end will sum up these various aspects of grief for the bereaved parent whose child was an adult at the time of death.

In the next chapter, an overall pattern of grief is described, allowing the reader to glimpse how some people view the process bereaved parents go through during their so-called grief work. Perhaps it might be referred to as an attempt to cut a path through that "dark wood" in which we may have lost our way in the first terrible days after our child died. It prepares us for our first attempts at reentry into the world after our child died.

CHAPTER 2

Four Phases of Grief

The death of a loved one places survivors in a situation they have never experienced before. Emotions come crashing down upon them, casting even the most mundane events into a setting the bereaved may not understand. Suddenly they are mourning; grieving.

The words mourning and grief, for those formerly spared the pain of loss and thus unfamiliar with their true meaning, may need definition. The dictionary tells us that to mourn means to be sorry, to feel or express deep regret, to look or act unhappy, to be sorrowful over a death, to grieve for someone who has died, to be distressed over, to bewail, protest or utter mournfully. Mourning is a ritual observance accompanying a death, a demonstration of grief. Grief is defined as suffering, pain, or distress. To grieve is to be in pain of mind on account of an evil, to feel a lashing mental suffering.

You did not need a dictionary to tell you that; you knew it already. What you probably did not know is that the dictionary does not begin to tell you how multi-faceted grief is. It does not tell you that grief is a process, not a settled state. It may be difficult for those who are newly thrust into bereaved status to realize that their feelings, their suffering, pain or distress, will change as they attempt to cope with their loss, that they will go through various phases.

Those who are reading this chapter may find it helpful to take time out to refer to books that deal with grief and its phases as they are described by professionals. I am neither a psychologist nor a psychiatrist, and it is not my intention to play the professional here, to serve up someone else's research slightly warmed over. Rather, I wish to describe my own experience and the experiences of other bereaved parents whom I know through my questionnaire or who are personal friends. By now, after many letters back and forth, my respondents, too, seem like personal friends. All of us are still making our way through the process others may have explained to us, but each of us has experienced in his or her own way.

In referring to psychologists and psychiatrists and other professionals who treat the bereaved, including grief counselors, I want to make it clear that I do not consider bereavement a pathology. Loss (in this case, death) is precipitated by something outside the self, with an effect somewhat analogous to a natural catastrophe like an earthquake, tornado, or being struck by a car.

Something happens which hurts the individual. It is not self-inflicted or genetic or pathological. The person may or may not need professional help coping with the injury. But whether or not professional help is sought should not carry a stigma when viewed by the general public.

Common knowledge tells us that each person who sustains a loss also suffers reactions to that loss. In dealing with the reactions, the parent whose child has died passes through stages in order to heal, just as a person recovering from surgery must have hospital care for a certain period of time. Or one's broken leg needs protracted immobilization and perhaps a plaster cast, physical therapy, crutches, and a cane in order to mend.

This step-by-step progress through grief applies to all types of loss: jobs, income, body parts or physical function, divorce, as well as death. It is important that bereaved parents know this; sooner or later, they must go through their grief, stage by stage, and not avoid it. Avoiding it is a great temptation; alcohol, drugs, denial, and being over-busy are some avoidance mechanisms applied by grieving people.

Passing through stages of grief after the loss of a loved one, however, is not an orderly progression, as it is when a physical injury occurs. No "six weeks in a cast, and then your broken leg will be ready for physical therapy and maybe a cane." Wildly erratic, the sensations which descend on the bereaved parent fluctuate from one phase to another with disconcerting frequency. People who have lost a child are in such emotional turmoil that they may never have an honest answer to the question, "How are you getting along?" If you asked them yesterday, they might have said, "Pretty well." If you ask them tomorrow, they may say, "I was doing all right and then something happened . . . I don't know what it was . . . and I am having a really bad day today."

Although this is a book directed toward the parent who has lost an adult child, in this particular chapter it is difficult to find many differences in the patterns of grief between the parents who have lost an adult or a young child. There are varying degrees of intensity and certain dangers along the way for bereaved parents of adults which will be pointed out, but essentially the stages hold true for grievers of any age bracket.

The back-and-forth nature of parental grief has made it difficult for professional caregivers to deal with bereaved parents who come to them for consultation. More or less arbitrarily, the experts have tried to impose order on this chaos by formulating a model, with names for the stages or phases of grief which can fit some but not all mourners.

These stages begin immediately after the death but do not arrive neatly packaged with labels:

1. The initial stage, characterized by shock or numbness and denial.
2. The second stage, anger and guilt.
3. A third or acute stage, characterized by intense sadness, may also include erratic behavior, illness, depression, yearning and searching, withdrawal from family and friends.
4. The fourth stage, reality or acceptance: a realization that the loved one is dead and is not coming back; internalization of that fact.

Sadness and pain will lessen somewhat after these stages have passed, but the parents of a dead child will never be quite the same as they were before their loss.

As enumerated above, these four stages of grief, rather than arriving within any given time frame, descend on the bereaved parents in one cataclysmic lump at the moment of the child's death. The parents are shocked and numb. They are in denial. They feel guilty because they did not prevent their child's death. They are angry at God or the doctor or fate. They are overwhelmingly sad, with fits of weeping and wailing. They get sick or can't face the people who come to comfort them. It may be impossible to distinguish one stage from the other.

In the beginning, the first two stages (shock and denial, then anger and guilt) will show themselves as predominant, but the other two (the acute stage, with intense sadness, erratic behavior, illness, depression, yearning and searching, withdrawal and then the arrival of reality) are always lurking in the background, soon to replace the first two as the major focus.

The meetings of the local support group I attend always begin with this routine: going from one after another of the parents seated in the circle, asking each to say that his or her child is dead, telling how the child died, and who the survivors are. At first, the parent cannot bear to say the word "dead," breaks into tears and passes without saying anything. Everyone expects it to happen and accepts it. Eventually, maybe months later, that parent will be able to say the child is dead, a first step toward that painful realization. Saying that dreaded word aloud needs to be practiced over and over before reality is possible.

My husband and I attended our first session of *The Compassionate Friends* less than a week after Cathy's funeral. At that first meeting, I sat in the circle in a daze, hardly hearing the recital of all the catastrophic events which brought these bereaved parents to the meeting. I kept saying to myself over and over, "these people have also experienced the death of a child, and they are still alive. Maybe I can stay alive too."

For me, bereavement occurred several years ago and I have only glimpsed the end. But I am now in stage four—reality. That is, most of the time.

Although somewhat useful in gauging the progress of grievers toward healing, the concept of four stages of grief has often been misused and misunderstood.

The most glaring of all distortions I have encountered was revealed in a talk to our local bereaved parents group by a well-meaning priest who came to one of our meetings. He related an episode which ostensibly happened to him when he saw a mother on the street, weeping over the body of her four-year-old son. The boy had just been struck by a car and the priest accompanied her in the ambulance as they drove the child to the hospital. Upon their arrival, the little boy was pronounced dead.

The priest stayed with the distraught mother for several hours, during which time he prayed with her, talked her out of her denial and anger, comforted her by saying she must not feel sadness because her child was happier with God in Heaven, and convinced her to accept the death as God's Will. In those few short hours, Father M quite proudly asserted that the mother went through the four stages of grief, implying that his skill in pointing out the way to her was responsible for this victory.

Those of us who were listening to his presentation sat in silence after the priest finished his message. No one wanted to be rude or confrontational, yet we could not respond positively to anything he said. For Father M was not lecturing to a lay audience. He was talking to an assemblage of experts; some fifty parents whose children had died. These bereaved parents had already encountered a wall of misunderstanding from everyone around them, including friends, relatives, doctors, and clergy. Their lives were in disarray, their spirits broken, their bodies and minds were not functioning properly. Some were hopeless, even considering suicide.

Father M was telling us that a mother whose little boy died had completed her grief work in a matter of hours. And we, his audience, were still struggling with our grief months, even years, after the death of our child.

He hadn't the faintest understanding about the four phases of grief. He didn't realize that it takes years of tremendously hard work to get through those stages of grief and that some never make it. We in his audience looked from one to another and rolled our eyes, thinking the words our leaders spoke aloud when he left, "Poor Father M. He means well, but he just doesn't get it!"

Yet we know those four stages are a valid concept. When the newly bereaved arrive at a meeting of *The Compassionate Friends*, we assume that they will be numb, in shock, denying that the death happened, just as I was at my first meeting. This numbing, this denial, is the narcotic which allows the parent to go about the necessary business of selecting the coffin, purchasing the burial plot, notifying friends and relatives, getting through the funeral, and all the while operating in a kind of dreamlike fog.

Eileen Byrne, one of the mothers who responded to my questionnaire, spoke of feeling that a veil or cloud descended on her when her daughter died. Eight months later, that veil just lifted and has been gone ever since. Not that she stopped grieving; her grief merely entered a different phase after those first eight months.

As the newly-bereaved parent begins his or her grief journey, numbness and denial protect the individual from the enormity of the realization that the loved one is dead. This seems to happen to all grievers, not just to those who have lost a child. It's the phenomenon of "I just can't believe it" or "There must be some mistake," or "This can't be happening," or "I'm sure he'll call me on Friday as usual," or "Soon I'll wake up from this nightmare."

Although this phase is usually short-lived, some people get stuck in the denial stage. A phenomenon particularly applicable to bereaved parents of an adult child, the denial can happen only when the child had not been living at home full time. Pretending the deceased is away at college or on a trip, or visiting friends, a parent hung up on denial may stall the natural grieving process for months or years. It is this kind of response which spawns poems beginning, "I am not dead, I am just away. . . ."

But no, the child is not just away. Even though the parents' daily lives may not have changed outwardly in any perceptible way, intense pain has suddenly injected itself into those lives. To cope with the pain, the parents may deny that the death occurred. Like a strong dose of medicine, it makes the parent feel better to pretend the child is still alive. Denial, in such cases, acts as the narcotic which gets in the way of progress and is to be avoided like any drug or alcohol, for it is among the greatest deterrents to healing.

After shock and denial, anger and guilt soon become the main focus of the parents' grief. They can get trapped in this stage too. It is obvious why some parents whose children were murdered or killed by drunk drivers focus on their anger. The same phenomenon is found among some of the parents whose children died in the crash of Pan Am 103 over Lockerbie, Scotland. It has been difficult for them to resolve their anger toward the terrorists who blew up the plane and toward our government's unsatisfactory initial response to the tragedy. Anger goes on so long that the parents may fail to deal with the sadness and subsequent phases of grief, deferring a completion of the grief process they must inevitably go through.

Parents are sometimes plagued by guilt because of something specific they did or didn't do at the time of their child's death. There may also be a general and non-specific feeling of guilt which is sometimes referred to as existential guilt. It often plagues the bereaved parent because he or she was unable to prevent the child's death. This aspect of guilt is dealt with more fully in Chapter 7, "Theme and Variations."

Phase three, the acute stage, is characterized by intense sadness as well as erratic behavior, illness, yearning and searching, depression, and withdrawal from family and friends. I wish there were a better name for this stage. I have thought of calling it "Limbo," but that has too many theological overtones. "The Pits" is more descriptive, but too flippant. This wretched stage builds during the first year and often reaches its peak during the second year after the child's death. The bereaved parents, expecting to feel better by that time, instead feel worse. The novocaine of shock and denial has begun to wear off and the surviving parents are faced with the painful truth of the finality of their child's death. The worst phase and the hardest to get through, this stage has dangerous life-threatening pitfalls described in greater detail in other chapters.

As we gradually and painfully work our way through phase three, sooner or later we will admit that yes, our child is really dead. Not away; not traveling; not in college: dead. Our child is not coming back. Not ever.

After internalizing the bitter truth that the child is indeed dead, we are faced with the task of going on, of restructuring our lives without that child. This fourth stage is often called "acceptance," which is certainly a misnomer if there ever was one. No one can ever accept a child's death. What is accepted is the reality that our child is dead.

And nobody reaches that fourth stage in a few hours, as the mother did in Father M's story. Listening to him and believing him, would have cast those troubled parents into even deeper trouble. If they indeed believed him, they would have judged themselves by his story. They would have wondered why they kept crying, or visiting the cemetery, or tossing sleepless at night, or suffering physical problems and depression. In that sense, the priest was not only mistaken, his talk was destructive, an example of harm done by someone who meant only to do good. And perhaps it represented a certain arrogance in a person who thought he had knowledge he didn't have. I am reminded of one of the sayings of Will Rogers, a popular entertainer during my youth, who remarked that you can no more know something you don't know than you can "return from somewhere you ain't been."

Reaching acceptance of the reality that your child is dead often takes many years, and progress is forward and then back, not direct. Parents are not weak or unstable when they vacillate from one phase back to the beginning}numbness and denial. They are merely acting normal. It is important for them to realize that they will be a little farther along the road to healing the next time they make some forward progress. The bad days will be fewer; the good days more frequent; the regression next time will be less painful.

Perhaps regression is an inappropriate word for the phenomenon which might better be called reversion, or a complete return to an early phase of grief after considerable time spent in a later phase. To illustrate, let me describe what happened to me more than eight years after Cathy died.

The date was September 1995. By that time, I had reached a plateau allowing me to function with a certain rhythm of equilibrium in my daily routine; body and mind operating without serious disruption. I was not constantly grieving.

"I am in a bad place," I wrote. "Maybe it is because I am ill again and worried about the possibility that my cancer has returned. I am longing so terribly for Cathy. Tears are close to the surface. I cry often. Other aspects of fresh grief are present.

"For example, I have tried to read but am simply unable to concentrate. Our Wednesday Philosophy Club is studying Karen Armstrong's *A History of God*. This week I tried again and again to do my reading assignment but had to give up because I could not concentrate. The material is interesting to me and I had had no problem reading previous assignments. It is not a matter of will. I just can't do it. My mind won't cooperate, won't operate.

"I know that my inability to concentrate is one of the expected grief responses I had suffered in the early years after Cathy's death and which had made it so difficult to read at the time. In fact, the only reading I could accomplish then dealt solely with grief literature. I had not realized how much I had improved in that department until the inability to concentrate suddenly descended on me again this week.

"Wise survivors of this phenomenon we call bereavement have warned me that this will happen. They use the analogy of a roller coaster to describe the progress and then failure, good days followed by bad days; good months followed by a bad month; good seasons followed by a bad season.

"What is 'bad?' It is a time, a feeling, a place in your life which jeopardizes the body and the mind and threatens to undo the careful work you have already done to restructure your life after the death of your child. It is discouraging. I am angry that the symptoms of early grief have reappeared; frustrated that what seemed to be a step ahead now has turned into two steps . . . many steps . . . back."

Rereading the above paragraphs at a later date, I recognize and appreciate the new insight I gained in September 1995. I hadn't realized how completely a person could revert to a bad place and all its attendant problems, even after many years of bereavement. Since then, I have identified the trigger which set it off: it was worry about my health.

The most cruel of all reversions can occur when an already bereaved parent suffers the loss of yet another child, as did one of my respondents, Marlene Patrone. Her son, Richard, a thirty-three-year-old doctor, died on April 17, 1993. Exactly three years later, to the day, her son Alfred died of cancer. A handsome man of thirty-eight, married and the father of three young daughters, Alfred had a warm winning smile; his mother sent the photo distributed to the mourners at his funeral. Inevitably, Marlene has been thrust back into the earliest stages of grief yet again. Her August 17, 1996 letter says:

> It is four months today since Alfred died and it seems like it has been forever. I feel barely alive, going through the motions of living but feeling nothing. It seems harder to deal with Alfred's death because he left a wife and three children. When I am with them I feel sadness and pain thinking of their growing up without their Dad. Richard was not married so there was no one to remind me of him.
>
> I was at the shore with my two daughters and their kids for a month. Sharon, Alfred's wife, and the three girls came down, but it was sad to relive the things we did with him last summer and revisit those same places.

I haven't gone back to The Compassionate Friends meetings; I don't know if I will return next month. There is no one in the group who has lost two grown children. *I do feel different from the rest!*

If bereaved parents can slip back into an earlier and more painful stage of grief, whether because of further loss or without immediately understanding why, they can also progress into a later phase without noticing. Carol Marshall, another respondent, writes:

> I talked on the phone one night last week to a mother whose nineteen-year-old died six months ago of cancer. As I listened to her talk it was like listening to myself for at least three years. She asked me if she would ever feel better and for the first time I could answer "yes" and feel that I really meant it. I don't know exactly when this happened to me. I think it is such a slow, painful process that we really don't know we are starting to heal. Of course it is a scab that will always bleed when we least expect it and the tears will flow, but that's OK. I loved my son Allen with everything that is in me and will always love and miss him. But now I can think of his life instead of always thinking of his death. I even find myself smiling sometimes when I think of him and what he meant to me.

If Carol Marshall is surprised to realize that she is, indeed, beginning to heal, it might be analogous to my own experience trying to recover from a hip replacement. While on vacation in Italy in December 1995, trying to escape Christmas at home without Cathy, I fell and broke my left hip. I had surgery and spent three weeks in the Venetian municipal hospital. Even after returning to the United States, long weeks of pain stretched into months of restricted mobility. I almost despaired of ever walking normally again.

Suddenly one day, I realized that I had lost my cane. If I had lost my cane, that meant that I was walking without it. Yes, healing had taken place without my having been aware of it. I had slipped into that phase of physical healing without noticing my progress.

If the concept of four phases of grief is helpful to the professional trying to guide bereaved parents through the rocky shoals of grief, then it serves some purpose. For the bereaved parents themselves, it may be an added comfort to realize that progress through those stages is necessary and normal, that the stages themselves can be described in such a way that they fit what may seem to be the parents' aberrational responses to their trauma.

There are precious few sources of comfort for those whose children die. Just to hear from another bereaved parent a reassuring "Yes, I have felt the same way, but I feel better now," may help, or for someone to tell you it is all right to experience your strange reactions. In the bleak world of the bereaved parent, those reassurances may seem slight, but they may be enough to make a difference in that parent's ability to go on, to make the necessary effort to persevere, and to reinvest in life.

CHAPTER 3

The Condolence Call

I wonder whether sympathetic friends and relatives who attend your child's funeral or come to call afterwards realize how extremely comforting their presence is. For our family, the sight of a familiar face, of someone who had flown in from afar or driven hundreds of miles to be with us was a kind of balm, a blessing. There were many of them. Just showing up at our time of need was all that was necessary to make us feel loved and cherished. At the funeral, they could spend only a few moments telling us they were sorry, the only appropriate thing they could say. The flowers, fruit, platters of food, the notes of sympathy, the long-distance telephone calls, the cablegrams from our overseas friends, all meant so much, even though we were in a kind of trance from the shock of Cathy's death all the while.

However, the subsequent mourning period with its condolence calls, with many people coming and going, is the time when bereaved parents get lots of free and often very bad advice. Some instinctively wise folk know the only thing they can do is express their sympathy, give you a hug, and share your tears. Others, equally well-intentioned, are anxious to help you to "fix it," but if they have not also lost a child, they often do not have a clue about how to do so. Nevertheless, this does not deter them from offering various prescriptions for complete, rapid, and permanent recovery.

It is very important to them that you recover completely, rapidly, and permanently, for the death of a child scares everyone, particularly other parents, who want you to return to your old self, preferably within a couple of weeks. They cannot abide the thought that a child can die, and seeing you grieve reminds them of that terrible possibility. Even after several years, you may never be able to recover completely, even though you will probably improve over the early stages of your grief.

They may say the following things to you:

> You are fortunate to have your spouse. This terrible tragedy will
> bring you closer.

Actually, if you have your spouse, you are fortunate, but this terrible tragedy will not necessarily bring you closer. It may, in fact, drive
you apart. Your spouse is as deeply distressed as you are and can't be
counted on to help.

> You have other children; they will help fill the void.

Your other children are suffering too. They may not be able to deal
with your pain; they may become estranged from you and from each
other because of that or because of a hundred other reasons. Their
presence may remind you of the void in your family circle. When your
surviving children are around, you may feel even more sad, making
them avoid being near you because you are so mournful. For they are
too painfully reminded of their loss when they are with you, thereby
complicating their own grieving process.

> You have all those wonderful memories and photos of your dead
> child to comfort you.

It is too painful to think of the good times, now gone forever, for
memories to bring you any comfort. Looking at the pictures makes you
cry and reinforces your sense of loss. In the earliest stages of your
grief, you may be unable to summon up an image of your child, which
terrifies you. In fact, it is so unnerving to realize you have no clear
recollection of your child that you begin to wonder if you have lost
your mind.

> Life has to go on.

Not necessarily. Many bereaved parents have to make a conscious
decision about suicide. The pain is unbearable and life doesn't look
very attractive after the death of your child. When the parent is elderly
and there are no surviving children to care for at home, the wish to go
on with life may not be strong.

> Try not to think about it.

It is impossible not to think about it. There is a powerful mental
video which plays over and over in your head and cannot be shut off by

any means. It is a symptom of grief, programmed to rehearse the details of your child's illness and death, the times you built up your hopes, and the times when those hopes were dashed, the last moments of your child's life, the awful realization that your child is dead, the purchase of the cemetery plot, the funeral, and on and on. These events and feelings come unbidden into your mind at all hours of the day and night, whether you are alone or with a multitude of people. That unwelcome script cannot be stopped, even while you are asleep. For more than a year after Cathy's death, no matter when I went to bed, no matter how fitful or restful my sleep, I awakened with a start each morning at 6:35 A.M., the time of Cathy's death on that Sunday in Boston.

The only way you can avoid thinking about your child's death is to take pills or get falling-down-drunk to find oblivion and that is not such a good idea, either.

You have to keep busy.

If bereaved parents keep too busy, they may be trying to avoid their necessary grief work. That grief work will wait, demanding your attention by manifesting itself as an ulcer or a broken leg or depression. Although you may find your enthusiasm for outside activities at an all-time low, maintaining a somewhat structured life is probably a good idea. My husband and I enrolled as auditors in courses at the nearby State University for Tuesday and Thursday morning classes for several years after Cathy died. We are fortunate; New York State allows senior citizens to do that without cost at all state universities. Each of us took nearly forty courses, sometimes alone and sometimes together, ranging from the sciences (geology, physics, chemistry, epidemiology), the arts, the classics, literature, history, archaeology, philosophy, and Shakespeare's plays over the years. The modified routine, the distraction of the lectures, helped get us out of the house on a regular basis and kept us on a more or less even keel as we dealt with our sorrow.

However, overworking yourself is counterproductive. If anything, you will probably experience a tremendous falling-off of energy. Driving yourself to keep busy may be prelude to a crash. A crash, in bereavement lexicon, means you experience a severe and almost disabling emotional and physical upheaval. It sends you back to *square one*, which is a bad place because it means you have to laboriously trudge through all the early grief stages again.

God never gives you more than you can handle.

There are many bereaved parents who are never again able to function normally after their child's death. Physical and emotional problems, accidents, and suicide, are not uncommon among bereaved parents. It takes real work to summon the will to continue living. Parents who responded to my survey enumerated many such problems suffered after the death of their children.

> It is God's Will that your child died. He needed another angel in Heaven.

That's supposed to comfort me? What about my needing my daughter here with me on earth? If there is indeed a Heaven, there must be plenty of angels there already. Parents who are believers have a hard time not being angry at God. A friend, seeing her priest in the hospital soon after her son's death, found herself thinking, "Father X, if you're representing God in this matter, you'd better get out of here before I tear your collar off!"

Then there is always the person who thinks it is helpful to remind you there are worse losses than yours so get on with your life. One so-called friend admonished me to stop grieving for Cathy because I should feel fortunate that she had to suffer for less than three weeks after her breast cancer was diagnosed. I was grateful that Cathy did not suffer for long years, but I was still sad that she died.

Another said her own daughter had been raped, which was worse than dying of cancer. Yes, she actually said it was worse! If I hadn't been so wounded by that remark, I might have reminded her that her daughter, a young mother, was still alive and living in Cleveland with her family. I had a hard time rejoicing at my daughter's good fortune regarding that. Another said that rather than feeling sad, I should be concentrating on the long and wonderful association Cathy and I were privileged to enjoy.

What the people who make condolence calls need to know is this: they cannot tell us how to grieve; they cannot cheer us up, no matter what they say; they cannot fix it. But they can give us hugs and weep with us, say they are sorry and ask us what we need from them.

We will probably reply that we need to talk about it. Talking about my child's death became an obsession with me in the early days of my bereavement. Once, after the repair man left the kitchen after fixing the dishwasher, my husband said to me, "Jeanne, the plumber does not need to hear that Cathy died!" He did not need to know, but I needed to tell him. I needed to tell everyone, over and over, how our child died, how we felt when we heard the news, how terrible life seems without our child, how unfair, and how we wished this or that had been done differently. And we don't want them to change the subject when our child's name comes up. They seem to think we won't be reminded of our loss if no one brings it up. We are thinking of it all the time, even if nobody reminds us. Even as we converse with our friends, we are speaking to them through the film of that mental video mentioned previously, trying to hear what they say but distracted by our anguish.

It is important to remember that the advice we get from those who have never experienced the death of a child is well-meant, but sometimes harmful. The non-bereaved have no way of knowing that the parents may already be greatly disturbed by their strange reactions, both physical and emotional. What the mourners are experiencing is not at all what those who come to express their sympathy assume.

The latter come to proffer their condolences; some also bring along their advice, advice designed to stop our grieving. The bereaved cannot react as non-grievers expect them to react, immediately accepting their prescriptions for recovery. The hurt is too great; the event too cataclysmic.

It is at this moment that the bereaved parents may become more distressed. They may not feel good about their memories—they can't even find their memories. Their spouse and their surviving children are no comfort. They cannot summon the energy to keep busy or even to get up in the morning. Life has lost all its savor and doesn't seem worth living any more. God seems to have let them down; He is the enemy.

Therefore, the bereaved parents may assume they are surely behaving abnormally: they have lost their minds; they are inadequate, of defective character, not courageous, and not worthy. Above all, they must be behaving differently from all other bereaved parents, for the stock answers they get from non-grievers tell them so.

Grateful for the sympathy extended to them by those who come to pay a condolence call, the grieving mother and father try hard not to offend or embarrass those callers. They may, as I did, nod their heads in agreement when all these unhelpful things are being said, chastising themselves secretly for their inability to follow proffered advice.

Someday they will learn to speak up, but this early in their grief, the parents are novices and don't know how. If they are anything like me, their self-confidence has departed. They don't trust themselves. They tend to believe anything and everything they are told.

Condolence callers can be roughly divided into two groups: casual friends and those who are more seriously involved in our lives, such as longtime associates and family. If the casual friends cannot deal with our attitude, they can and often do drift away. That solves their problem with us and ours with them.

Longtime associates and family members seldom have that option. They are thrust into our company long after the mourning period is supposedly over, on holidays and other special occasions such as weddings, graduations, birthdays, and anniversaries. They are constantly reminded of our tragedy and may be uncomfortable with our grief.

Sometimes we bereaved parents talk among ourselves about this problem. We are aware that family members are angered by our seeming refusal to return to our old selves, as though it might be perversity or stubbornness on our part. Their anger prompts them to adopt a pattern of behavior designed to stop all references to our child, to our child's death, and to the fact that our child ever lived. In other words, "Until you bereaved parents stop talking about your dead child, you are out of order and your behavior is not acceptable in this family. We are not going to listen to you any longer." This project is an almost concerted effort, a plot if you will, to deflect any reference to our dead child. I remember long-ago occasions when I cut off my cousin's constant references to her dead son, which, to my non-griever's eye, seemed to persist much too long after he died. I didn't want to hear about it. I wish I could beg her forgiveness for my insensitivity, but she is dead.

So how do bereaved parents react when someone cuts them off that way? They may get angry, resenting the unfeeling responses of their relatives and declining invitations to family celebrations.

As these occasions multiply, more tension develops. More resentment streams from all parties. Family ties no longer bind us in love. One bereaved mother said, "My sister is the worst. She hangs up on me when I mention my dead daughter." Or "You'd think my mother at least would understand. But she is just as bad as the others." My own brother, now dead, kept telling me Cathy wouldn't want me to grieve. I should stop it; I should shape up. Is this part of the project? Ignore, scold, cut off the bereaved parents until they come to their senses?

In the interests of family harmony, there ought to be a way to defuse the anger and hurt feelings. It behooves the bereaved parents to make their needs understood, but in the climate of fear and denial among the non-bereaved, it is nearly impossible for them to be heard if they speak up.

The bereaved parents, hurt, angry, and grieving, can hardly summon the necessary effort and skills to negotiate such a truce. Counseling might be an answer, but how many families—uncles and aunts, parents, cousins, in-laws, siblings—would consider such a drastic and expensive measure? No, let the bereaved parents stop misbehaving and spoiling all our family celebrations.

The first thing we bereaved parents have to do is care for ourselves and realize that the non-bereaved who treat us that way are misbehaving. We must not allow others to tell us how we should feel. We must remind ourselves that we resemble the person whose leg has been broken and then is urged to ignore it and get up and walk. We can't get up and walk just yet. Those who would urge us to get up and walk when one of our legs has been broken are misguided and wrong. Even if our leg were injured, we would have to be immobilized until the bone knitted and then use crutches or a cane. In that case, people would have no trouble realizing that we would have to spend long hours and weeks learning how to walk again. But somehow they can't envision why our healing after the death of a child is taking so much time. It is helpful to discover the comforting fact that many of our seemingly antisocial reactions to grief are often shared by other bereaved parents.

Probably the most crucial thing to keep in mind is that the death of a child of any age is the most devastating thing a human being can experience. It brings reactions which are almost impossible to deal with, and it takes tremendous strength, courage, and hard work to rebuild their lives.

Having said that many bereaved parents experience similar reactions, I realize it is important to note that there are significant differences between the death of a young child and that of an adult child. For the parents of an adult child who dies, the circumstances are necessarily quite diverse and the means of coping with them are also diverse. Suggestions about rebuilding their lives that apply to bereaved parents of young children are often not applicable to those of bereaved parents of adults.

Because most members of support groups I have attended over the years have lost young children, those differences again make the older parent feel left out, defective in character. Whether intentionally or not, we are made to feel somewhat out of place in seeking solace. In a sense, it might resemble the *Condolence Call* translated to the support group, with negative vibes sent out to the older bereaved parent. At meetings of *The Compassionate Friends* I have stood by while other, younger bereaved parents, have been introduced to newcomers and I have been passed over and ignored. Rather than nurse hurt feelings, I step in on such occasions and introduce myself, saying I'm also a bereaved parent.

Ageism, dealt with in another chapter, sends us the message that bereaved parents of adult children are out of order grieving. For didn't our children live a relatively long life compared to that of small children? With all the wonderful years we had together before our child died, why are we grieving? Our child had left home, established his or her own home, and was no longer present in our daily life. If there is grief, it is the daughter-in-law, the son-in-law, and the grandchildren who are the most sorely bereft.

My survey indicates that the widows and widowers of the adult child who died sometimes remarry very soon after their loss; the parents do not heal so readily. The remarriage of their child's spouse increases the bitterness of the parents, who had initially suffered just as painfully but had been cast aside in the grieving process. The spouse who remarries seems to be able to get on with life while the bereaved parents continue to suffer.

The responses to my questionnaire tell me we are not alone. Parents whose adult children have died are bonded in a special way, and I find it a great comfort to know that there are others who understand my pain, who empathize with my struggles to stay afloat, and who want to help each other make some affirmation.

Those who have to deal with bereaved parents, those who come to pay a condolence call, must be helped to understand us. Now that we have been changed by our tragedy into entirely different people, are we their friends any longer? Are we embittered by their behavior toward us, angry that they don't understand?

Although some of them are too anxious and frightened by our condition to continue the friendship, others are genuinely interested in being supportive. Bereaved parents must let the former go gracefully; the latter may continue to be friends. If so, they must accept our condition as being unfixable for a long time. We have to be frank with them, telling them exactly how we feel and how they can help us.

If they can live with their discomfort and frustration, the truth is that just being there for us is the only thing we need. We do not want advice or cheering up. We want to talk about our child who died, so they should not change the subject when it comes up. In fact, they should bring it up by saying, "Do you feel like talking about your son/daughter?" Or ask what we need or, "What can I do to help you? Can I drive you somewhere—shopping—to the cemetery?"

Making bereaved parents feel that their telephone calls are welcome when they need to talk is fairly simple. Just dialing a number may be as much as a bereaved parent can do in the beginning. But the need to talk is so great that a telephone conversation may make a big difference in whether or not the day is bearable. If the parent doesn't phone, the friend should be alert to the possibility that depression is setting in and should initiate the phone call.

The above prescription for being a friend to a bereaved parent is emotionally demanding and may sound tedious and unrewarding. But those wonderful people who love us enough to persist, to stay the course with us, are indeed among the blessed of the earth. We bereaved parents will never be the same as we were before our loss, but I have faith that someday we will be companions worthy of their devotion.

CHAPTER 4

Fair-Weather Friends

When friends come to pay a condolence call, they often attempt not only to comfort us but to repair the wounds caused by our child's death. They have, shall we say, an urgent agenda. Having once been one of those calling on the bereaved rather than a bereaved parent as I am now, I have a wide perspective from which to view the scene. I have been both places. This chapter might well be subtitled "Mea Culpa," for I was surely among the worst of friends when it came to someone's loss of a child, particularly if that child was about my children's ages.

The words "friends" and "friendship" are bandied about casually, often without any clear understanding of their true meaning. Some friendships, our earliest close connections with others outside our nuclear family, are apt to have been formed when we were very small. Based on random contacts with our peers, the ones we "hung out with" and called our pals, those were the friends who helped make our childhood enjoyable. A few of these early friendships last through the years, but they rarely survive because each of those young friends has lots of growing and changing to do.

Adult friendships may fall into the same category of randomness and propinquity, with slight common interest of any lasting importance: a neighbor, someone you encounter at the supermarket or at a meeting, a fellow churchgoer, parents of your children's friends whom you met at a Parent-Teachers' Association event.

Other deeper relationships develop through shared ideas, interests and activities. Those relationships lead to socializing and real affection. These are true friends; bosom friends; best friends; friends even more significant in our lives than some relatives. The importance of such friendships to our sense of well-being can hardly be overemphasized.

Although there are no guidelines for friendship, everyone expects a friend to be there, to help in some way when tragedy strikes. With this expectation, it is disappointing to discover, as my respondents reported overwhelmingly, that friends dropped out of the picture after their children's deaths. Not all friends; just the fair-weather friends, those who could not withstand the storms accompanying our grief.

Such an abandonment represents the shattering of one more illusion: that friends are loyal sources of support in times of trouble. Other chapters discuss the destruction of illusions about the fairness of life, our religious faith, our philosophy, and the integrity of the medical, legal and military establishments. Previously held illusions about such matters were at least challenged if not totally destroyed, perhaps to be replaced by cynicism in the aftermath of our child's death.

If we are faced with yet another disillusionment as we see our friends flee from our sides when tragedy strikes, it might be well to seek some understanding of what motivates them to distance themselves from us, to disappoint us when we need them during bereavement. These are the same friends who would not have abandoned us in any other crisis but would have visited us in the hospital, brought food when we were sick, picked up the daily newspaper, and tended the garden when we were away.

But the death of our child—that's something quite different. Hearing news of that death may have elicited a counterreaction among those friends who also had children. As a former fair-weather friend, I can testify that just hearing about a child dying, being near a parent who had lost a child, sent me into a flight pattern in the years before Cathy died. Afflicted with existential terror, I could convey my sympathy initially, but my contact with them stopped the day after the funeral.

I was not alone in that reaction; rather, it seems I was in the majority. Few friends will step forward with ongoing sympathy and support for bereaved parents. Strangely enough, it is not the depth of the friendship, its longevity or its importance in our lives that determines whether a particular friend will drop us after our child dies. Often a mere acquaintance will suddenly become a strong and supportive presence while a dear and trusted friend will defect. No one can anticipate who will be the fair-weather friends and relatives, the ones who abandon parents after the death of their child.

Just the mention of parental loss may throw another parent into a panic, as illustrated by my encounter with Laura a few summers ago. She stood behind me as we waited to register at the International Women Writers' Guild Conference at Skidmore College. A good-looking woman in her early forties, slender, and stylishly dressed, asked if she was in the right line for registration since there were four unmarked lines.

"I hope it's the right one," I replied. "It doesn't appear to be very well organized."

As the line moved along, stopping and starting, Laura and I began to chat. I sensed from the bits of conversation she shared with me and the woman behind her that she might be going through some kind of personal crisis. At one point she turned to me and muttered fretfully, "I don't know why I'm here." I never discovered whether my hunch was correct or not, for after our next encounter I never spoke to her again.

By lunch time, registration was accomplished and baggage stowed in the dormitory room I was sharing for the week with my friend Ann Eberle. At noon the two of us pinned on our food tags, trekked across the campus, located the cafeteria, and loaded our lunch trays from the vast array of foods.

As Ann and I settled at a table, I spied Laura across the room, alone and looking lost. I waved and beckoned for her to join us. After introducing Ann, I asked, "How's it going?"

"Oh Lord!" she exclaimed. "You won't believe what just happened to me. I saw this nice woman and we started to talk and I asked her why she would come all the way to Saratoga, New York, from California for this conference. Well, it turns out that she had a couple of airline senior coupons to use up. She had been flying back and forth from coast to coast while her daughter was ill and the coupons were left after her daughter died. She decided to use them on this conference. Can you imagine? How sad! Her daughter died! Oh, I didn't know what to say. I was so mortified that I had brought it up."

There was a long moment of silence. Finally I said, "You tell her, Ann."

"Laura," Ann began, "Both Jeanne and I are bereaved parents, too. I lost a son; Jeanne lost her daughter."

"Oh no!" she moaned, both hands clasping her head. "How could I say that? I mean, I'm so sorry. Oh, please forgive me."

Laura was so contrite that Ann and I began to laugh. We assured her that it often happened to us when somebody found out about our children's deaths, that we understood how she felt.

I don't know whether or not Ann was formerly as upset as Laura to hear about someone whose child had died. But I recognized myself in Laura's reaction. My story about our friends the Weavers will illustrate just how upset I used to be.

My husband and I traveled a lot after our children grew up. Our longest trip took place after I received my Masters Degree from New York University in 1970. The vacation was a reward for several years of study to complete my college education that had been interrupted when we married during World War II.

On that trip, Bob and I spent four months in Europe, starting in England, then flying to Rome and on to Greece. We met the Weavers for the first time in an obscure restaurant in Athens, where they too, were struggling to make sense of the menu. In desperation, the four of us finally went to the kitchen and pointed at what we wanted. Even then we weren't sure what we had ordered, but it tasted good.

A generation older than we, Houston and Eva were a handsome, jolly, and urbane pair from a suburb of Albany, New York. We enjoyed chatting with them during the meal, saying cordial good-byes at its completion.

The next morning Bob and I set off to drive around Greece, heading toward a far-off corner of Thessaly to see the strange region of Meteora. Justly famous as one of the earth's geological wonders, Meteora resembles a forest of gigantic rocks in the shape of needles or swords, some tipped in threatening positions like the Leaning Tower of Pisa. Our goal was to visit the brilliantly painted fourteenth-century monasteries built atop the pinnacles by various religious orders.

The lone hotel in the area, Xenia, was situated at the base of the rocks—remote and isolated. We rented a room on the second floor; no elevator, no porter, no frills.

Our bathroom immediately presented us with a problem we could not solve. An inexperienced maid had carefully waxed the toilet seat. By the time we arrived, the wax had dried to a stubborn and sticky sheen, making the seat unusable. My efforts at scrubbing it off came to nothing, so I went to the desk to complain to the concierge. Wax on toilet seats is not a situation usually dealt with in a language textbook and the poor man, who spoke minimal English, was unable to understand what I was talking about. He smiled a lot but I never did succeed in my mission.

And who walked in as we were involved in that hopeless endeavor? Eva and Houston Weaver! They shared our near-hysterical laughter.

Later we joined them for dinner in the hotel dining room. The next morning we invited them to go along with us to explore the monasteries on the heights of Meteora, spending the day and subsequent evening meal with them as well. They were interesting and fun. We learned that they had not been married long. Eva had been Houston's secretary and they married after his first wife died. They were members of the Unitarian church in Schenectady, New York, near Albany. We still lived in Mount Vernon at the time, some 150 miles away, but because we were also Unitarians, it was another link to them. Having become friends by this time, we met again on the road in Greece by prearrangement.

After returning to the United States, letters and visits between Albany and Mount Vernon cemented our friendship with Eva and Houston.

By this time you may be wondering why, in a book about bereaved parents, I have spent so much time telling you about a chance encounter with two Americans in Greece. It is because I wanted to make clear that the Weavers were not just casual acquaintances. They became our great friends, charming, gracious people we had learned to love, with common ideas and interests—friends we associated with for a long time.

Several years after our first meeting, we got a letter saying they were very upset because Houston's twenty-ish grandson had been diagnosed with brain cancer and was dying.

Bob and I had three children in the same age category. We didn't want to hear about the possibility that people that age might die. Existential terror took over. I sent a letter to say we were sorry. Eva wrote a few times to report on his progress but I never answered.

I am ashamed to say that we dropped them. We just couldn't deal with the news that a young man the age of our children was dying. We didn't want to hear about it or get near them. The death of a child is contagious you know. As one of the *Compassionate Friends* said, "We bereaved parents are toxic." If you avoid hearing about it, thinking about it, getting near anyone who has a child who died, it won't happen to you. Obviously I was never conscious of the reason for my decision to break off our association with the Weavers. There was no thinking involved. It was probably my subconscious that told me to flee from them.

Some ten or twelve years passed. By this time our older daughter, Laurel, had received a Ph.D. in Art History from the University of Michigan, married, and moved to Albany to teach at the State University. In 1981 she had a baby boy, our only grandchild at the time. We visited them often, and with each visit I thought about the Weavers, wondering if I should contact them. After so long, and after such cruel neglect, perhaps not.

Laurel eventually became a single parent, so when we left the New York metropolitan area, we relocated to Albany to be near her and little Paul. The Weavers were still on my mind and still in the phone book, but we never called them.

Less than a year after our move to Albany, our younger daughter, Cathy, suddenly became ill and died of cancer. The day after her death, we purchased a burial plot in the beautiful and historic Albany Rural Cemetery. Standing in the blinding July sun at the gravesite, I watched as my husband wrote a check to the cemetery director. The date: his seventy-first birthday.

Cathy's gravesite at Albany Rural Cemetery has now become familiar to us. We visit it often, clipping and tending the plants which we change seasonally.

One day a few years ago, Bob left me alone at Cathy's grave as he wandered about the cemetery. He came back some minutes later.

"I made a discovery," he said hesitatingly, putting his hand on my shoulder. He pointed toward the east. "Someone we know is buried just a few yards from here. Houston Weaver. Eva's stone is in place with no death date on it."

We walked together to Houston's grave, as we have done many times since then—sad and contrite. Although we knew Eva was still alive, we never contacted her; too ashamed. One day I saw her obituary in the local paper. She was eulogized as a kind and compassionate person, beloved by all who knew her, a woman who lived out her later years (she was in her 90s) in a nursing home. Now she too, lies in Albany Rural Cemetery, not far from our Cathy.

Each time we visit the Weavers' graves, we are made painfully aware that once we shunned those who needed us because we were afraid to face the thought that a child, maybe our child, could die.

How well I understand those who used to come up and talk to me before Cathy died but now avoid me or rush past, calling out, "Hi, how are you? So glad to see you! You look great!" (Why is it people tend to end their embarrassing encounters and hasty greetings with "You look great!"? It has happened to me so often that it has become a source of amusement.)

I recognize those people as the anxious parents we used to be. I try not to be too hard on them because I have had to forgive myself for this callous behavior. I have to forgive uncaring friends and relatives too, and hope they never discover that turning away from any contact with people whose child died will not protect them from the same fate.

As I mentioned earlier in this chapter, although some of my respondents reported that their friends had rallied 'round them after the death of their children, more than twice as many said they had not. Most of their friends had either shunned them altogether or had not been understanding and comforting. Some of these parents said they felt bitter about losing the support of their longtime friends.

That great majority might appear at first to be insensitive. But I know, having once been one of them, they were not primarily insensitive: they were just scared. They were frightened to be in a world where there is a possibility that children, perhaps their own children, could die before parents.

Some fair-weather friends abandon bereaved parents for reasons other than fright. The boundaries of friendship are unclear and will differ among each group of friends: casual, neighborly, long-term, or "best friends."

In times of trouble, some of the least committed will become more supportive; the closest may drop away. This dropping away can be explained in part by the emotional dependency of the bereaved parent on the friend. The emotional drain can take a heavy toll on the one who is not grieving. The sister-in-law of one of my respondents once shouted in anger, "Your constant dwelling on your dead son is offensive to me!" A sister, on the telephone, said to another, "I'm sorry, but I can't call you any more. It's too depressing to hear about your grief. It's getting me down."

During the memorial service for my friend Ed, a man who had lost his adult son many years before, one of his friends rose to speak. "Ed and I were friends for a long time before we had a falling out," he said. "It was after his son died; he was so angry! He and Betty got divorced. Years later, Ed and I resumed our friendship."

My own brother, now dead, used to scold me each time he called, "Cathy wouldn't want you to grieve like this. You have to get a hold of yourself." I wondered how he knew what Cathy would want and how I was supposed to get a hold of myself.

Real friends would not abandon the bereaved. They would just be there—just be there to listen. I have been abundantly blessed with such friends.

Many others have slipped away, never to be heard from after Cathy died. Those are fair-weather friends, and I gladly wave them good-bye.

CHAPTER 5

Crying at the Supermarket

Because the reasons are subtle, the response so unexpected, it may be hard for the bereaved parent to understand why it is so difficult to function, to get back to daily life after the funeral. To the bereaved parent, an attempt to resume daily activities represents a reentry into a world that may seem the same, yet is not the same as it was before our child died.

In today's society, bereaved parents are usually expected to take off a certain time from work, say a couple of weeks, and then return to the job. Being away from the house all day, among non-grievers in the workaday world, forces the working parent to function at least on some level, if not very effectively.

Tasks at home are another matter, however. Many of us, particularly those who have had the major homemaking job in the family, experience unfamiliar and unsettling reactions when we attempt to resume simple daily chores such as personal care, shopping, cooking, and socializing.

The initial response to bereavement is typically this: you don't want to get out of bed in the morning. When you do get up, you don't want to get dressed, and if you do manage to get dressed, not to get "dressed up" in clean and neat clothing, not to be well-groomed. I heard one bereaved parent say to another who was having a particularly bad time, "Don't be too hard on yourself. You got out of bed today, didn't you? That's a real accomplishment!"

However, even the most despairing among us knows that it is a morale booster to face the day by caring for our bodies. If we can't, after the earliest days of grieving have passed, then we may need professional intervention to treat possible clinical depression. A fellow philosophy club member, Imogene Scheer, once said to me, "I look forward to the day when you walk into a meeting looking less than 'well turned out.' Then I will know you aren't working so hard on your morale."

For parents of an adult child who died, with no young children at home to care for, the temptation to lie abed, to neglect to wash and dress oneself, can be very great. The reverse side of the same coin would lead one to assume that a return to normal activities should be easier for the older parent: no one at home to care for; and no dramatic changes in the household routine, the arrangement of bedroom, playroom, etc.

The expectation that you can resume daily activities automatically may sandbag you. Sandbagging is a term we bereaved parents use a lot: you're not expecting a particular thing to upset you so you aren't prepared for it when it happens. It's as if someone hit you from behind and knocked you down. One of the reasons sandbagging occurs is that nobody told you a return to normal activities was going to be difficult. You knew you would cry a lot, but who told you the little, ordinary, day-to-day tasks would loom so large?

Take, for example, the simple chore of shopping. We must eat and to eat, we must purchase food. So the time comes, soon after the funeral, when all the casseroles and cakes contributed by sympathetic friends and neighbors are gone. We must set out for the supermarket with a shopping list.

Going to the store sounds so easy; something we have done all our adult lives. Yet it is fraught with difficulties we do not expect to encounter. Shopping forces us to realize that everyone else around us is functioning normally and we are not. It comes to us almost like a physical blow to see that their lives have continued as they did before our child's death. Our lives are shattered and seem to have stopped.

Pieter Brueghel, a Netherlandish artist who lived and worked in the sixteenth century, conveyed his understanding of this phenomenon in several of his works. One of his paintings, "Census in Bethlehem," which hangs in Brussels, shows a village center where people are going about their daily activities. It is a crowded, busy winter scene: wood-gatherers, hunters, diners clustered in a restaurant, chickens pecking in the snow, children playing games, and men and women hurrying to and fro. In the distance, skaters glide by on a frozen river.

Among all the bustle, in an obscure corner, not even noticed by anyone else, is a woman, pregnant and riding on a donkey, led by a man. Looking closely, you will recognize Mary and Joseph, headed for the stable where the baby Jesus will be born—a momentous event in history, yet no one pays them any attention. Instead, those on every side go about their daily tasks heedless of what is going on.

Another Brueghel painting, "The Fall of Icarus," is in the same museum, the Musees Royaux des Beaux-Arts in Brussels. Icarus, the mythological figure whose ambition to fly led him to his own destruction, is shown falling to his death in the sea. If you look at the painting however, you will not notice Icarus at first. Instead, your attention is drawn to the foreground, where an elegantly dressed farmer, his head turned away from the death scene, tills his field on a bright sunny day. In the distance, a handsome ship with sails unfurled is sailing out to sea. And nearby, in a mere splash, Icarus plunges to his doom in the blue-green water. No one watches. No one cares. The whole world is oblivious to his plight.

Icarus, like a bereaved parent, is alone in an indifferent universe which continues on its accustomed way, uncaring of his suffering.

When we see life going on after our child's death, we want to say, "Stop! Stop!" But activities continue as before, in spite of our loss.

That first simple task in our return to normal life—the initial shopping expedition after our child's funeral—finds us confronting these unexpected feelings. It may be the first time we have been out in public. It is a shock to see so many people going on with their daily chores, reminding us that life does continue. And we don't want it to go on as it always did. We may not even be sure that we want it to go on at all.

Shortly after we arrive at the store on our first shopping trip, select a cart and start rolling it down the aisle, we reach toward the shelf which holds the first item on our list. Suddenly we may feel slightly nauseated; our eyes fill with tears. We may even break into sobs. This prompts startled looks from other shoppers. One woman, in response to my tears, said to me, "Oh, dear, it can't be that bad!"

What causes bereaved mothers to act this way? Looking at all the foods on the shelves and in the fresh produce bins, we are reminded that we and all the shoppers around us are buying food in preparation for eating meals. And our child lies in the cemetery, dead, never to eat again.

In the first few days and weeks after the death of our child, we find ourselves trying to deal with the physical fact of that death, going over and over in our minds what it means, trying to process it. For as parents, we have been profoundly connected with the physical presence of our child. We feel the warmth of the sun or a cool breeze; we know our child can no longer feel. The sound of laughter or shouts, a bird song or a melody wafts through the air; our child can no longer hear or speak or sing. Our eyes glance toward a passing car or we look at the clouds sailing by; our child can no longer see.

And now we have entered the supermarket for the first time since our child died. Seeing all the groceries, the people shopping for food at the market, has a tremendous impact as we continue to process the fact that our child is dead. Food, the very fuel of life, shelf after shelf piled high with food, fresh produce spilling from the bins, the aroma of breads and cakes baking: everywhere our eyes dart, we are over-whelmed with the realization that our child is dead and will never eat again. This realization is a visceral response to our loss, a gut reaction. It literally nauseates us.

Perhaps at this precise moment, when our defenses are low, we see a tired mother, her nerves frayed by excessive demands on her time and energy, slap her cranky toddler or abuse the child verbally. Ordinarily we might cast a disapproving glance in her direction and go on with our shopping, but now we react with physical revulsion. With our newly-reinforced knowledge of how precarious life is, we cannot abide the sight of a mother abusing her precious child.

That does it! We bolt toward the door. Our partially-filled shopping cart stands abandoned in the middle of the aisle. We beat our retreat, perhaps to return when we are more calm or perhaps not to return at all.

For a long time thereafter, our shopping may consist of rushing into the store, picking up a few necessities and leaving before the tears start.

It is easier to connect this behavior to a grief response in the mother of a young child who died than in the mother of an adult child. At our bereaved parents' group, tales of shopping disasters and inap-propriate purchases abound: stocking up on case after case of peanut butter because it was the child's favorite food, for example. Buying peanut butter feeds the parent's need to deny the child's death, to pretend the child is still alive, waiting at home to eat peanut butter and jelly sandwiches. Or if not at home, maybe soon to return, at the end of this bad dream. If we buy the child's favorite food, we are able to cling to that child, however symbolically, yet a little while longer. This happens too, when we postpone laundering the last garment our child wore or delay disposal of his or her belongings.

Yet why do I, whose child left to establish her own home many years ago, have such difficulties shopping for food? I think it is because the sight of food reminds me of all the meals I prepared for my Cathy and which I will never prepare again; part of being her mother and nurturer. When I pass the display of fresh rhubarb, I remember that I can't surprise her with her favorite strawberry-rhubarb pie next time she arrives home on the bus from Boston. She is never coming home again. I, the old woman who has already lived a full life, am still alive, still buying food, while my young and vigorous daughter is dead.

Marilyn Heavilin, one of the speakers at a *Compassionate Friends* national conference in Charlotte, North Carolina, said that after her teenage son was killed, her kitchen was closed. Sounds of nervous laughter throughout the audience told us that nearly everybody understood what she was talking about. The preparation and eating of food has, for many bereaved parents, taken on a new and unpleasant dimension, reminding them that life is going on all around them in spite of their loss, that they are not sure they want to go on with life in view of their loss, that their child is no longer a part of the physical scene which surrounds them day-by-day and cannot participate in the simple activities necessary to maintain living organisms.

One of my favorite activities, actually a hobby, had been cooking, experimenting with new recipes, and preparing meals for my family and friends. Before we settled into our recently purchased home in Albany in July of 1986, our Italian friend Giorgio Rizzetto came to visit us from Venice. We showed him around the empty house. Seeing the newly-remodeled, well-appointed kitchen, he turned to me with the solemn pronouncement: "Madame, your kitchen is a temple!"

And until Cathy died, I took full advantage of its convenience and modern appliances to concoct sumptuous meals—the more complicated, the better.

After Cathy's death, I had to force myself even to enter the kitchen. And when I got there, the dinner hour at hand, I had no appetite. I couldn't think of anything to cook.

Bob, my husband, sensing my inability to come up with a menu, began doing the shopping, bringing home groceries for me to prepare so that I didn't have to make any decisions or do any menu-planning. (Decision making is one of many skills which may depart with the death of a child.) This has continued to a lesser degree until today. I recognize it as a tremendous favor. However, he seldom checks the cupboard or the refrigerator before going to the store. (I know; he is grieving too.) As a result, he brings home fresh supplies of items we already have, which makes extra work for me in finding ways to process the perishable foods before they spoil.

There has been a running battle with peppers in particular. Red or green peppers appear rarely in my repertoire of foods. Perhaps because my father found them hard to digest, Mother never put them into the food she prepared. Yet Bob has me constantly supplied with a host of rotting peppers. "Stop buying peppers!" I shouted in exasperation not long ago. "It complicates my life when I have to think up ways to use them."

I still find grocery shopping unpleasant and I often feel the urge to leave the store before the job has been accomplished. But I know I am improving because I am now able to walk the seven or eight blocks to the supermarket without crying all the way there and back as I did at first.

Another hidden hazard at the supermarket might be called "The Left Turn." If you live in a fairly small community where you have many casual acquaintances as well as close friends, you may experience this uncomfortable problem. Some acquaintances have heard of your tragic loss but have not as yet called you or sent you a card. Seeing you at the supermarket for the first time since your child's death is a shock for them; they are embarrassed and don't know what to do. Should they stop and express their sympathy, thereby prompting a scene with tears? Or should they pretend they don't see you and make a left turn with their shopping cart in order to avoid you? Of course you have already seen that casual friend before he or she makes a left turn, and your feelings are hurt yet again. Anger, always near the surface during early bereavement, may flare anew.

Shopping for clothing, another mundane but important chore we must accomplish, is an activity I often share with my surviving daughter, Laurel, and which I shared with Cathy in the years before her death. Clothing is high on my gift list for my children. Out of respect for their taste, I preferred to let my daughters and my son select what they liked and then pay for the purchase rather than making a choice which might be a mistake.

I must admit that shopping with Cathy was sometimes more of a chore than a joy. Because she was an artist, she had definite ideas about what she wanted. Color, shape, size, cut of garment, had to be exactly right. Her standards of perfection were hard to meet and considerably higher than mine. There are occasions when I am out shopping for clothing these days and come across a garment I recognize as one she would find really smashing. Those occasions are so rare that I am not prepared when I encounter them, and invariably I begin to weep.

Looking back to her childhood, I realize Cathy was always that way, fretting at the perceived unsuitability of the store's offerings, spending hours at the selection process. Yet the adult Cathy, confident of her taste and determined to select the perfect item, helped me sharpen my aesthetic sense.

This was true not only while shopping for clothing but also while viewing art at a museum, another activity we shared. Her refined sense of form and color enabled her to interpret art, giving me a richer experience than if I had been viewing it alone.

Because visits to museums have always been associated with Cathy, it is a bittersweet experience to go to a museum since her death.

The paintings remind me of her facility with a brush, her keen and insightful ability to delve into the psychological depths of a subject. And then I am overcome with regret and anger that she died. "What a waste for her to die!" I say. "She was such a good artist with so much to give."

In addition to the above-mentioned grief responses, we parents of adult children who died are sometimes perplexed by a more subtle and insidious change which has taken place in our daily lives. Because we have lived a longer time than parents of young children, our tastes and predilections are less flexible. We are, as they say, more set in our ways. And yet our bodies and minds may switch off after the death of our adult child, refusing to carry on not only basic tasks like shopping, but also the leisure time activities we used to enjoy, like museum visits. I, who for years accumulated the volumes of diaries lined up on the shelves of my study, found it almost physically revolting to pick up a pen and write after Cathy died. Writing had been a source of real pleasure prior to her death. Grief counselors often recommend writing as a comfort and a healing tool, yet I could no longer record anything in my diary. Even going to a writing workshop at one of the national conferences of *The Compassionate Friends* found me unable to complete more than the first sentence of a simple exercise. I spent the entire allotted time weeping instead of writing. (One of the comforting aspects of a national conference of *The Compassionate Friends* is having permission to sit and cry unashamedly and without reproach instead of doing a writing assignment.)

Bereaved parents are always examining their strange responses, and that episode in the writing workshop started yet another in a long series of inner chastisements. This tiresome exercise always begins with, "What's wrong with me?" and concludes with "I'm losing my mind; I'm worthless, destroyed."

No matter how many times it happens, I always forget that beating myself in that way stems from the basic premise that a parent is supposed to protect his or her child from harm. My child is dead, therefore I failed to protect her; therefore I am a failure as a mother. Unrealistic in the extreme, it is an ever-present feeling just the same. This feeling is explored in greater detail in the chapter on Theme and Variations.

Several bereaved parents who answered my questionnaire have given me further insights into the phenomenon of rejecting former pleasurable activities. These respondents have told me their experiences correspond to mine. One woman, seriously handicapped by polio, said her favorite recreational activity was reading. She had been a voracious reader prior to her daughter's death but couldn't pick up a book for three years afterwards. If she did try to read, she experienced a panic attack.

Another said, "I used to read but I can't read any more; I just can't do it." By her inability to read, she is expressing a revulsion toward an activity she formerly enjoyed. For the same reason, a mother whose daughter died of drug-related sepsis said she has only recently been able to begin reading some of the books available at The Compassionate Friends library, even though she had known they would help her.

One problem I face is my growing impression that most cultural pursuits, whether art, music, theater, movies, lectures, or festivals, seem trivial to me in the face of my tragedy. It has forced me to reorder my priorities, including not only a new approach to culture, but a disdain for status and the accumulation of wealth or possessions.

A changed response to cultural pursuits looms more significantly for older adults, both in expenditure of time and money, because they have probably reached a stage in their lives when they have more of both time and money to indulge an interest in the arts than young parents.

Perhaps, some weeks or months after the funeral, you will not only attend the theater or a movie, there will come a moment when you will have conquered your reluctance to go to a party or other large gathering where you do not know everyone present. In chatting with various guests, the inevitable question will come up: "How many children do you have?" Furious calculations will begin in the bereaved parent's mind. Do you want to answer truthfully, revealing the death of your child, and cause discomfort to the questioner? Yet the need to include the deceased in your response may be uppermost in your mind. It is of paramount importance to me. I can never leave Cathy out. Therefore, when I am confronted with that question, I devise my answer to satisfy both my questioner and myself. In this matter, the bereaved parent whose child was an adult at the time of death has an advantage because the deceased was already grown. I have perfected my own response: "My husband and I raised three beautiful children; two girls and one boy. Tell me about your children." This allows me to toss the conversational ball to my questioner. If the exchange continues and the occasion seems appropriate, I can then reveal the fact that one of my children died, but if it remains a casual conversation, I do not. My needs are satisfied; so are the questioner's.

Another stock answer that has saved me from embarrassing explanations has been my response to "How are you?" Sometimes I am having a really bad day and I can say, "I'm fine, and I'm lying." This is usually accompanied by a laugh, which tells my questioner the truth but defuses the sadness.

A few bereaved parents, both male and female, have had problems reentering the workplace. Some have been threatened by firing or actually been dismissed for poor performance on the job after their child's death.

Although my husband was considering retirement before Cathy became ill, he was still going into his office in New York City a few days a week. After Cathy's death, Bob went back to work for only a short time. He sold his business in New York City and retired. Perhaps one factor in his decision was his reluctance to leave me alone for two days a week in my precarious emotional state.

In all the above manifestations, demonstrating our reluctance to resume life as we knew it before our loss, are we bereaved parents responding to some inner voice? A voice telling us not to go on with life without our child? Are we in fact committing a pseudo-suicide after we have wrestled with and discarded the idea of actually taking our lives? This phenomenon is discussed more fully in the chapter entitled "Whither Thou Goest, I Will Go" (Chapter 8).

As one of our friends said in a sympathy letter, with the death of our adult child we have lost a psychic pillar in our house of life. Trying to rebuild that house is a real challenge; each aspect of that rebuilding involves drudgery. It must begin in a mundane way by setting about to repair and restore the daily routines which keep us alive, the getting up and going to bed, the washing of our clothing and our bodies, shopping for food, preparing and eating regular meals, maintaining our surroundings, and keeping up our human contacts.

Each step of the way, the wounded psyche says "NO!" We must find ways to cajole that psyche into compliance. Reordering priorities, summoning energy and the will to persevere: those are first steps.

The introduction of some sort of regimen into bereaved parents' lives may be a helpful part of our reentry into the world, though we must take care not to overextend ourselves at a time when our energies are at a low point.

Some people volunteer to do charitable work. For my husband and me, it was an advantage to be old enough to be considered senior citizens and thus eligible to audit classes free at the State University near our home. As mentioned before, we took just about everything available on Tuesday and Thursday mornings for several years, each of us having audited nearly forty different courses so far. That routine forced us to get up early on school mornings, to dress neatly, to read our lessons, and to report to class on time. During those hours of classes, we were distracted from our grief, continually reminded that there is a world out there still going on, still worth knowing about. Gaining that knowledge—not so much what is taught in the classes but the knowledge that life goes on—was a necessary part of the rebuilding of our day-to-day lives.

Throughout this chapter, bereaved parents have been introduced to the problems attendant on their reentry into the world immediately after their child's funeral, at the moment when they are faced with the day-to-day chores necessary for life to continue. This reentry is forced upon the parents when all their emotions are new, confusing, and painful. Many of these emotions have to do with the need to process the physical fact of death, of separation from our child.

The first important step of bereaved parents' forays into the world after our child's funeral is recognizing that it is not the same world as it was prior to our child's death. We are dealing not only with our intense sadness, but with a whole universe of changed emotions which we may be unable to encompass so early in our grief.

Because bereaved parents find it hard to accept the fact that life goes on as it did before, we devise subtle methods of prohibiting its progress. This phenomenon may partially explain why we are reluctant to get up in the morning, to dress neatly; why we balk at purchasing and preparing food; why we experience sadness in routine encounters with cultural activities as well as with friends; and why we switch off former pleasures.

Somewhere along the pathway of grief, walking step by painful step, most of us will find our own way to reconstruct our lives in this new and different world. Listening to the assurances of others who have stumbled and groped their way along that pathway, we can hope for some measure of healing for ourselves.

The healing may be so slow as to be imperceptible. Test yourself after some time has gone by: are you still crying at the supermarket? You may be surprised to discover that you are not!

CHAPTER 6

Why?

The first question many parents ask when their children die is "Why?" It rings out in a plaintive wail at a wake or in a bereaved parents' group as the new members sob out their pain. "Why did this happen?" they say over and over.

In a sense, the question is moot because they don't really mean "Why did our child die?" Unless there is a truly mysterious reason, the parents already know the answer to the question of what caused their child's death: their child died of illness, murder, suicide, an accident, a military episode, or somebody's mistake.

What those parents are really asking is not a causational but a philosophical or theological question: why did God/Life/The Fates/The Powers/The Universe let our child die? Bereaved parents spend a lot of time wondering and talking about "Why Questions." And because it is a phenomenon most evident in the very early stages of grief, asking "why?" is hardly ever unaccompanied by tears: wailing, sobbing, moaning tears.

At the same time they are considering the theological or philosophical questions, some bereaved parents also ponder the "Why Didn't I?" questions "Why didn't I realize how sick she was?" "Why didn't I go to the hospital with him?" "Why didn't I forbid him to take that trip?" "Why didn't I call her?" "Why didn't I notice what was happening?" "Why didn't we get a second opinion?" "Why didn't I say something?" "Why did I say what I said?" On and on and on. . . .

Then there is the "Why Me?" question. The "Why Me?" question voices an underlying bargain most people make with life, which goes something like this: "If I play by the rules and take good care of my child; if I love and nurture my child, nothing bad will happen. In view of my having kept my part of the bargain, why did this disaster, the death of my child, the most painful thing in the world for a parent, happen to my child and to me?"

For me, hearing someone answer the "Why Me?" question with another question: "Why NOT me?" was important. As parents, we may have thought we lived a charmed life, that some magic would spare us the tragedies others experience.

Although we now realize our charmed life was a delusion, perhaps the delusion was necessary for us to live without what some people call existential terror as we raised our children. For after becoming parents, loving our children made us extremely vulnerable.

With our child's death, we now know that there was no magic which would save us from the pain and sadness of loss, even if we played by the rules and did everything right. It is a bitter lesson to learn. Because parents whose adult child died have lived longer with the illusion that our lives were charmed if we played by the rules, the awakening is a particularly rude one for us.

The "Why Questions" often take up most of the grieving parents' time and thoughts at first. A recital of their child's virtue, intelligence, beauty, and importance to the world, will find parents wondering why their child died. Why, with all the criminals running loose on the streets, with elderly and infirm patients lying like vegetables in the nursing homes, did their young and promising child die instead? My friend wept bitterly as she kept saying, "Why did my son die? He was so good. He was needed by his children. Why didn't I die instead?"

Voicing the "Why Questions," parents are mired in the earliest phases of grief: shock and denial, guilt and anger. Pushed aside are the really important questions about how to go on after their child's death.

Even though parents did the best they could for their child given what they knew at the time, some dwell exclusively on what might have changed the outcome. This fits in the category of lament called "If Only . . . ," another tiresome and fruitless enterprise which occupies much time after the child's death.

At a certain point, those "Why?" "Why Me?" and "Why Didn't I?" questions have to be settled and put aside. There is no way to change the basic fact that our child is dead. If we keep on with those "Whys," we will be stuck on the road we have to traverse toward some degree of healing.

The truth is if we could answer those questions, we still would not feel any better. Answers to questions do not bring peace and healing. If we cannot figure out the answers, we must realize that it would not help, even if we knew the answers to every one of our "Why Questions." There would still be the emptiness, the pain, the sorrow, knowing our son or daughter is gone forever and we will never see him or her again.

Nevertheless, having said that, I realize that the basic need to know the exact details—factual, not philosophical—of our child's death compels bereaved parents to pursue these nagging questions. We accord an important place to the basic need to know as we seek to resolve, to process our grief. Protecting parents from the cruel facts of their child's death may seem to be a kind thing to do, but such protection gets in the way of healing.

I shielded myself from the truth about my daughter's medical treatment, the mistakes which caused her death, until we went to trial in Boston in a malpractice case; an attitude left over from my earlier denial, perhaps. Each wrenching, excruciating detail of missed opportunities to save her was recited one by one. Believe me, hearing it for the first time in open court was not easier. I completely lost control and began to sob. I had sensed that I needed to know, but I couldn't face it before.

In addition to finding out the factual reasons for our child's death, understanding why the child died, in the deeper philosophical sense, is also a compelling question for some parents. Gaining that understanding must be included then, as another difficult part of our grief work.

Coming to terms with one's philosophy of life, one's religious faith, is not only compelling, it may also be dangerous. Perhaps wrestling with the question will destroy that religious faith. It is a risk bereaved parents feel almost forced to take.

After the death of her daughter, my friend Martha said that she was glad she did not believe in God. She didn't have to contend with the question of why God allowed this to happen or whether God was punishing her for some misdeed, as some of her friends had done in the face of personal tragedy.

I didn't have to concern myself with that question either. To me, existence is a great mystery; it just "is." Events are caused by physical forces and just happen. No vengeful God snatched my daughter away. She died because she had cancer, and two doctors failed to treat her cancer properly until it was too late to save her.

With the above recital, it will be evident to the reader that life seems to me absurd, with no purpose. That conclusion doesn't upset me, though some others have said they could not continue if they felt life had no purpose. Even without purpose, I still feel life has meaning and is infinitely worth living, pain and all. In spite of sadness, remorse, tears and grief, love endures and makes me want to go on; love for my daughter and others who have gone before; love for my surviving children, my daughter-in-law and grandchildren; love for my husband and relatives and friends; for the beautiful earth and its creatures; and for music, art, and human kindness. Love, glorious but tinged with sadness, sustains me without purpose. That may not be enough for some, but it is for me.

This may be too stark a vision for those whose belief in God is strong. If so, they may wish to consult a clergyperson or someone versed in philosophy for help in resolving the doubts which may arise after the death of their child. There are more books offering comfort to the traditionally religious than to those like me, without a conventional religious faith.

One of my cousins told me she couldn't go on with life if she didn't think God had a plan and that the death of a child was part of that plan. "Yes, you could; you could go on," I answered, quite confident of the truth of my answer. A threat to their belief structure may present grieving parents with challenging emotional and spiritual struggles, but they can work them through.

This is most difficult for older parents whose long and comfortable lifestyle had never been subject to a serious assault before their adult child died.

During the question and answer period at a *Compassionate Friends* national workshop on parental grief, I was present when the wife of a minister stood up to make a statement. She was responding to a clergyman's lecture about the comfort offered by religion during bereavement.

She began by speaking about the many times her minister husband had been called to the bedside of a dying child, about how he had read portions of scripture, held the parents' hands, prayed with them and shed tears.

Then his own son died. Suddenly, all the gestures he had made as a minister presiding at the death of a child seemed a charade to him. He was enraged at himself for having responded in a conventional way to his parishioners' grief. He was angry at God. He left the ministry; he left the church. The minister's philosophy, his belief structure, his career; all were totally shattered.

St. John of the Cross called such upheavals "the dark night of the soul."

No matter how difficult, bereaved parents have to face a crisis of meaning if it is presented to them at the time their child dies. All bereaved parents have to make a choice: to go on or not to go on, no matter how or why their child died or what they believe about life and death.

Some of the respondents to my questionnaire have been sustained by their belief in God. Others have said religion has no place in their lives. Each attitude and all shades between the two extremes show up among the respondents.

An anonymous mother wrote, bitterly, "There is no religion; only opinions." "I feel it is all chance, not God's will," says Lydia Eis. Phyllis Crizer believes she must live a good life in order to see her son Dave in Heaven when she dies. Cheryl Gentile is not observant but her belief in God is firmer. Jeane Van Aken, who died soon after answering the questionnaire, found some peace from her religion. Mr. David feels his faith has deepened; he knows he will see his daughter and his late wife when he enters the Eternal Kingdom. Marlene Patrone, who has lost two adult sons, no longer goes to church. Carl and Josie Malitsky have a greater appreciation for their religion than before their daughter's death. Evelyn Guiliani wonders if God has a master plan which might make some sense of this terrible experience.

No matter how their belief system may have changed after their tragedy, the strength of will which allowed these and other parents to decide to go on with life exists in believers and non-believers alike.

The Compassionate Friends, as an organization, wisely recognizes this fact and makes certain that religion seldom enters into their meetings. If it does, it does so as a neutral factor.

An author has more leeway, and sometimes religion plays an important part in books about grief. When it does, it may represent a barrier to healing for the non-religious bereaved. If a paragraph ends with, "I feel I couldn't have gone on without God's help," or "I turned all my grief over to the Lord," then some readers who are non-believers are going to be lost; certainly they are not helped.

As you read the verbatim records of the respondents to my questionnaire, there will be many such responses. That is fine for them, but it does not fit every bereaved person. Atheists and agnostics must not be abandoned in the grief process. According to a recent poll released by "Free Inquiry,"[1] the International Secular Humanist Association magazine, in the summer of 1996, 92.1 percent of Americans describe themselves as believing in some kind of God; from 7.9 to 12 percent say they are either atheists or do not believe in a conventional God. This latter statistic represents a minimum of well over twenty million people. Surely some of them are bereaved parents who also deserve consideration as they cope with their grief.

We Americans respect each individual's right to his or her own belief. We recognize that there is no one way to believe. The mystery is there; interpret it as you will. Being judgmental is not helpful.

Grieving parents, as they wrestle with the "Why?" questions, may really be facing a crisis of meaning, of what makes life worth living,

---

[1] Statistics used by permission of "Free Inquiry."

what values we hold that give us personal satisfaction, what makes us feel that our having lived has had some significance, that our lives count for something, that the major investment of our energies has been worthy.

The major investment parents make can be and often is in the lives of their children. Over the years, parents worked at molding the character, shaping the values of their children as they were growing up, hoping that the children would adopt the parents' values as their values too. How well the parents did these tasks, how deeply committed they were to the lives of their children, are overwhelmingly important because they affect how the parents view themselves, their sense of self-esteem.

In this matter, the grief work for some parents, most of whom lost adult children, is more complicated than for others. These are the parents who suffer from what I call "Disallowed Grief." Their children were suicides, crime victims, were killed while serving in the military or died of AIDS. Because the general public may respond judgmentally to such deaths, the bereaved parents are placed in an awkward position.

I recall having received a phone call from someone I hardly knew, asking me to serve on a committee, shortly after Cathy's death. After I declined, saying my daughter had just died, I noticed a slight hesitancy when my caller asked the cause of Cathy's death. When I told her it was cancer, I sensed her relief. Cancer is a perfectly respectable way to die; the best people are doing it.

The best people are also dying of suicide, murder, and AIDS, but their bereaved parents sometimes feel stigmatized because of the way their child died. They may be shunned or at least receive less sympathy than other bereaved parents simply because the public feels uncomfortable about such deaths.

Those surviving parents may struggle with a feeling of guilt attached specifically to Disallowed Grief. An unreasoning, nagging voice echoes in the parent's lonely, sleepless conjectures: was there something I did or did not do to cause my child to take his or her life, to get involved with dangerous companions, to contract a sexually-transmitted disease? If my child was homosexual, is this wrong? Was it my fault? How can I pretend to be proud that my child died in the service of his or her country when I feel bitter and sad instead?

One of my respondents whose son died of AIDS says, "I regret having to deal with society's rejection regarding his having AIDS. Because of this I am not able to share my feelings openly."

As a result of Disallowed Grief, some parents are forced to reexamine their parenting skills, even their whole lives, in order to find the answers to perplexing questions: What was it in their birth family that formed them, that made them bring up their children as they did? Where did they get their child-rearing ideas, their morals, their values, and their attitude toward the world?

In 1990, Doug DeFord, the son of Beverly and Mike DeFord, was found shot to death in a remote area of rural Indiana called Wildcat Creek. Although Doug's parents believe his death was murder, the authorities ruled it a suicide. The case has all the overtones of a criminal coverup because it was preceded by labor troubles in which Doug was involved as manager of a store. Doug was killed by the gun which he had inherited from his war-hero grandfather.

Doug's death forced his mother's deep probing of her past in order to secure the preliminary knowledge some of us need in order to come to terms with the death of our child. This probing, for Beverly, is vitally connected to the shadow of violence which colored her childhood. Her letters sometimes arrive with clippings of letters she has written to the newspapers urging an end to violence.

Beverly's father was a twice-wounded, highly decorated veteran of World War II. He was so traumatized by his wartime experiences that the family felt a day-to-day connection to those experiences all through Beverly's childhood. As in so many cases of terrors unspoken, the shroud of terror hung over them all the time, even at every meal. Beverly writes:

> About my dad, Virgil Thomas Campbell. I don't know what all the medals he received were. I saw them when I was small. But I wanted to shut out all the war stories in those days and just be a child. I grew up in a very depressing household and had to be the cheerleader, so to speak. I didn't realize at the time that I was a one-person support group for an emotionally damaged soldier.
>
> Dad kept his medals in an old ammunition box. If anyone came and wanted to talk about that stuff, Dad would get the box out. I'm going out there soon and look at the medals if Mom will show me. She's so moody, I never know how she's going to react.
>
> My Dad was a sergeant and was in the Battle of the Bulge. He captured a large troop of Germans singlehandedly. He was wounded once in Germany and once in France; his back was still full of shrapnel when he had triple bypass heart surgery in 1980. The doctors talked a lot about it when they looked at the X-rays.
>
> He suffered from depression. I think he felt he had killed someone he shouldn't have killed. While he was in the service overseas he thought he would never see home again, so when he got home he never left. He was there! We lived in the most remote 200 acre farm in the county and we didn't go anywhere, just to relatives and to

town once a week. Dad would get very upset when a car drove up our two-mile driveway.

When I was a kid, we had to be careful at mealtime about the way we turned our knives and forks. If the glare on our silverware caught Dad's eyes, he would have to turn his head away from the table and cover his eyes with his hands.

He got better by the time I was fifteen years old. The government took away our land to construct an artificial lake; paid us very little for it, and the folks were angry. But it turned out to be good for them. They had to move to a place closer to civilization. Dad began driving a school bus. Being with the kids helped to heal him. But even after many years, he couldn't face the idea of letting our German exchange student visit. About four hours before Mike and I were to leave for dinner at the folks' house, my mother phoned. 'Your Dad says not to bring the German boy out here.' I was surprised that Dad couldn't be with a German after all those years. I often wondered what terrible things were part of Dad's past.

Perhaps it was because Beverly DeFord's son Doug was killed by a gunshot wound from his grandfather's weapon that she was impelled to delve so deeply into her childhood. His death was linked to the violence of war which entered her family even before her birth. Doug's murder forced her to come to terms with all the suppressed terrors she inherited from her father.

Another facet of Disallowed Grief which younger parents do not have to deal with is ageism, which is discrimination against the elderly merely because they are old. Perhaps because youth is glorified in our culture, it naturally follows that the old are relegated to an inferior status. A form of denial not dissimilar to the general public's fear of bereaved parents, it implies that if we do not think or hear about old age or the death of a child, it won't happen to us.

Because ageism is prevalent throughout society, it is no surprise to find it in bereaved parents' support groups. For the parent whose adult child died, the most unfortunate aspect of ageism is a tendency among other bereaved parents to discount or devalue the intensity of the older parent's grief. The implication is that we elderly parents should be grateful for what we had, not grieving for what has been taken away. Aren't we almost greedy to have wished that we be given more time with our child after having had a rich, full experience with him or her as an adult? Our child was able to make choices, have an independent career, and perhaps even a family. We shared long years of joy with our child. Why then are we grieving? What more do we want? We had everything; their young child never had a chance to live a full life. They had nothing but a promise.

Sometimes my husband and I exchange knowing glances when bereaved parents speak disparagingly about the aged grandparents of their dead children. Not realizing that we are even older than the grandparents in question, the young parents imply that their pain cannot be understood by their own seventy- or eighty-year-old parents. Why did the grandparents survive in their decrepitude and senility when that darling little grandchild died? They do not suspect the truth: the decrepit, senile grandparents are bewailing that fact, too. Survivors' guilt, the "I should have died instead" syndrome, is played out with added intensity by those whose lives were already long, including the parents.

There are two important misconceptions here. The first is the matter of gratitude. All parents are grateful for having had their children, no matter how long they lived. Our lives were immeasurably enriched by our children. Because they had reached a point in their lives where they related to us on an adult level means that perhaps we elders are even more bereft than young parents. As one respondent to my questionnaire said, "I had my son for thirty-two whole years. Thirty-two years to love. Thirty-two years to do things together, to respect and appreciate."

We have been talking about Disallowed Grief, largely peculiar to bereaved parents who were very old or whose adult children have died from some cause which makes the general public uncomfortable, thereby complicating the grief work the parents must do. Disallowed Grief emphasizes the parents' probable diminished sense of self-esteem, which is shared to some extent by many other people whose children have died of illness or accidents—deaths which the public views with some neutrality and without judgment.

A further probing of this loss of self-esteem, this loss of the thing in which we invested our all, may bring us to a consideration of the lives of others who have invested, not in their children, but in something else of overwhelming importance in their lives.

As a woman who once aspired to a career on the stage as an opera singer, I have followed intently the careers of the famous sopranos who attained that goal. In particular I have been captivated by perhaps the most glorious and controversial of them all: Maria Callas. Her voice, her acting ability, her interpretation of the music, earned her a place as perhaps the greatest singer of the twentieth century. No matter how many times I hear her recordings, they never fail to reduce me to tears by their sheer emotional impact.

I remember having seen a framed photograph on the wall of a Venetian apartment we once rented: Callas in a long, flowing white gown, walking across San Marco Square. Her stride had been interrupted by one of her fans, a young man who knelt at her feet to kiss the hem of her dress. She was looking down at her admirer with a startled expression, her arms slightly outstretched. Yes, she was a goddess to him and in some respects to me.

Maria Callas was born in the United States to Greek immigrant parents in 1923. Her mother took Maria back to Greece when she was in her early teens and enrolled her in an intensive program to study singing. Music was an obsession with Maria. Nothing else had any meaning for her, and her hard work paid off when she became a famous star of the opera stage at an early age.

I remember hearing her and agreeing with the critics that, although her voice was transcendently lovely, it was flawed. Her high notes were uncertain, even unattractive. She tried to overcome the flaws by force, which further strained and damaged her voice.

All the while, even though they were aware of her problems, her fans flocked to her performances. She tried to cure the faults by training and practice, but it was to no avail. Her singing got worse and worse. She began taking off long periods from concertizing.

Friends who visited her noticed that she had let her fingernails grow long. That meant she was no longer playing the piano and thus no longer spending much time practicing. She got depressed. Her great and good friend, Aristotle Onassis, left her to marry Jackie Kennedy, the widow of John F. Kennedy.

Her voice, that magic voice, was the only thing that had meaning in her life, and now it was nearly gone. She knew better than anyone else that there was no hope of repairing and retrieving that voice.

Although a heart attack was announced as the reason for her death at the age of fifty-three, friends wondered if it was in fact suicide. Meaning, the very reason for her being, had departed from her life with the loss of her ability to sing. Maria Callas could not go on.

The tragic life of Maria Callas, her inability to continue life without its most essential element, may help us understand the devastation a parent feels in the loss of a child. A consideration of some others whose lives have been seriously damaged will give us another perspective from which to view the loss of value and meaning for bereaved parents of an adult child.

The January 16, 1996, issue of the International Edition of *USA/Today* carried a story about the difficulties of Bosnian War refugees, some of whom are now resettled in Atlanta, Georgia. The International Rescue Committee's Marge Flaherty says, "These people had good lifestyles, and when you have something and lose it, it can be more difficult. Starting over can seem insurmountable." Many have lost family members killed or missing. Their homes were destroyed. Those in ethnically mixed marriages can never go back to Bosnia again. Women who were raped during the war found the humiliation too great to bear and many have committed suicide. Some refugees, says a fellow Bosnian, are frozen in despair. If they lose everything, they don't believe in a future.

If parents lose an adult child, they are in a situation comparable to that of a Maria Callas or those refugees who lost the element that gave significance to their lives.

Some people find meaning by devoting their energies to an ideal: a political or religious movement, educational and societal reform, or elimination of poverty and crime. For many parents, their children's lives are the ideal to which they gave their predominant, if not complete, devotion.

Some ideals fail. Their devotees are psychically wounded; they become cynical or apathetic, concluding that they had been deluded in their attachment to that ideal.

Bereaved parents are much more tragically wounded by the deaths of their adult children than those who have lost an ideal. They too, may be disappointed in life, having lost a sense of meaning and purpose. Because they may feel they are too old to start over, to reinvest, the parents' grand project, their life work, has died with their children. The sense of sadness and defeat, the loss of meaning, is similar to the loss of faith in a great ideal.

One big difference exists, however, between the loss of a child and the loss of an ideal. Parents will never chastise themselves for having invested so much love, time, and effort in their child who died. If asked whether they would still want to have had that child, knowing the loss they would suffer, they would surely answer in the affirmative.

To miss all the experiences the parents shared with the deceased, from babyhood and early childhood, through adolescence to maturity, would be to miss what gave meaning to their lives.

With others who have faced a crisis of meaning in their lives, bereaved parents have the same temptation to opt for bitterness and suicide. Can we reinvest in life after the death of our child? Can we transcend our grief to forge new meaning in the years we have left?

Those who have earlier walked the road we are on have assured us that we can. They have given us no clear prescriptions, only sketchy guidelines and slogans to cheer us on: "Hang in there;" "You'll feel better;" "Don't give up;" "Lean on others if you need to."

The two co-leaders of our local *Compassionate Friends* chapter, Vicki Crozier and Margaret Syrett, tell us at the beginning of each meeting that we can get better. "You may not believe us," they say, "But look at us. We're proof. We are no longer grieving, but you should have seen us in the beginning. We were both basket cases. You can't imagine how bad! If anybody like us can get better, so can you!"

But they have also told us, very definitely, that it is not going to be easy.

CHAPTER 7

Theme and Variations

As we journey through life, from childhood to adulthood, we pick up attitudes and assumptions which allow us to function smoothly in our day-to-day activities. Most of these assumptions, though they may be largely unexamined, serve us well. Some attitudes, tucked away below the level of our awareness, never surface. But they are there, all the same, and they can cause havoc when a crisis occurs in our lives.

Psychologists tell us we have an unconscious, defined as representing the "greater part of the psychic apparatus accumulated through life experience that is not ordinarily integrated with or available to conscious behavior." Coupled with that, sometimes overlapping and considered by some experts to be the same thing, is the subconscious. The subconscious is defined as "mental activity just below the level of consciousness. It affects thought, feeling, and behavior without entering awareness. It exists in the mind but is not immediately available to consciousness."

One of the foundations on which many of us built our lives are these subconscious/unconscious assumptions: parents are responsible for a child's health and safety. If something bad happens to a child, it is the parents' fault. If anyone dies, it is supposed to be the parent, not the child. These assumptions are still operating when our child dies and suddenly present a threat to our sense of self-worth, to our very reason for being. For we have failed in our most basic duty. Therefore, we are unworthy.

If something so unreasonable can be called reasoning, this is the theme: my child died; therefore, I am a bad parent because I failed in my primary obligation to my child. My unconscious tells me that it is my duty to keep my child alive. Everyone may say I had nothing to do with my child's illness or accident or murder or suicide, but I know it is my fault. I did not prevent my child's death. Therefore I am a terrible parent, a worthless person.

It is easy to understand why the parents of young children who died might feel this way, even though it is equally irrational. Those parents have had complete custody of the child and responsibility for his or her care.

However, by the time the child has grown to adulthood, the parent has supposedly relinquished this responsibility in almost every aspect of that child's life. Yet there is a subtle sense in which parents never relinquish responsibility for our children, no matter how old they get or how old we get.

When our adult children predecease us, that feeling of responsibility presents itself afresh. No matter how many years have gone by since they were in our care, we are still operating under the old assumption that our duty as parents is to protect them from harm. Feeling that we have failed as parents if our child died creates a barrier to our healing and must be dealt with. That barrier has a name: guilt.

Society has a way of reinforcing our subconscious feelings about parental guilt. When a person dies prematurely, we naturally wonder whether trouble could have been foreseen and prevented. With hindsight, all situations which caused a death look dangerous, even though they did not appear so earlier on. The parents, intent on reconstructing the details leading up to the child's death, now lapse into a series of futile conjectures, usually beginning with questions like "What should we have done that we didn't do?"

When a bereaved parent begins to sort out the reasons for the death, this new, focused, surface guilt mentioned in the above paragraph is added to the unfocused "existential guilt" lurking in the subconscious.

There are many variations on the guilt theme. Some bereaved parents are reluctant to speak of their guilt feelings because such thoughts and feelings seem bizarre. That is a grief response which may make bereaved parents think they are going crazy and is the reason the subject is voiced only in the privacy of a self-help group or with a counselor.

Examples: One of my respondents who prefers to remain anonymous said, "If I had married someone who had better genes, then my son wouldn't have contracted cancer and died. I love my husband, but I knew when we married that disease runs in his family. He has genes with that disease and passed them on to our child. Yet now I know I should never have married him if it meant our child would die. I know it sounds stupid, but I really feel guilty about it."

Another: "My husband and I were having difficult domestic problems and then we got a divorce and that may have caused our son to get sick. At any rate, I feel I might have paid more attention to the early symptoms and maybe consulted the doctor earlier. It's my fault that he died."

My own ruminations included thoughts such as this: "If I hadn't been such a worrier as a mother, my daughter would not have concealed from me the appearance of a lump in her breast. Then I would have suggested that she see another doctor and she would still be alive." (Never mind that I too, would probably have listened to the two doctors who misdiagnosed her cancer. After all, they were the experts, not I.) "If we had lived closer to her, seeing her more often, I would have noticed that she was sick before it was too late. We looked at houses in Boston and Albany but chose the latter because our daughter who lives in Albany is a single parent. We thought she might need us to help care for our grandchild. We didn't realize Cathy was going to get sick and need us even more. We should have moved to Boston instead of Albany."

Another mother: "They called to say my son was sick and in the hospital. It was snowing so hard the roads were closed and we couldn't get through to the hospital. So we waited until the next morning to go. If we had gone that night, right after they called us, maybe we would have realized how sick he was and done something about it. If I had been there, I would have been watching him; I would have known. They thought he had the flu. They didn't pay any attention to him and just let him die. I feel so guilty that I wasn't there when he died."

Another friend: "My son had a congenital heart condition. When he was a little kid, I took him to the doctor regularly. But when he grew up, he didn't want to keep on checking with the doctor. He was supposed to; he knew he was supposed to. And he was a grown man, so it was his obligation, I thought. But I should have insisted that he see the doctor and I didn't. Now he is dead and it's my fault."

A father: "Our son got in with some undesirable friends and got shot. Why didn't we intervene before it was too late? I was supposed to be taking care of him and I didn't do it."

A mother: "No matter what you say, I feel guilty that my daughter committed suicide. I was her mother and supposed to take care of her and she took her own life. I must have raised her wrong. I failed."

Another respondent: "My son got in trouble with the law for drinking and driving. He was stressed because he had family problems and had lost his job. When he was growing up, I worked hard and spent a lot of quality time with both my children and made certain they went to church and had good values. I did the best I could, raising him without a father after my divorce, but I failed."

One of my friends says: "If we hadn't been living here, there would have been no accident. If I hadn't married my husband we wouldn't be living here. I shouldn't have married him."

The guilt responses above do not deal with the instances where parents were at fault and actually caused the death of their children: a father who accidentally shot his son in a hunting accident and then killed himself in despair, for example.

I know parents who caused their children's death. Their burden of true guilt is quite reasonable and nearly unbearable. This type of guilt is not considered in this chapter, which deals with unreasonable, irrational guilt.

The first approach toward changing or at least softening the feelings of unreasonable guilt is to examine the theme: If you are a good parent, your child will not die. If your child dies, for whatever reason, you are not a good parent.

Looking at it in such simple terms shows immediately how irrational the theme really is. As parents, we have limited but not absolute control over what happens to our children. Parents are human beings who make mistakes, but they usually do the best they can on the basis of what they know and understand at the moment of any given decision. For their ignorance, for their mistakes, they must forgive themselves because those mistakes were made in good faith. They must not allow that basic and simplistic theme to control their thinking.

Bringing unreasoning guilt out into the open, admitting and examining it, may be the first step toward removal of a barrier to healing. If parents spend their grief time (in other words, all the time) chastising themselves for causing their child to die because they are worthless, stupid, wicked parents, who ought to have died instead of their child, then they are stalled in a bad place.

Let us admit that we have little control over what happens after we have done the best we can to protect our children from harm.

In making this admission, we can supplement that guilt theme with a positive variation: I did the best I knew how as a parent but my child died in spite of that. Life is not fair. I have to learn to live with that fact. Now I must find a way to go on without my child.

The void in our lives is the hardest to deal with, not whose fault the death is, what a failure we are as parents, or what actions would have been necessary to change the outcome. After the remorse, self-chastisement, anger and guilt, and all the attendant sadness, we come to the fourth phase of our grief: the realization that our child is dead and we cannot change that fact.

In this phase of grief, all comforting illusions are gone. Arriving at that place in our grief does not mean that the other three phases are finished. There will be times when disbelief, denial, anger, guilt, and all the accumulated sadness will take first place in our thoughts and feelings. But when we have periods of realization that our child is dead and we can't change that, then we can begin to fashion a way to live day after day with the absence of our child.

Even after reaching that point, there will still be tears, but the parent will not be stuck in a "Why me?" or "If Only . . ." or "I can't believe she's dead" place. At least those periods won't last as long when they do recur.

Much unpleasant, drudgery-type work has to be done in restoring physical and mental health, in restructuring daily living, revising our philosophy to fit the facts of our new knowledge, and mending relationships with other loved ones. Getting beyond the earlier stages of grief is necessary in order to do that work.

I'm there right now, many years after the death of my daughter. Things are better, but I sometimes slip back into a worse place. I expect it, but I know it will not last as long as it did before.

How many of us have healed to a certain extent and still have not dealt with that existential guilt? Is it still rattling around in our subconscious, gnawing at our self-esteem? How do we exorcise it? Is it too seemingly ridiculous to talk about, thus forcing us to keep it under wraps and unrecognized as a deterrent to further healing?

I have heard a mother say, "You know, I feel so guilty because I couldn't prevent my child's death. I know I shouldn't feel that way, but I do."

That mother has broken the first rule: no matter what her feelings are, she must accept them. The parent may be ashamed of having such feelings. But irrational feelings have a destructive force which must be reckoned with, and the longer they are kept repressed, the more destructive they can be.

Is there, as a hidden part of existential guilt, yet another variation on that theme which many people carry throughout their lives? Not fashionable these days, there exists nevertheless the idea of sin, which used to get more attention.

I am not speaking of original sin, or the Seven Deadly Sins, theological concepts not applicable here. The kind of sin I am talking about is an aspect of guilt connected more closely to magic thinking, superstition or old-time religion.

The Bible refers to sins of the fathers visited upon the sons to the seventh generation. That idea is very old indeed. Primitive, a relic of prehistoric magic, it was already well established in ancient Greece during the Bronze Age. We know of it through our study of the Greek myths.

Those of you who are familiar with the classics will immediately think of the House of Atreus with its line of descendants tainted by the sin of murder: blood guilt. Guilt from murder poisoned the lives of this family through many subsequent generations.

Dr. Blanche Brown, my professor of Classics at New York University, who knew everything there was to know about the ancient Greeks, used to begin a response to a student's question about a Greek myth with a deep breath and a sigh. "I hesitate to start," she would say, "Because one Greek myth leads into another and there is no graceful place to stop."

Nevertheless, this never deterred her from embarking on an explanation, and it will not stop me.

If you go to Greece, you can visit the ruins of the ancient city of Mycenae on the Peloponnesus, as my husband and I have done several times, once with our son, who raced out the city gate while we photographed him reenacting the flight of Orestes after the murder of his mother, Clytemnestra.

Mycenae is the locale where Atreus was king, some thirty-three centuries ago, in the Bronze Age, the age of the Greek myths. Atreus was the son of Pelops and therefore suffered from a curse which had been laid on his father.

Atreus brought an even greater curse on himself and his sons, Agamemnon and Menelaus.

Atreus' brother, Thyestes, seduced Atreus' wife. Atreus, infuriated, murdered three of the four sons of Thyestes, then cooked and served them to their father at a feast. Thyestes thereupon laid a curse on the house of Atreus.

Atreus himself was later killed by Aegistheus, the one son of Thyestes to escape being served up in the stew after the earlier murders. One catastrophe after another befell the descendants of the House of Atreus.

Menelaus, Atreus' son, was the King of Sparta. His wife, Helen, was stolen by Paris, a Trojan prince. Her kidnapping started the Trojan War: the famous Helen, whose face launched a thousand ships. History blends almost undiscernibly with legend, but scholars agree that the Trojan War was indeed, a historic event which probably took place between twelve and thirteen centuries before the Christian Era.

If this is one story about the origin of the idea that sin is the cause of misfortune, that idea itself has lived on for a very long time indeed. The conviction that misfortune is caused by sin was still very much alive in my small home town when I was a child in the 1920s.

A nice, respectable young couple, friends of my parents, gave birth to a beautiful baby girl. It soon became apparent that the child could neither hear nor speak.

Some of the townspeople began to speculate. What, they wondered, had that couple done to cause this terrible affliction? Surely it must have been retribution from an angry God for some hidden sin they had committed. Or wait! Maybe it was one of their parents or grandparents who had committed a terrible sin!

Everyone knew their parents and grandparents, of course, knew everything about them. But there appeared to be no reason why this had happened. Nevertheless, it was common knowledge that God punishes people across the generations when they do something sinful. If no one could discover the hateful act, it must have been secret sin.

Somebody in town pointed out that the mother had had all her teeth extracted during her pregnancy. He ventured the opinion that maybe the anesthetic had a deleterious effect, but that was generally discounted as the cause of the baby's impairment. No, it must have been sin.

If it had happened today, very few people would have suggested that the affliction was caused by sin. I don't think that kind of reasoning is prevalent any more. But like all outmoded ideas, old wives' tales and folk wisdom, they may linger in the subconscious.

When my daughter died in 1987, didn't I, the highly educated, relatively unillusioned, and sophisticated individual who prides herself on her rationality, entertain a few fleeting thoughts: "What terrible thing did I do for which this is punishment?"

I don't believe in this for a minute. But there it is, another variation on the theme of guilt, lurking in my idle thoughts, in my subconscious, waiting to be dealt with.

CHAPTER 8

Whither Thou Goest, I Will Go

From time to time a small news item will record a pathetic story, such as the one which appeared in my local paper early in July 1995. It told of a Florida woman whose only child, a fifteen-year-old girl, was killed in an auto accident. The distraught mother applied for permission to purchase a gun, waited the necessary three days to buy it, then shot and killed herself.

Those who lose a child experience such extreme anguish that suicide is a real possibility for them. In fact, it is so common to consider suicide that most of those who answered my questionnaire admitted they had thought of it as an option.

Recently our newspaper reported a discussion about laws to make doctor-assisted suicide legal for terminally ill patients. Proposals for these laws were prompted by the activities in Michigan of Dr. Jack Kevorkian, the so-called suicide doctor. One exception proposed in the legislation caught my eye: bereaved parents would not be allowed permission under the law to get help committing suicide. The phenomenon of bereaved parent suicide appears to be generally acknowledged, even by legislators.

Sometimes we talk openly about suicide at our bereaved parents' support group. One woman carried the premise to its logical and ridiculous conclusion. "I thought about it a lot," she said. "I realized if I committed suicide, then my parents and my husband would be devastated. I don't want to inflict further pain on anyone, so I would have to kill them, too. Then the relatives closest to them would in turn be devastated. In order to spare those people any further grief, I would also have to kill them. How can I possibly kill all those people?"

We laughed nervously at the sick humor but it got the word "suicide" out into the open for discussion. And the urge to commit suicide must be defused if possible, for it is not an acceptable solution.

I know that consideration of suicide is not unique to parents whose adult children die. Yet there are subtle differences which bear on whether or not those parents will actually carry it out.

The most obvious difference lies in the family situation. Although some single parents lose an only child and some couples lose an only child, a young child who dies is more apt to have surviving siblings who demand the parents' day-to-day care. Obligations to other loved ones, in such cases, function strongly to overrule the parents' urge to end it all.

Adult children who die, who did not live at home and were not as completely dependent on their parents as are young children, or who may even have established their own homes and families, are quite another matter. Independent adults who die do not present their grieving parents with the same deterrent to suicide as the young child.

Another difference lies in the length of time during which the older parents have associated with their child who died. They can look back on the task of raising a child to adulthood, something the parents of a young child have not as yet experienced. The investments in that older child's training, education, and character have been tremendous. The sense of victory when our adult offspring become good citizens, good friends, mature human beings, is a source of joy and accomplishment which gives older parents a certain serenity. It is as though we have reached the pinnacle of our existence.

It was enjoyable for my husband and me to exchange thoughts and ideas with Cathy, to share holidays and vacations, and to have frequent family reunions. Her friends were our friends and vice versa. Our tastes in art, music, movies, and literature were similar. She would phone if there was a good book she wanted me to read. She once called me long distance, saying there was something on Public Radio she wanted me to listen to. "Mom, they are doing an analysis of Rachmaninoff's Third Piano Concerto. I know it's one of your favorites. Turn on the radio right away!" Then there would be a request for a recipe or she would ask for a menu suggestion for a party she was planning. If she needed advice, she phoned and talked over her problems with us. We were friends and enjoyed being together. The days of fractious childhood and adolescent conflicts were long past, even forgotten.

Over the years Cathy had become a mature woman, rich in wisdom and compassion, concerned for her parents, just as we had been for her in the earlier days. She was worried about our safety when we traveled to the Soviet Union; after her death, several of her friends confided that she had expressed her concern for us while we were on that trip. She wondered whether we were using too much salt in our meals.

Having earned a Masters Degree in Counseling at the University of Massachusetts, she picked up some clues when something was amiss at home. She consulted with her siblings and made suggestions for solving a personal crisis that erupted between her parents.

And when she lay dying, she tried to protect us, first from the knowledge that she would die and then from the physical and emotional strain. Her father and I were with her when the diagnosis of cancer was announced. As we each held one of her hands, we felt a kind of electric shock from her body when she heard the bad news. A moment of silence and then she spoke. "Oh, Mom and Dad, I'm so sorry for you." Then a pause and she spoke again. "Well, better me than Laurel." (Laurel, her sister, had a six-year-old son.)

The last night of her life, she insisted on hiring a private nurse because she said, "It's getting too hard on you, Mom." The nurse was hired for two nights, but her services were needed for only one. Cathy died at 6:35 the next morning, her parents, sister, and brother keeping a vigil beside her through the night.

One of my correspondents from Pennsylvania, Frances Phillips, a woman whose two sons were killed by a drag racer, said something all parents who have lost adult children must feel: "Just when you think you have them raised and everything is OK, then pow, they are dead!"

Is it any wonder, then, with such an overwhelming loss, at such a late date in their lives, that bereaved parents might seek a quick end to their sorrow? Their situation is unlike members of the general public who commit suicide, who for the most part are considered mentally disturbed.

However, bereaved parents' thoughts of suicide have an added, hidden, and mysterious component outside and beyond the classification of mental illness and despair. And it is as difficult to comprehend as it is to explain.

In Chapter I of the Book of Ruth, the Bible tells of the love and loyalty Ruth feels toward her mother-in-law, Naomi, who is about to leave for her native land after the death of her two sons. "Entreat me not to leave thee," says Ruth, "Or to return from following after thee; for whither thou goest, I will go."

Ruth's love for her mother-in-law transcended all the physical and emotional difficulties which loomed as probable results if she abandoned her native land. Yet because of that love, she left her homeland, its security and its familiarity, to follow Naomi to an alien place and a future fraught with uncertainty and danger.

In a way, this story has relevance to my condition as a bereaved parent. It has taken me a long time to understand this peculiar aspect of my love for and attachment to my dead child. I once thought it applied only to me, but I now know that many other bereaved parents have had to wrestle with the same response after their children died.

It is a phase of my grief which is now over, a part of phase three, the acute stage, the most painful and dangerous stage of grief, the time when suicide is most likely to occur. As I look back on it now, it seems appropriate to call it the "zombie stage."

My dictionary, in two of its definitions of the word, says a zombie is (1) a person resembling the walking dead or (2) a person markedly strange or abnormal in mentality, appearance, or behavior.

During my zombie stage, I had a desperate, overpowering need to be with my daughter, wherever she was. I wanted to lie down beside her grave, go to sleep and never wake up. I didn't want anything or anybody else but my daughter. I had no clear conception of what that meant, where I had to go, or how I could get there. But if it meant being dead, so be it.

This feeling, conscious or unconscious, is what underlies so many social, physical, and emotional changes which befall bereaved parents after their child's death. Because it runs so completely counter to all we know about the natural human instinct to stay alive, it makes bereaved parents feel they are going mad.

Just as wild animals are seen in nature films watching over, standing beside, and protecting the bodies of their dead babies in the face of danger to themselves, bereaved parents must wrestle with this primitive biological urge to cling to their dead children. They become zombies, members of the walking dead, disconnected from the world, turning away from routine activities. They are indifferent to their surroundings, to their surviving loved ones, and to their own health. They cling to the dead child's belongings: the underwear which smells of perspiration; the shoes with slightly rundown heels; the comb with the child's hairs in its teeth; the smudged eyeglasses found in a bedside drawer; anything which reminds them of the physical presence of that beloved person, now dead.

With this urge, this strange disconnection from life, there comes a siren voice which keeps sounding in our ears: stop functioning as you used to; don't cook; don't eat; don't socialize with your friends; go to your child; go with your child, wherever he or she is. The magnetic call to the gravesite and the shutting out of all other human contacts are dangerous indications that the bereaved parent may resort to suicide.

My friend whose son died in an auto accident said, "Oh, Jeanne, if there had been a gun in the house, I would have used it to end my life. I wanted so badly to be with him." You will notice she did not say she wanted to be relieved of her agony. She said she wanted to be with her son.

The important thing for bereaved parents and their caregivers to understand, I think, is that the parent is not only anxious to end the pain of his or her loss; the urge to be with the child is just as great as, perhaps even greater than, the need to end the pain.

One of my respondents, Carol Marshall, lost her son on August 16, 1990, when he was killed in a car accident. Carol says:

> Our marriage has suffered because of our son's death. I always wonder how a child you both loved so much can tear you apart. Other people think you should become closer, but that doesn't happen. The pain and grief are so great that you are each dealing in your own way and in your own little world.
>
> I didn't want anyone else in my world except my son and me. Not even my two daughters; I still don't understand that part of my grief. My husband wanted the girls included in everything we did, but I wasn't ready to let anyone into my world of grief: not my daughters or anyone in the family. I wanted to be left alone. I did just what my feelings said, even if it hurt others in my family.
>
> My husband always hit things head on, but not me. Of course we were both new at this. Losing a child is not something you know about; how you will react takes you totally by surprise. Sometimes you think, "Is this really me or someone else in my body?"
>
> My husband was always there to take care of me and I expected too much of him when our son died. He couldn't take care of himself and me, too. It took me a long time to realize this.
>
> It has been three and a half years without our son. We have both changed and our life will never be the way it was before. So we have to start a new life, a life with a part of us missing. But we have to go on with what we have left: two wonderful daughters, a grandson, and each other.
>
> I experienced all of the problems mentioned on the questionnaire except overeating. I lost thirty pounds in three weeks and had to have my gall bladder removed. They could have taken everything out of me; I didn't care. It would help us bereaved parents just to know we are normal with these feelings.

When I read what Carol Marshall experienced, I empathized with what she was saying. On February 22, 1992, I had surgery for the removal of a large growth the size of a lemon. When the surgeon phoned to report that it was malignant, I hardly reacted. I asked him to tell me about the disease, something rare called Merkel Cell Cancer. He said he had never heard of it before and had to look it up before he called me. Less than 500 cases had been reported at that time. I asked what the life expectancy was (about 8 years) and where I could find out more about it. But I didn't cry or carry on.

Maybe that surgeon thought I was brave, but in reality I just didn't care; it didn't matter much if I lived or died, because if I died, I would be with Cathy. That was what I really wanted.

It matters to me now, however; in the intervening time I have decided I want to live. No, not decided; rather, the feeling that I want to live has come back to me. That is the important message of this chapter. You stop being a zombie after awhile.

While I was in that "I don't care," zombie stage, I had to deal with many tasks. My husband and I had to clear out Cathy's apartment in Boston and move the contents to our garage in Albany before the end of the month of her death. Our cousin, Edward Parish, flew up from Atlanta to drive and load the rental truck. Our daughter Laurel went with us. A dozen of Cathy's friends congregated at her apartment in Boston and did all the work. Mother and Dad stood around in a daze most of the time, giving some token or other: a dish, a book, an article of clothing to a friend. We followed directions given by the others. An unreal time. Totally unreal. Its unreality and the loving concern of Cathy's friends made it bearable.

It took several months before I could launder the last garment Cathy wore before her hospitalization. How I wept as I washed away all traces of perspiration! When the counselor I was seeing at the time couldn't understand, raising his eyebrows with that "Do-you-realize-what-a crazy-thing-you-just-said?" look, I knew I had to quit seeing him. He was reinforcing my feeling that I was losing my mind. Even though I was in bad shape and hardly able to reason, at least I had enough sense to realize that counselor was not helping me.

While we parents are hanging on so desperately to our dead child, withdrawing from life, wrestling with this irrational need to join the child, we are alienating our closest loved ones. Our spouses and friends worry that we will kill ourselves; our surviving children get the idea that the child who died was our favorite and that they, the ones who are left, are not as important to us as the dead child was. "Doesn't it mean anything that you have two other kids, Mom?" Or similar hurtful thoughts.

Yet as we progress through our grief journey, we can conclude, with Carol Marshall, that we have to start a new life, a life with part of us missing. We can't afford to turn away from life; we have too much to lose that is precious to us. We have to learn how to go on with what we have left. And I, too, have reasons to go on living: a wonderful husband, two wonderful children, a wonderful daughter-in-law, wonderful grandchildren, wonderful friends, and relatives. I realize now that they are indeed wonderful and precious to me. And if I have overused the word wonderful, it is because the concept is something I have relearned, a renewed sense of wonder, after my zombie days. Yes, in spite of all the grief and pain, there is still something worth living for.

As bereaved parents, we reach a point when we no longer have to listen to that destructive voice telling us to leave the land of the living. We can and we will stop being zombies.

We will no longer feel compelled to say, "Whither thou goest, I will go."

CHAPTER 9

On the Road to Damascus

One of the most dramatic of all the biblical stories painted and repainted by artists over the centuries is called, "On the Road to Damascus." Taken from an episode in the New Testament, the painting is usually characterized by great contrasts: a brilliant flash of light against a brooding dark sky.

The scene illustrates the conversion of Saint Paul, who began life as Saul, an energetic persecutor of Christians shortly after the crucifixion. A great zealot, a fierce fighter against the new religion, Saul concentrated his efforts on apprehending the followers of Jesus and bringing them to justice.

At a certain time, the Bible tells us Saul presented himself to the high priests, requesting letters permitting him to seek out Jesus' followers in Damascus. He was anxious to arrest them and bring them, bound, to Jerusalem for trial.

After receiving authorization to carry out his mission, Saul set out on the road to Damascus. At some point along the way, he was thrown from his horse by an overwhelming force. This force, whether an earthquake or violent storm, was accompanied by a brilliant light and a vision of Jesus. Some paintings show Saul cast to the ground, his arms upstretched in fear.

With the vision came a voice saying, "Saul, Saul, why do you persecute me?" Saul, trembling in fear, asked who was speaking to him and what was required of him. The voice told him to stop fighting against Jesus' followers and join them instead.

After the vision disappeared, Saul discovered that he was blind. This temporary blindness which ensued during the vision made Saul dependent on the people who were journeying with him. They had to lead him into the city to the home of a man named Ananais, where Saul's sight was restored. Saul's name was changed to Paul and henceforth he became a Christian.

Converting to Christianity was an experience in which Saint Paul's life was completely turned around. Before this dramatic event, he had been violently opposed to the followers of Jesus. After the vision on the road to Damascus he became an influential and important advocate of Christian teachings. Scholars agree that he was the one individual most significant in keeping the Christian faith alive. St. Paul spent the rest of his life preaching, writing letters, and carrying the faith throughout the known world, ultimately dying for his beliefs.

Although few among us are saints, bereaved parents can find a metaphor here without a reference to religious or doctrinal implications. They can easily see a parallel to St. Paul's experience and their own. At the moment their children died, the lives of the newly bereaved parents turned completely upside down, never to be the same again. This is universally true for all parents who lose a child, not just for parents of adult children who die. Those in the latter category must contend with a host of changes just as great as those experienced by younger parents who lose a child, though different.

These changes, however, do not involve restructuring their day-to-day living arrangements, so are not immediately evident. There is no bedroom to turn into a TV room or home office, no closet to empty. There are no photos or posters to take off the wall, no dolls and toys to pack away, and no school papers to dispose of.

Although physical changes in an older parent's surroundings are hardly perceptible, the psychological change is monumental. And, being closer to the end of life than the younger parent, the one who survives the death of his or her adult child is overwhelmed with survivors' guilt, the thought that it should have been the parent rather than the child who died.

I remember the exact time and place when such a change took place in me, though there was no flash of light or vision. It was the moment when I realized that everything I had believed about life suddenly and completely collapsed.

It happened a few days before Cathy died in St. Elizabeth's Hospital in Boston. Her sister Laurel was with Cathy in her hospital room; her father and I had left our bedside vigil to get a breath of fresh air and some exercise. We stepped out to take a walk around the block in the warm sunshine of that July afternoon.

The oncologist had just given us the latest report on Cathy's cancer, which he had called "very aggressive." The report was pessimistic and I was scared. Suddenly I felt my whole world falling apart. For the first time, my cheery denial left me and I faced the rude and terrible fact that perhaps my daughter was dying. I clung to my husband, sobbed and wept, mumbling all the while, "I can't give her up! I can't! I can't!"

Yet I knew that I would probably have to give her up, that she would die. All my faith in the fairness of life, in the assurance that things would go well for me and my family if I followed the rules, was dashed to pieces.

I remember saying to myself with distinct and terrible clarity: "I am sixty-seven years old. Today I grew up. Today I also grew old."

That day I also stopped wearing my contact lenses, for from then on the tears were never far from the surface. When I began to go for hours without those tears, several years after Cathy's death, I decided to start wearing the contact lenses again. Alas, when I peered into the case, they were twisted, dried up and wrinkled, completely unusable.

Bereaved parents can readily identify with the drastic changes brought about by St. Paul's encounter on the road. They need only observe how different their lives are now, compared to the way they were before their child died. But there is an additional analogy, one that is perhaps not so readily evident as the changes a child's death wrought in one's daily life.

Recall that Paul was not only thrown from his horse, he was struck blind after he had his vision of Jesus. Although his blindness was only temporary, it rendered him completely dependent on others, helpless and confused as long as the blindness lasted. Unable to find his way, he was ministered to by his companions, on whom he had to rely totally. They led him to the house of Ananais where he rested until he could see once more.

Again, the experience of a newly bereaved parent is analogous. When a child dies, the shock is so profound, so all-encompassing, that it might be said to have rendered the bereaved parents psychically if not physically blind. At least for awhile, the parents may feel they have lost their reason for living. Their self-esteem, their composure, nerve, courage, and their memory may disappear. Their health suffers. They can no longer put words together in a sentence.

Like St. Paul, surviving parents may be temporarily dependent on others immediately after the death of their child. Evelyn Guiliani, a respondent to my questionnaire whose daughter was stabbed to death, said, "One person told me that for two weeks I didn't put a sentence together correctly. My husband told me I didn't do anything 'crazy,' I just didn't remember I had said something. I experienced memory loss, physical problems like loss of appetite, and headaches. I lost touch with old friends and don't see anyone."

Some bereaved parents, including me, listened to everybody who offered advice because our ability to think rationally was greatly damaged. As illustrated in Chapter 3 "The Condolence Call," we may have been treated with tenderness and sympathy, but we may also have been given misguided advice which subsequently damaged us.

Some of the psychological effects I suffered were themselves almost physical and immediately apparent in my awkward sense of confusion, an inability to find my equilibrium. I had a sense of terror, of dread, loss of control, of utter chaos which permeated my every waking moment. It is hard to explain this to non-grievers, who can logically point out that I had already experienced the most dreaded thing I could possibly experience. Why was I overwhelmed by a sense of dread? What worse thing could happen to me? Yet there it was, that frantic flailing about to regain control.

There were mindless attempts to establish some order in my life: alignment of the silver when setting the table, moving furniture to stand symmetrically in its place, unreasoning insistence on correct storage of supplies on the shelves, fits of weeping when some insignificant thing went wrong with the laundry or the stove, if someone forgot to turn off the light or the radio, if a bit of food fell on the floor, or a vase of flowers tipped over.

Outside the home, while shopping, I made inappropriate purchases in order to forestall, to be prepared for, an unnamed emergency. I later discovered that I shared these irrational responses with other bereaved parents. At our local support group, tales were told of buying new curtains for non-existent windows, extra TV sets purchased without thought of where they would be placed, gifts bought and then forgotten, and new appliances added before the parents recalled that they had already bought the same appliance a few weeks previously.

I realize now that this behavior indicates a need for bereaved parents to regain control over their shattered lives. When it happened to me, I interpreted it as a sign that I was demented.

Unlike St. Paul, my psychic blindness did not go away in a few days or even in a few years. Looking back on my grief journey, I realize I was trapped in a bad place for a long time.

The germination of the idea for this book took place during that bad period. After I came out of that earlier stage, during which my whole personality seemed shattered, I could recognize and even reject bad advice, which I couldn't do previously. Instead of chastising myself for my inability to appreciate or follow a suggestion given to me by a non-griever, I could say, "No, that's not the way it is," or "I'm sorry, but that is not a helpful suggestion," or even "No, I don't think God needed another angel as much as I need my daughter. And I don't feel that she is with me always. I wish she were, but she is dead and I feel bad about that."

That may not appear on the surface to be a victory, but it is for me. In the bad days, I would have nodded my head in assent on hearing those pieties, hating myself for not being able to accept that reasoning or for not speaking up.

I feel good when I am honest about my feelings. I feel good when I can educate some well-meaning person who is totally wrong in his or her approach. I can do it kindly, prefacing my remarks with, "I know you want to be comforting, and I appreciate that, but what you are saying is not comforting and is not applicable to my situation." (Job had comforters, too; they were not comforting either.)

I had made some progress. I could identify and trust my feelings. I was able to leave those conversations without the sense of self-loathing I used to have.

When the mind begins to clear, when the wildest aspects of disorientation begin to subside, sometime during the reality stage of grief, the sense of self gets stronger. Bereaved parents realize then that many changes have occurred in their lives, changes not directly connected to their grief.

Everyone who responded to my questionnaire reported a reordering of priorities after their child's death placing a greater emphasis on appreciating their surviving children. They no longer have any regard for trivial concerns like status, keeping up with others, or accumulating possessions or wealth.

Judy Sturchio, one of the respondents, says, "Everything about my life has changed: religion, friends, and my attitude about life itself. Not a grain of sand on this earth remains the same as it was before Christopher's death."

For adults who had already grown old when their child died, the loss also brings about a subtle change in their response to cultural pursuits. Perhaps they had reached a stage in their lives when they had more time and money than young parents have to indulge an interest in the arts. I realize that I missed a whole generation of good movies, plays, books, concerts, and art shows because I was tied down caring for my youngsters, too poor and too tired to seek outside entertainment.

I always had an intense interest in the arts. In college I studied music and had illusions about a career in opera. I received my Bachelors Degree in Art History. Yet I put my interest in the arts "on hold" while raising my three children.

When the children grew up, I was able to go out more, to travel, and to attend many cultural events denied me in my earlier years.

Since my daughter's death, I find myself less tolerant than the general public of trivial art. Fads, show-off productions, titillating, or shocking displays: these unworthy efforts are distasteful, even offensive to the consumer of art who is also grieving.

This has been particularly evident in my reactions to theatrical productions. Although I used to enjoy the theater, now I hardly ever have any interest in what is being produced. Most of the time I find myself leaving the modern theater slightly angered by the pretensions, emotional blindness, and downright silliness of the plays I see there. The classics, Shakespeare or the Greeks, always prove a moving exception.

As for literature, I often find myself putting down a supposedly "good book" without finishing it. Themes of unrequited love, power plays and ethnic tension, money-grubbing, and betrayal seem worthless in light of my present insights. I sometimes talk back to the author or playwright: "What you're telling me may be true for you, but it has no meaning for me and is irrelevant to my condition."

A best-selling book has been going the rounds in my circle of friends and was the selection at several book clubs. It is discussed frequently; people loved it. I feel uneasy and even unperceptive when I register my dislike of the book. But recently I forced myself to reply when someone asked me why I didn't like it. "It seemed callous to me," I said. "The characters' behavior offended me." "Well, yes," someone replied, "I suppose you're right. But didn't you find anything to like?" At that point, I couldn't let myself say that such books don't speak to me in my present condition. I feared my listeners, who are also my friends, might interpret my remarks as judgmental, so I dropped the subject.

But I have been thinking about it since then. I discovered that I didn't like that book because it dealt largely with things which mean nothing to me: angry encounters with neighbors, incestuous relationships, failed business ventures, and murders. My daughter's death cut me off from enjoyment of much of popular culture. That loss enabled me to distinguish what is really important: the nobility of the human spirit and the enduring power of love.

On the other hand, poetry, which used to be fairly low on my list of reading material, has become particularly important since Cathy died. Not just any poetry—the kind that is faddishly obscure—but poetry that deals with the deepest human emotions: love and loss and longing, courage and awe.

I sense that this is true of grieving parents in general. Our *Compassionate Friends* newsletters abound with small, heartrending poems. I wrote a few myself, awkwardly-crafted and liberally-watered with tears.

I searched the poetry anthologies after my daughter's death, trying to find something to touch my anguish. It was a compelling need, something I had never felt before. I skipped over the odes to sunsets and noble trees, to the lips and hair of the beloved. I found comfort in Wordsworth, in Shakespeare, and in the small poems of Emily Dickinson. Or in this excerpt from "Remembrance" by Emily Bronte:

> When the days of golden dreams had perished,
> And even Despair was powerless to destroy;
> Then did I learn how existence could be cherished,
> Strengthened and fed without the aid of joy.

My "Road to Damascus" experience has left me with a challenge to cherish existence without the aid of joy. Philosophically, one of the residual effects of my bereavement has been the loss of my illusions about the fairness of life. It is as though an invisible veil were lowered over my eyes, with no prospect of its ever being raised to let the sunshine of pure joy come in again. The bare minimum for my happiness is gone: my family is no longer intact.

On a birthday or Mother's Day, I used to wait around for all the children to check in with a phone call. When the last one had called, my husband would grin at me and say, "There, are you happy now?" To be really happy, I need to have my children alive and well, and I will never have that again.

I cannot, like Saint Paul, devote myself to a new and fulfilling life of dedication to a great and wonderful cause. My challenge, it seems to me, is not to search for joy. My challenge instead, is to fight off bitterness, hopelessness, and cynicism. Several of my respondents said, "I'm trying not to become bitter."

If I should become bitter, hopeless, and cynical as a result of my loss, it would be a betrayal of my daughter Cathy's legacy to me and to the world: her concern for others less fortunate than herself; her wonderful artistic and musical talents; and her love for her family and friends.

If I should become bitter, it would be a betrayal of the love I feel for her and for her survivors. Dealing with an ill-tempered, bitter, pessimistic old lady is something I don't wish on them. I hope to reinvest in life more gracefully.

I have recently become aware of another change in me since Cathy died, which some of my respondents say they share with me. I have developed a strong reluctance to kill anything: a flying insect, a mouse or rat, a vagrant plant, or even a weed. I have felt the fool as I work in my garden, crying because I must pull up some tiny plant in order to give the others room to flourish. "Thinning," gardeners would say. "Killing," I say.

The very fact that life exists seems an overwhelming miracle. How could I take it away? These thoughts remind me that Cathy's life was cut off prematurely. Life, pulsating, tender life, it is so fragile, so precious!

The changes brought about by the death of an adult child may have the effect of forcing parents to reexamine other matters. In another kind of Road to Damascus upheaval, they can start a probing of personal events in the past. Parents may have unresolved problems which surface during the grief experience, demanding with troubling insistence to be looked at when the bereaved parents are least capable of looking at them. It may be something in their early lives, perhaps, which shaped the moment they are now facing, which determined how they dealt with crisis situations, how they related to parents, siblings, marriage partners, and friends. In fact, some parents have a compulsion to see with greater clarity just how they became the people they are. Perhaps bereaved parents can better understand this need to find clarity in their own lives as they read Saint Paul's first letter to the Corinthians, verses 11 and 12:

"When I was a child, I spake as a child, I understood as a child; I thought as a child; but when I became a man, I put away childish things. For now we see through a glass, darkly; but then face to face. Now I know in part; but then shall I know even as also I am known."

The urge to add the last verse is almost irresistible:

"And now abideth faith, hope, and love; these three. But the greatest of these is love."

Many centuries ago, Saint Paul's life was turned upside down after a traumatic encounter on the Road to Damascus; quite a change from Saul the persecutor to Saint Paul, who finally recognized the overwhelming power of love.

Bereaved parents have learned how such a change can occur. They already knew about the power of love.

CHAPTER 10

Gender and Grief

In all the literature I have read about grief, and in endless discussions about grief, there is no subject more shrouded in mystery than the differences between the ways men and women grieve.

"They grieve differently but they come out the same in the end," I heard a lecturer say, immediately posing the question about just where "the end" is and exactly what "they come out the same" means. This flippant commentary trivializes an extremely complex problem. It is almost like saying, "Don't worry about it" when the doctor gives you a diagnosis of cancer. The differences between the way males and females grieve is a subject of tremendous importance, worthy of attention.

The bereaved parents of the deceased child are the people most intimately connected emotionally and the people most devastated by the death. If they are married and living in the same house, thrust together on a daily basis, wracked with pain and sorrow, confronting the most difficult situation parents must face, they may lack the resources to deal with it. It is indeed a cause for serious concern. The viability of the marriage may be at stake.

Some marriages emerge intact from the loss of a child. Others collapse under the strain. The statistics tossed around in bereavement self-help groups tell us that 80 percent of marriages dissolve after the death of a child. Though many divorces result from the stress, that percentage seems an exaggeration. However, in spite of the differences in the ways men and women grieve, it is imperative that husbands and wives find some understanding of each other in order to live together with a minimum of conflict during the mourning period and beyond. The marriage partners both win or they both lose in this endeavor.

Professionals feed us myriad prescriptions: "Remember, there is no energy left in either partner to help the other." "You have to talk about your dead child." "Give your partner space and permission to grieve in his or her own way." "Express yourself, but bear in mind that men are taught not to cry, not to show emotion. They don't know how to handle it. Women have to assume men are grieving, even though there are no outward signs." "Be kind to each other."

These recommendations look very good on paper and sound sensible in a lecture hall. But there is a point at which all this advice is unheeded and wasted: the first year or two, for starters. Many newly bereaved parents can't even hear what is being said. They are probably in shock, vacillating between denial and anger. How can they think of being kind or giving their partner space? How can you talk about your child when you cry every time you open your mouth? Or what you say is blubbering nonsense: "I wonder . . . did she die? Why do I think she died? She couldn't die! Tell me she's not dead. I don't want her to be dead!" Some conversation! If you are the wife spouting such words, you will probably drive your husband to another room or out of the house. In our culture, most men don't want to see their wives cry; it makes them feel helpless. Their job is to fix things, to make them better, to take care of their loved ones. The death of their child cannot be fixed. The father may regard this as his failure, affecting his relationship not only to the family but to the outside world.

At the same time the father is leaving the room, distraught at his wife's behavior, the mother may be concluding that he is angry or unfeeling, which adds to her own distress. The rift starts to widen. She gets the message: if she has to cry, she'd better make sure her husband does not see her. But then she wonders why he does not feel sad too. Perhaps he didn't love their child as much as she did. She may begin to resent him as a cruel, unfeeling man.

In such cases, anger and misunderstanding escalate. Two people, crazed with grief, only half aware of themselves as human beings, are now snarling at each other for reasons they barely understand. Raw emotion rules their every encounter.

The male and female parents who lose a young child also experience differing grief styles. But their problems are in many ways unlike those of parents whose child was an adult at the time of death. Bereaved parents of a mature individual, one who had probably already left to establish his or her own home, must deal with a terrible emptiness. They may have lived alone in their house for many years, but their child came home from time to time. Even with an empty house, there was comfort in knowing the family was intact. The death of their child now accentuates the void and becomes an emptiness in their lives. The very fact of their aloneness with each other, an aloneness untempered by the presence of other children in the house, makes their situation more unrelievedly stark.

If the house of older bereaved parents seems suddenly more empty because their adult child is dead, the doors to that house become more appealing as escape routes. Those doors are the same ones which might remain safely closed in the homes of parents who lose a young child. Escape is not an option when there are other children still living at home. But in the house uninhabited except by two grieving parents, the doors are not secure. The grieving parent may be tempted to flee the pain and sorrow.

I have friends in Italy whose daughter died of a brain tumor. The youngest of three adult children, she was the only one still living at home. After her death, the father could not bear to come home. Each day after work, he would enter the house where his child had died and become violently ill. His business drew him every day to a downtown shop. Upstairs from his shop was an empty flat, which he moved into. This state of separation from his wife, who was left dwelling alone, dealing painfully with her grief and sense of abandonment, went on for several years. Eventually he was able to return. But some bereaved parents may leave and never return.

Many bereaved parents of adult children are at least middle-aged. Many are senior citizens, their life-work (which includes rearing their children) and their life journey are nearly finished. Contemplation of their future, in which their children had been the loving, supportive center, is almost unbearable. I have heard several elderly parents remark that they are glad they are so old. They don't have many years left to endure the absence of their beloved child. Some of my correspondents have expressed a fervent wish for their own death.

Add to this aloneness and despair another potent ingredient: sex. I have sat through a two-hour workshop on grief and marriage and not once heard the word "sex" mentioned. Yet sexual expression is paramount in most marriages and undergoes profound changes after the death of a child.

Depression, probably an almost universal response to grief, tends to lessen the desire for sex. For those not experiencing depression, the need for comfort during bereavement may heighten the desire for sexual contact.

For many married couples, sex has strong emotional connections to their grief, for it is through the sex act that they conceived their child and they identify their loss with sex, making them reject the very idea of intercourse. Others feel guilty enjoying anything after the death of their child and eschew sexual activity because of its connection with pleasure.

Although the death of an adult child implies that the parent no longer has the expectation or even the capacity to have another pregnancy, younger parents sometimes abstain from sex because they fear having another child who might also die. (This is an important difference between the death of a young child and an adult.) Some parents have indicated that they are reluctant to engage in sex because they feel the presence of their dead child.

I am painting a grim picture because I want to make three points. First, it is important that we not be unrealistically optimistic. There is hardly any way the partners in a marriage can work together rationally and lovingly in the early days just after the death of their child. They have to hang on until some semblance of rationality dawns in their lives. Meanwhile, they must be assured, either by a professional or by those bereaved parents who are farther along in their grief, that such a time will come. While they are waiting for that to occur, they should be careful to avoid permanent hurts.

Second, I want to emphasize the fact that most of the advice the professionals give bereaved parents is sensible and good. As mentioned above, they tell us we must remember that neither of the marital partners has enough energy to help the other; that it is helpful to talk about our child; and that each of us must give the other space and permission to grieve in his or her own way. Grief counselors say it is important to express the emotions we feel, but women need to realize that men are taught not to cry, so it may be hard for them. We must be kind to each other.

Bereaved parents may be able to follow this advice well along on their grief journey. But by that time a lot of damage may have been done to the relationship with their spouse; indeed, it may be too late to save the marriage.

My third point is this: as we gain greater understanding of each other, our differences in responding to the death of our child, we men and women will make allowances for those differences. We will cease to judge each other by our own standards, will become more tolerant, and once again become the loving partners we were before the tragedy struck.

In this chapter on gender and grief, there are two sets of excerpts from my questionnaire. The first set will describe the experiences of other bereaved parents regarding the differences between the way the father and mother grieved after their child's death. The second group will report on sexual problems of bereaved parents.

It might be significant to bear in mind that most of the questionnaires were filled out by mothers; only 10 percent were sent in by fathers. How accurately the observations of females who answered the questionnaire correspond to the actual grief experiences of their male partners is hard to determine. Perhaps that accuracy may depend on how close the partners feel after their bereavement and whether or not estrangement has set in.

Some of the illustrations which follow may seem cryptic or incomplete—they are recorded almost exactly as written on the questionnaire. Even in the families where the parents are not divorced, the person responding may not have mentioned the other spouse's way of expressing grief, which in itself is a commentary.

1. Parents of a twenty-five-year-old son, although divorced by the time their son murdered his girlfriend and then took his own life, experienced even greater stress and anger in the family because the father leaned heavily on the surviving son for emotional support.

2. The parents of a thirty-year-old daughter, who were divorced fourteen years prior to the accident which killed her, had never been able to communicate without feeling stressed. Since her death, they have talked at length. Some years after his daughter died, the father is beginning to grieve openly, with feelings of depression and not wanting to go on with life.

3. Parents of a son electrocuted on his job find it hard to talk about their son; each time they do, they both cry. Because the father and son were best buddies, working together on building projects, the father misses his son terribly and can't sleep at night. He has to keep busy all the time.

4. The thirty-five-year-old son of parents married thirty-nine years was killed in the military. They felt their marriage was coming apart and couldn't tell each other how they felt until they took a vacation away from everyone. They talked and talked about their son and made a determination to get better. The wife was having the hardest time with her son's death, sometimes having to seek help for panic attacks at a hospital emergency room some years after his death.

5. Before his death of a massive heart attack just a year to the day after his son's murder, this father had been very supportive of the mother. They had never been closer.

6. The twenty-two-year-old son of sixty plus parents was killed in an auto accident. The mother and father still have a close relationship, though the father has difficulty expressing himself verbally.

7. Their twenty-six-year-old daughter, mother of two children, died of leukemia. Her parents have difficulty communicating and can't talk about their deceased child.

8. After the death of their forty-year-old son, killed while fighting a fire, his parents feel they would be lost without each other. Though the father tends to grieve privately, he encourages his wife to grieve in any way she needs to.

9. The mother of a twenty-seven-year-old son who was murdered found it impossible to get any support from her husband. Her marriage to this second husband, who is not the father of her deceased son, did not survive.

10. The parents of a married son who died of leukemia talked about his death for awhile afterwards. The husband becomes angry if his wife cries in front of him so she cries only when she is alone. As far as she knows, he has not expressed his grief.

11. Parents of a son, nineteen, killed in a mountain-climbing accident, found that the first several years were lonely and depressing. They considered separation. Because the husband grieved alone and silently, the wife felt particularly lonely in her grief. Even though they have been bereaved for many years, they sometimes talk and cry over their son's death, but usually avoid it.

12. The father of a thirty-three-year-old son, also killed in a mountain-climbing accident, says he and his wife have experienced some stress in their marriage and sometimes have difficulty communicating. There is really no significant difference in the way they grieve. There is an occasional flare-up.

13. Her eighteen-year-old daughter was stabbed to death. The mother was divorced from the father many years before their daughter's death. She was supported in her grief by her second husband.

14. These parents lost their twenty-four-year-old son to substance abuse. Because the father feels a strong sense of guilt, whereas the mother does not, they find it difficult to communicate about their dead son.

15. The mother of a thirty-five-year-old son who died of a heart attack says she and her husband have differing grief styles. He seeks comfort in alcohol. There is absolutely no communication between them.

16. While away at college, the twenty-two-year-old son of these parents committed suicide. The father cried constantly and became extremely withdrawn and depressed. He died a year after his son's death. As a result of grief and family complications, the mother lost her job.

17. Although they grieve differently, the relationship is good between the parents of a twenty-four-year-old son who died of leukemia.

18. The parents of a twenty-four-year-old son, killed in an auto accident, say the pain and grief were so great they had many difficult times in their marriage. Each of them dealt with it individually and were unable to help one another.

19. When their eighteen-year-old daughter died of viral pneumonia, these parents had disagreements about how to handle their grief. The mother is on a slower, more passive route to healing. The father is active with a support group.

20. Married to a widower with three children, this thirty-year-old woman died of scleroderma. Her parents live together but don't communicate much. The father never mentions his deceased daughter's name and does not participate in annual memorial excursions to the cemetery with the mother and siblings on the date of her death.

21. The mother of a thirty-three-year-old son who took his own life has no communication with her husband. Their relationship was not good before their son's death. While the father goes to church and the cemetery almost every day, the mother has not been to either place.

22. Although divorced, the parents of a twenty-two-year-old son who was murdered, have become good friends since his death.

23. The parents of two sons killed in an auto accident are close and supportive of each other. However, they find it difficult to discuss those who died.

24. The twenty-three-year-old son of divorced parents (mother is remarried) died of cancer. The father and mother retain a cordial relationship but he became too dependent emotionally after his son's death. The mother is grateful for the loving support of her second husband, who is also grieving for his stepson, whom he knew since boyhood.

25. Although the mother of a thirty-one-year-old daughter who died of drug-related sepsis feels she and her husband have become closer, they have trouble talking about their deceased child. The mother goes to the cemetery alone on her daughter's birthday; no one else even mentions the birthday.

26. An only child, this thirty-eight-year-old woman had been ill with lupus for twenty-five years before her death. She was married and the mother of two children. Although the parents cry together, the father doesn't want to talk about his daughter.

27. These parents lost their twenty-nine-year-old son to AIDS. The parents have become closer. The father, who has many regrets because his relationship with his son had been strained, cries openly.

28. At twenty-one, this one of three children in the family died of suicide. His parents felt that there was a distance between them at first due to differing ways men and women grieve. The mother couldn't talk about her son, but after awhile they cried and talked and felt better. The father needs to ventilate a lot more but it will take a long time. The mother has learned not to bring things up unless he is ready to talk.

29. These parents lost both a twenty-four-year-old daughter and a six-year-old granddaughter (child of a different daughter) in an auto-truck accident. Family relations are difficult, with the double loss compounding everything. Husband and wife have grown closer and have the time to talk and cry together. The mother needs to read everything she can about grief.

30. The thirty-six-year-old married daughter of these parents was killed when her stopped car was hit from behind at a toll booth. The parents feel they have grown closer since their daughter's death.

31. These parents lost a twenty-two-year-old son in a bus/pedestrian accident. At first they were so involved in their own pain, they couldn't help each other, but they feel closer now.

32. At twenty-five, married and the mother of a young son, this woman died of heart failure. The parents had a good relationship and feel remarkably compatible in their grief styles.

33. The mother of an eighteen-year-old boy killed in an auto accident, says she and her husband have often cried together. He never gave any indication of embarrassment; his pain was a heartrending release. It hurt her to see him this way, but it was also a relief to know that he could express his grief. His outbursts were like flash floods in the desert. She, on the other hand, cried for hours and days and what seemed weeks on end.

34. Although it has been several years since the death of their thirty-eight-year-old son, the mother cannot mention his name in front of the father who either leaves the room or says, "That's enough!" He will not allow anyone else to mention his son's name either, though from time to time, a surviving daughter will corner him and insist on talking about her brother.

Having culled from the responses to my questionnaire all those relevant to gender differences regarding the way men and women grieve, it appears that most women find it easier than men to express emotions of sadness. They give themselves permission to cry often and to talk freely about their loss.

Men tend to be more private in their expressions of grief. Some are fortunate enough to be able to cry, but the common comment by my respondents is that the fathers of children who died must get off by themselves from time to time in order to grieve privately. They do not feel comfortable sharing their wives' tears or in talking with other men about their loss. It is difficult for the leaders of our grief support group to keep a circle of men focused on their grief rather than talking about sports or politics during a meeting.

What would happen, I wondered, if fathers sat down with us mothers and told us their feelings? Maybe they would write them down or tell some interviewer (I offered to hire a professional), so we could understand what is going on with men and grief. Or perhaps fathers would answer a questionnaire about the way they grieve.

Not so! My questionnaire aimed specifically at bereaved fathers was cast aside, unanswered. The mothers responded: "Sorry, he won't do it;" "He doesn't want to answer it;" "My husband isn't interested;" "It's been so long he just wants to forget." The wife, in every case, was the intermediary.

In addition to describing their grief styles in the questionnaire I distributed throughout the United States, the bereaved parents also answered question number seven regarding their sex life after their child's death. They were promised anonymity in this matter. Thus the respondents' frank disclosures pertinent to this chapter were deleted from their individual stories and taken out of context in order to respect their privacy.

The following quotes exclude the many who chose not to answer the question, those who are divorced or widowed, and those who gave monosyllabic answers.

1. "I wouldn't say sexual problems, but our sex life has definitely changed. Before our son died we made love with passion; now it's compassion. We never laugh any more."

2. A mother who is one year bereaved: "I've lost interest in sex, but I feel I have started to regain some life back."

3. A couple whose child committed suicide: "Sex is almost non-existent since our child's death."

4. A mother: "We have sexual problems, but never at the same time."

5. Mother: "Sex? What's that?"

6. A father reports: "My wife and I had problems for the first three or four years after our child's death."

7. A mother says: "My husband and I did not have a good relationship before the death. Now we have no sex at all."

8. Quoting a mother: "We were overwhelmed by our son's death and for the first year were tentative about sex. We felt very close to each other, but struggled to find our way back to our normal love life. There was more tenderness, more sensitivity to each other's moods. It was a sad and difficult time. Now two years later, we seem almost back to normal."

9. A father says: "We had sexual problems for awhile."

10. A couple who have been bereaved four or five years: "We had sexual problems at first, but now they are resolved."

11. Bereaved mother: "I just lost interest in sex."

12. Mother: "My husband and I had problems for about three years but we are OK now."

13. Mother: "At first, every time we tried to have sex, I started to cry. I am sorry to say that, although the crying has stopped, things are not much better."

14. Mother: "I must admit that for a long time, maybe five years, I had no interest but my husband did. I slowly began to realize that my lack of interest in sex had more to do with my own depression than anything else."

15. "You asked about how the death of our daughter affected our sex life. I think we went a year and a half without intimacy, and we seem to go months and months before intimacy again. It makes no difference to me one way or another. Before, it was important; now . . . When I hear of someone losing a child and then they have more kids later, I wonder how all that came about."

Of those who chose to answer the question regarding their sexual relationship, there were few who did not experience problems. Most of them were temporary however.

Differing response to the sex drive is only one of many ways in which men and women are out of sync after the death of their child. Brief mention was made above of the way husbands escape when their wives begin to cry. It was a thread running through many of the responses to my questionnaire. These escapes were often accompanied by visible anger on the part of the husband. Although undoubtedly the husband is responding to his frustration at the death of his child, the wife usually interprets the anger as directed at her. If the anger is not visible, it sometimes manifests itself in silence.

One of my respondents was bereaved for a year and a half before her husband would even speak their son's name. Returning from each day's work, he would grab a bottle of liquor and retreat to the garage for the evening. His wife, feeling abandoned and furious at his drunkenness, was ready to seek a divorce.

One day she came into the house carrying a chrysanthemum plant. She was startled to see that her husband was already at home, sitting in a chair.

"What are you going to do with that plant?" he asked.

"I'm taking it to _____'s grave," she replied.

"I'll go with you," was his surprising answer.

When they reached the cemetery and planted the chrysanthemum on their son's grave, her husband began to cry and shout hysterically, pounding the ground and screaming.

It took a year and a half. But it was, at last, an expression of grief.

In some of my reports, the tendency of men to want the grief period to end, to put the whole agony behind them without ever coming to terms with their need to grieve, has placed their wives in an untenable position. The father assumes that life should be back to normal; the mother is still grieving. The implication is that she should shape up, which is what the general, non-grieving public tells her. And that is impossible.

I want to close this chapter with a personal story about my so-silent family.

I was ill, recovering from a hip replacement, partially bedridden and feeling sad on Cathy's forty-eighth birthday. I called my husband to my bedside.

"Help me," I said. "I am having a very bad day. I need to talk."

He sat on a chair in our bedroom and made some awkward remarks about the beauty of the flowers, which we had donated to that morning's church service, and made a few monosyllabic responses to my attempts to start a conversation. Then after about ten minutes of silence he left the room.

Not content to let my emotional situation deteriorate further, and slightly angry by that time, I laboriously pulled myself out of bed and, with great difficulty, got dressed. Then I called Bob, who was watching TV in the next room.

"I need to go to the cemetery," I said.

We drove silently through the snowy landscape to Albany Rural Cemetery. I sat in the car and cried while he placed a rose on Cathy's grave.

We drove away in silence, my frustration at a peak. Choosing my words carefully, in order to make sure I did not sound confrontational, I said, "I see that you can't talk about Cathy even when I need to."

"I'll try," he said, "but it's hard. So many painful memories about her illness and death. And about the wrongful-death trial. How sad I feel that she died. But I'll try."

Slowly at first, we started to speak about some of the good memories and the joyous experiences we had had with her on some foreign travels. We spoke about the worry we felt when we went into our hotel in Jerusalem and there was no word from Cathy, not even a note. We were supposed to rendezvous with her there after we had spent a week in Jordan and she had been traveling for some weeks on her own in Egypt, which had itself been a source of our concern for her safety.

Taking our bags down a long hall, the porter opened the door to our room. There, on the dresser, was a huge bouquet of flowers with a card saying, "Welcome to Jerusalem! Love, Cathy." Shortly thereafter, she appeared to greet us in the lobby.

Then we recalled that delightful week she spent with us on a barge on the French canals with some of our friends. As Bob and I spoke, I could almost see her stretched out on the deck, soaking up the soft sunlight of southern France, her slender, graceful body in its bikini, her dark hair bound up in a kerchief. We recalled with pride the day she stood in the midst of the adults, chatting in French like a native to the proprietor and then translating for us while we were all visiting a local winery beside the canal.

As Bob and I spoke, one anecdote led to another, filling her birthday afternoon with wonderful thoughts of her life, things I would not have thought of on my own.

You will not think this is remarkable until I tell you that this conversation, the first her father and I have ever had about Cathy which lasted more than a minute, took place on the ninth birthday since her death. Nearly nine whole years after she died!

Why did it take so long? Did we have to arrive at a point where we could put aside for a few minutes the painful memories of her illness and death, our anger and frustration about her poor medical care, and the disillusionment with the judicial system which cheated us? These thoughts were the triggers for our pain, the bottleneck which previously had prevented the good memories from coming through.

Was it really necessary for so long a time to go by before the good memories appeared? Could we have forced ourselves to try to talk about Cathy? I only know that, in the beginning, it was impossible to talk about her as she was when she was alive and healthy, relating to us as our other children do now, recalling daily activities and things we used to do together. In the early days and years after her death, talk degenerated immediately into incoherence and tears. As we tried to come to terms with the enormity of our loss, the sheer mention of former joys plunged us into despair because we realized those joys were gone forever.

Perhaps this should caution others to temper their remarks when they try to comfort us by saying: "You have so many memories." Sometimes memories can inflict tremendous pain, not comfort.

Alfred, Lord Tennyson, says in the poem Locksley Hall,

> This truth the poet sings,
> That a sorrow's crown of sorrow is remembering happier things.

But there is hope for us bereaved parents of adult children who died. Some day our memories will reappear in a new guise, bringing with them warm thoughts and smiles—not pain. Those thoughts will be many and they will comfort us. That host of memories is the reward for having had so many years before death ended the life of our adult child. In the sheer amount of memories, we are more fortunate than the parents of young children who died.

Those memories are also an assurance that we will never forget our child, which so many bereaved parents fear will happen with the passage of time.

Reinforcing the memories with talk cannot happen however, if the parents fail to communicate and to share the memories. Those who greet their spouse's requests for talk with silence are denying themselves and these spouses a source of comfort. Surely this is an unnecessary cruelty to pile on an already sad and burdened relationship.

Would that husbands and wives could face the pain of talk and seek to turn it into comfort for their mutual good!

CHAPTER 11

The Search

It was a December day sometime in the late 1950s. The snow had been falling heavily all night, promising the school children an unscheduled vacation the next day. While we parents may have fretted about the prospect of having to shovel driveways and sidewalks, a "snow day" was the best sort of holiday for our offspring, who were delighted at the prospect of a whole day of nothing but play with their friends. Our suburban neighborhood was amply provided with throngs of children, the babies of the Baby Boom grown to school age.

On that particular snowy day long ago, my two daughters and son were frolicking about the yard with their schoolmates. The sun shone brightly. The temperature was hovering near the freezing mark. The snow was soft and sticky. Conditions were just right for outdoor play, for making snowmen, forts and snowballs, for playing snow games, and chasing each other up and down the street. Laughter and shouts of joy brightened the neighborhood.

Playing right along with them, all day long, was a huge brown dog, an Afghan hound.

When it began to get dark, time for supper, I called the children into the house. They put their soggy mittens on a warm radiator, took off their wet shoes and boots, and hung their damp jackets in the laundry room to dry.

Instead of leaving when the children came into the house, the Agghan hound lingered outside the door, then stationed himself on the porch, looking wistfully at the children through the window.

After awhile, noticing that the dog continued to sit on the porch, I began to feel sorry for him. The temperature had fallen; it was now bitter cold. The wind was blowing and the snow drifting. Why didn't the dog go home? Was he lost?

I put on jacket and boots and went out to check on him. He was wearing a collar with a name, a telephone number, and an address. But it was not a local address. It was in a community miles away.

I called the telephone number.

"There's a beautiful brown dog at our house and his collar bears your address and telephone number," I said to the woman who answered. "He's been playing all day in the snow with my children."

" Yes, that's our dog," she replied.

"I'm concerned about him. It's getting cold and he's a long way from home—several miles actually, if the address is correct."

"Yes, he's a long way from home, I know. But he's all right. He'll eventually come home."

"Shall I let him into our house?" I asked, wondering why the woman didn't seem as distressed as I was. "It's very cold and the weather is getting worse."

"No, he wouldn't stay. That's just the way he acts. He finds some children to play with. Don't worry about him. He'll come home. We just let him roam because . . . well, we just can't control him. Sometimes he stays away for days at a time. You see, he's searching . . . searching for my little son, who died."

"Oh, I'm so sorry," I answered, choking on the words as I hung up the telephone.

Searching, like a wild animal in the forest or the jungle, or like that brown Afghan hound, we all do it when a beloved child dies, even though there is no hope that he or she can be found alive.

The urge to search for a dead child is a phenomenon with a long history. One of the most famous of the ancient Greek myths tells the story of the goddess Demeter's search for her lost daughter, Persephone, who had been stolen by Hades, the god of the dead in the underworld. Her search for Persephone took Demeter on a tireless journey all over the world. She was enraged that Zeus, the principal god in the Greek pantheon, had allowed Hades to kidnap her child and carry her to the land of the dead. In her wrath, Demeter, who was the goddess of growing things, withdrew her gift of fertility and caused the earthly plants to wither. Zeus was alarmed at the possibility that all humankind might be destroyed by her actions, so he persuaded Hades to return Persephone to her mother to prevent the destruction of agriculture. But because the young woman had eaten several seeds from a pomegranate while she was in the land of the dead, she was doomed to return to her captor for the winter months thereafter.

The story of Demeter and her daughter Persephone eventually entered the body of Greek myths. It was used to explain the changing seasons. Demeter, the mother, came to symbolize the ripened harvest;

Persephone symbolized the new, young grain. As queen of the underground, Persephone also symbolized death and rebirth.

The Search, a wartime film starring soprano Zinka Milanov and the Hollywood actor Montgomery Clift, told the story of a mother whose little boy was separated from her during the exodus of populations in Europe toward the end of World War II. She began to wander with the teeming groups of refugees, searching for him, walking for miles, for days on end.

At a certain point along the way, the mother is told that the little child, who escaped from captivity in one of the death camps, was chased into a river by his Nazi pursuers, where the boy drowned. A witness came forward to give her his cap, found at the edge of the stream among some rushes, as evidence that he was dead.

In spite of the fact that she recognized the cap as belonging to her son, the mother kept wandering the countryside searching for him.

In the movies, things turn out for the best. There are happy endings. The mother found her little boy alive and well, and in the care of an American soldier.

As survivors of our children's death, bereaved parents must cope with the strange illusion that, although they may be dead, they are not really dead, in a final and irrevocable sense. Particularly in the early days after their deaths, we have that vivid sense of their presence which makes us feel they are coming back. Perhaps they are victims of some cruel mixup, are waiting to return, or waiting for us to find them. It is one of many irrational aspects of fresh grief to which perfectly sane and rational people fall prey. It may be a part of the denial mechanism which enables us to go on from day to day as we gradually absorb the truth of our tragedy.

A few weeks after Cathy died, my husband and I were in our car, leaving the driveway, when I saw Cathy running down the street toward us, waving frantically to catch our attention. Of course, there was the proof I had been waiting for: she was not really dead. I knew that; I had known it all along. What joy welled up in me! We stopped the car and I ran to her with open arms.

But it was not Cathy; it was her sister, Laurel. Same body configuration, shape of face, and flyaway hair. Laurel had not gone to her job as usual but had come to tell us something.

"I thought you were Cathy," I said. Then I burst into tears, not only with the realization that it was not Cathy but knowing how it must have hurt Laurel when she sensed my disappointment. She must have felt many times over the years that my overwhelming grief at Cathy's death was a reflection of my favoritism toward her sister. Common wisdom among bereaved parents confirms that surviving siblings often interpret the parents' grief as favoritism toward the dead, though parents know that is not the case. It is not favoritism; it is pure grief.

At that moment I was convinced that I was losing my mind. When a bereaved parent says "I thought I was going crazy," it may have been something similar to that wildly mindless incident which prompted the feeling.

It is not hard, then, to understand why we bereaved parents, seeing someone who looks like our child, begin to follow that person. Even though we know our hope is vain, we are drawn toward him or her by some strange magnetism. Maybe, maybe our child is still alive. Maybe we were mistaken to think our child was dead. Maybe it was all a bad dream.

We want desperately to speak to that person. Yet if given the opportunity, we have nothing to say. Imagine the response if you approached a stranger with, "I just want to look at you, to hear your voice, because you look like my daughter who died."

Every morning, in the days when I used to escort my grandson to elementary school, I encountered a young mother and her daughter. The mother looked so much like my Cathy it almost broke my heart to see her. Same lean, graceful body, and abundant dark hair. What a bittersweet experience it was to watch her bend over her little kindergartner, a tender smile on her face as she straightened the little girl's collar, tied her shoe, or gave her a farewell kiss. All the while I was thinking what a wonderful mother Cathy would have been, how she adored children and how they adored her, and how death had cheated her.

On days when that young mother was late, I withdrew across the street and waited for her and her little girl to appear, just to see them. One day, as I waited, the mother arrived at the schoolground on crutches. I was quite upset—really alarmed. I had been fantasizing so strongly that I felt a personal involvement in her well-being. I couldn't resist the urge to approach and ask if she had been hurt. Looking at me with a cold, puzzled expression, she mumbled a monosyllabic answer which made me embarrassed for having asked. She had no idea I had been watching her day after day and identifying her with my daughter. Surely she thought that I, a complete stranger, a nosey old lady, was out of order to intrude on something that was none of my business.

I remember hearing about a bereaved father whose adult son, Rob, died, leaving in addition a mother and sister as survivors. The father felt impelled to go out every evening after dinner to walk and walk and walk for hours. One night he returned from his walk to hear his daughter speaking to a neighbor who had dropped in and was sitting in the kitchen. The neighbor asked, "Where's your father?" His daughter answered, "He's out looking for Rob again."

That father remarked that he hadn't realized until that moment that he was searching for his son, though the rest of the family sensed that was what he was doing.

The search bereaved parents indulge in becomes less intense after the years go by, but the impulse to search is always there. We are subconsciously listening, watching, and waiting.

The same phenomenon finds me, year after year, attuned to the sound of the first robin as spring approaches. That song has enchanted me since I was three years old and watched a pair of robins raise a nestful of babies in a tree near our kitchen window in rural Wisconsin. I am never aware of waiting for it, yet suddenly, one chilly day early in March, I hear it and I am filled with joy. I recognize it as the song I had been waiting for all winter long, a sign that spring had come.

The same sense of joy greets my sight of someone who looks like, could be, or might be my dead daughter. Momentarily, before reason takes over, I think Cathy is still alive. Unprepared for the emotional impact, I burst into tears. It is one of those triggers which plague bereaved parents, destroying their composure.

The search for the dead child is shared by most bereaved parents, whether their lost child was very young or an adult. No matter how old or how young our children were, we all feel the need to fill the emptiness their death has left in our lives.

Elizabeth Philipps is the mother of a twenty-year-old daughter who was killed on December 21, 1988, a victim of the Pan Am 103 bombing over Lockerbie, Scotland. She is quoted in an interview in the Albany *Times Union* on October 31, 1995:

> I find myself still in a lot of ways looking for her. In the early days, I would be on a city street and see a young woman coming toward me and glance toward her and think, "Oh, Sarah! How wonderful to see you." And I still look for her. And I think other parents do that, too.

A meeting of *The Compassionate Friends* is hardly the place where a burst of laughter would be heard, but at our meeting a few months ago there was near hysteria. It was so unusual to hear laughter, in fact, that the men who were having group sharing in an adjacent room had to come into our circle to discover what was prompting the hilarity. We had been talking about the phenomenon of "The Search", and one of the mothers whose son died two years ago of a heart attack told us the following story:

She was shopping at the neighborhood supermarket when she saw a clerk who reminded her of her dead son. He did not have exactly the same physiognomy, but his mannerisms were just like her John's mannerisms. She stopped and gazed at him long and hard, emotions churning. Finally the clerk noticed her attention. He came over to her and said, "Lady, you'll have to stop coming on to me; you're too old for me!" The ludicrous nature of his comment was not lost on the assembled bereaved parents.

Occasionally the search for their dead child may make parents not only give the wrong impression, it may motivate them to try replacing the one who is deceased. Martha, a friend of many years who has since died of cancer, lost her teenage daughter when Meggie was electrocuted; her hairdryer fell into the bathtub while she was bathing. To assuage their grief, Martha and her husband tried immediately to fill the void in their lives.

Any bereaved parent could have told them to beware, that among the first capabilities to go after their child's death, would be their parenting skills. But Martha and Ted blundered into an impossible situation, one which had unfortunate long-range consequences. They adopted a brother and sister from the inner city. The children were about nine and eleven years old, abused and psychologically damaged. Martha tried in vain to deal with the two, who got into very serious trouble as they grew to adulthood in the affluent suburban community where Martha and Ted lived. There were school difficulties, run-ins with police, behavioral and addiction problems, and jail terms.

Meanwhile, Martha's marriage dissolved because of the stress caused by the adopted children and the parents' inability to deal with Meggie's death. Martha's life became even more of a shambles than it was on that tragic day when her daughter died. Many times over the years, Martha expressed to me her regret at having adopted those children. Perhaps it was yet another inappropriate response to the initial search we bereaved parents engage in in the early stages of our grief, an act of desperation to assuage the pain of loss.

Others who lost an adult child may at the same time be entering the period of their lives in which a mid-life crisis might be expected, even if the parent were not bereaved. A desperate attempt to regain lost youth may now be coupled with grief, which may lead to promiscuity or the complete abandonment of a former career. Such a distortion of the search for a dead child is potentially dangerous, particularly when the judgment of the bereaved parent is so severely impaired by grief—as dangerous as a resort to drugs or alcohol.

Dr. H. William Batt, an obliging friend who was always ready to come to my rescue when a problem arose regarding my computer during the writing of this book, related the following story to me.

Many years ago, Bill was a young college student who was undergoing the identity crisis commonly called "sophomore slump." In a particularly unhappy mood, he took off from his studies in Amherst, Massachusetts, during the spring break and set out to hike the Appalachian Trail by himself.

The first night on the trail the weather was raw and rainy. He located a lean-to in the woods, built himself a warming bonfire, and hunkered down for the night. Some time in the hours after midnight Bill's slumbers were disturbed by a rustling noise. He awakened, looked up, and saw an enormous man peering down at him silently. The intruder was clad in a shiny black raincoat and carried a walking stick. He appeared to be a man in his late fifties, had a scraggly red beard, was dirty and unkempt.

Bill was startled, then very frightened. Not knowing what to expect, and hoping to placate his guest, he said, "Hello. Can I fix you a cup of coffee? I'll put some more wood on my fire and heat it up."

The man sat down. He was gruff and wasn't much interested in coffee. Besides, he had brought his own bottle of liquor, having already drunk quite a bit of it. The two of them started to talk. Bill telling the man about himself, how confused and unhappy he was, and how uncertain and unpromising his future looked.

The older man's story then came out. He was, he said, the father of two sons. One was a ne'er-do-well, a disappointment to his father. The other, a brilliant, intelligent, earnest, and socially-conscious young man, was his father's pride. Young, idealistic, that son had gone to Cuba to fight alongside Fidel Castro in his struggle for power during the Cuban Revolution. He had been killed in that war.

By the time his story was ended, the older man was very drunk. He began berating Bill for being a weak, sniveling, self-pitying, and worthless human being. Why was Bill still alive while his own more worthy son was dead? He raised his walking stick and charged toward Bill.

Bill was able to dodge the blows. His drunken assailant fell down. Bill quickly took out a rope he had with him, tied the man up and then tied him to a tree.

By now it was nearly dawn. Bill took off at top speed to run to a nearby village. He reported the incident to the local policeman, who accompanied Bill back to the wooded spot and apprehended the man.

This scenario is not difficult for bereaved parents to understand. The almost uncontrollable anger fathers or mothers feel after losing a child is monumental in scope. The temptation to drown their over-whelming sorrow in alcohol is also immense. Getting drunk and beat-ing up a young stranger, however, is hardly the acceptable response to either anger or sorrow.

To hear that this episode occurred in the midst of a dark wood in the middle of a very dark, rainy night, far away from that bereaved father's home, is also an indication that he may have been engaging in a subconscious, irrational search for his dead son.

If it is a parent who has lost a young child, the search has another dimension not shared with those whose child was an adult at the time of death. However fraught with difficulties, the young parents who search for a way to fill the void left by the death of their child may have a hopeful option not open to elderly parents: they can sometimes have another baby.

In February 1995, we were awaiting with joyous anticipation the birth of a second baby to our friends Delores and Ronnie Campbell. When the phone rang on their due date, my husband answered. Hearing the name, I immediately picked up another phone and shouted, "Ron, your baby is here! I am so happy for you!"

"Wait, wait, Jeanne," cautioned my husband, "there is bad news."

Ronnie told us that although the baby's heart had been beating normally during the long delivery, it stopped immediately after his birth. Frantic attempts by the attendants started the heart beating after some time, but tests revealed that the little boy was brain dead.

For several days the parents, grandparents, and little sister kept a sad vigil until he died. Months of sorrow and anguish followed for those grieving parents. They wanted another child to fill their empty arms. Could they endure the possibility of another tragedy if they decided to have another baby? Their answer was a courageous "yes."

The next pregnancy was filled with tension and worry for both parents. Even Laura, who had been two and a half when her brother Kenneth died, expressed her concern that this baby might die, too.

This time the result was happy. Maria, a beautiful baby girl, was born twenty months after the death of her brother. Yet Delores, her mother, is torn with conflicting emotions. "I love this little baby to distraction," she said, "But I know we would not have her if Ken hadn't died. I feel strange about that."

Delores is expressing feelings never experienced by parents whose adult child died. For them, the possibility of reproducing is foreclosed by the passage of time; their biological clocks have run out.

If bereaved parents must continue searching for the child who died, they must beware of finding an inappropriate replacement. Whatever the temptation to find one, there really is no appropriate way to replace a dead child, particularly if the parents are beyond the age when they are physically able to have another baby.

Parents of an adult child who died must deal solely with their loss, and with the gaping emptiness in their lives which cries out to be filled. The void created by the child's death can never be filled. Life must be reconstructed around that void.

That is not only the hard part, but the only sound and sensible part as well. Being sound and sensible are not always the reigning attributes of bereaved parents, however. Years after their loss, and at a point when they are least expecting it, their dead child will suddenly appear, walking along the sidewalk up ahead. And the parents will once again follow her. "Wait! Wait! Talk to me!" they want to say. But they don't say it. This time the parents have no illusions that the child is really theirs, or anything like theirs except in appearance. Wistfully, they will realize that their feelings are only a sign that "hope springs eternal in the human heart."

CHAPTER 12

Conflicting Agendas: Adult Survivors

When a young child dies, the bereaved parents automatically become the focus of intense grief. There may be young siblings, grandparents, aunts and uncles, cousins and friends, but no one questions the primacy of the parents' grief. And only the parents are in charge of funeral arrangements, final decisions about a burial site, memorials, time, and place of mourning. The parents are completely independent of anyone else in assuming the authority to do whatever they see fit.

However, that is not true of the death of an adult child. There are usually several adult survivors, not just the parents, who had a strong emotional investment in the life of the deceased. Each of them has some input. Each of them has some claim to authority. Each one must handle the chaos resulting from the death in his or her own way. The decisions which are made in such circumstances often conflict with the emotional needs of the bereaved parents.

At the very moment of death, when no one is entirely capable of making intelligent decisions, someone is forced to make those decisions.

The very first question, then, is who is in charge? Is it the widow or widower, the survivor with the legal right? Is it the parents? Are the parents so devastated that an adult sibling of the deceased must take over? Do the siblings agree on what must be done? How much influence do the parents have among the others?

Funerals are notorious for spawning family squabbles—some petty and some serious. Even when events follow a natural order and it is a parent who dies, it is not uncommon for siblings to disagree when making final arrangements. In the case of the death of an adult child, when in-laws are vying with parents of the deceased, the potential for anger escalates.

We have friends in New York State whose daughter was living in California when she died of a heart attack. Their son-in-law insisted on burying his wife in a hand-hewn coffin. Though the parents preferred cremation, they deferred to his wishes. Their gracious acceptance of their son-in-law's decision enabled them to retain a good relationship with him, a relationship sustained for more than twenty years. It enabled them to share in the raising of their then two-year-old grandson, who spent part of each year in California with his father, part with his grandparents in New York. Perhaps this peaceable resolution to a potentially hurtful disagreement is an exception to the rule.

A few years ago I listened to a tearful mother from Florida tell me her story at a national conference of *The Compassionate Friends*. Her daughter was a victim of AIDS, acquired from a blood transfusion. After a painful, protracted illness, she died. Sensing that her son-in-law would soon remarry, the mother hoped to have her daughter buried nearby so she could visit her grave often. Instead, the son-in-law insisted that the burial take place in his hometown, far away from the mother's home. An estrangement grew up because of that. Now the widower has indeed remarried; the grave is unvisited and untended. The bereaved mother doesn't even see her two grandchildren any longer.

Funeral and burial details, alas, are sometimes only the opening salvo in a long-term battle among survivors of an adult child's death.

In addition to disagreeing about funeral arrangements, there is a temptation for survivors to engage in destructive behavior in their extreme distress. This in turn, prompts the anger and disapproval of all other survivors. In our self-help group, we emphasize the importance of avoiding negative responses to the death of our child. We are cautioned not to succumb to alcohol, drugs, promiscuity, and other irresponsible ways of coping with our grief.

Although we focus on ourselves as parents, we sometimes forget that the other adult survivors of our child's death are just as vulnerable to destructive behavior as we are. If those other adult survivors behave inappropriately, both personally and regarding the raising of grandchildren, complications develop and become an added burden for the bereaved parents as well.

I shared a workshop in Philadelphia some years ago with a couple well into their seventies. They faced serious problems trying to deal with the widow of their only son. Their daughter-in-law, devastated by her husband's death, had adopted a destructive life style. The mother of two preschool children, she had begun drinking and carousing, neglecting the youngsters and causing the grandparents to worry about their safety and well-being. The bereaved parents were both in precarious health and unable to get custody of the children.

Because bereaved parents are so preoccupied with their own condition, they may not be able to understand the motivations behind some of these actions on the part of other survivors.

The age difference goes a long way in explaining much of this aberrational behavior. The younger survivors are at a different place in their lives than the parents. Young widows, widowers, or "significant others" are faced with having to go on with their lives without the presence of their partners. Companionship and sexual and economic needs may loom as determinants in a decision to cut the deceased's parents out of the survivors' lives. For family members as well as in-laws, there may have been residual hostility in the relationship that came out into the open when the death occurred.

It might be helpful at this point to illustrate the types of situations faced by some of the bereaved parents who answered my Questionnaire. Following are some abbreviated responses to question 8: "What is your relationship with your child's survivors?"

A divorced mother whose daughter committed suicide replies: "I have had to take over the care of my teenage grandson. My son-in-law has not been a responsible father to him. Needless to say, my son-in-law and I do not have a good relationship."

Behind that terse sentence is a story of this mother's attempts to fill the void brought on by the death of her teenage grandson's mother. Piled on top of this, is her own grief and sense of failure over her daughter's death.

A mother whose daughter was killed in an auto accident in which the son-in-law was driving: "I resent his not having been alert, which caused the accident. We are not in touch very often. He has remarried now, which has been painful for us."

Parents whose son was killed in the military: "He was divorced, with two surviving children, ages twelve and eleven. Relations with our ex-daughter-in-law were quite strained at first because our son had had custody of his children. We, the grandparents, tried to get custody and lost. Things are now much better with our ex-daughter-in-law and just perfect with the grandchildren."

Mother of a murdered son: "My son was married twice. I have been friendly with his former wife. His second wife and I are estranged and I don't see my grandchildren."

The mother of a son who died of leukemia after a long illness: "His father and I got divorced during his illness."

Parents of a son who was electrocuted on the job: "We gave all our son's personal belongings to his fiancee, including his new car and a considerable amount of insurance money. She married his best friend. We are upset and resentful."

The mother of a son who died of suicide (suspected murder) in Indiana: "His live-in girlfriend made life miserable for us. She keeps after us for money." A surviving brother in this family has been divorced since his sibling's death.

A mother whose son was murdered while in military service: "My son's father and I were divorced many years ago and I had remarried. My second husband couldn't cope with my grief. He told me to shape up or get out. We are now divorced."

The mother of a son killed in an avalanche during a mountain-climbing vacation: "Another of our sons was also in the accident. He was badly hurt but survived. Both he and his ex-wife believe the trauma of that experience caused their subsequent divorce."

A father who also lost his son in a mountain-climbing accident: "Our surviving daughter, who was with her brother when he was killed, suffered from extreme guilt feelings. Although she is working this out, she has had trouble earning a living because of the emotional stress."

A widowed father who lost a son and a daughter within one year: "My daughter's husband was badly injured in the accident which killed her. He seldom communicates with my surviving daughter and me. He has moved and changed his phone number, which I do not have. My relationship with the grandchildren is OK, although I seldom see two of the three."

Mother of a son killed in an auto accident and a daughter who was murdered: "There have been lots of problems brought on by their deaths. The sibling closest in age to the dead children is behaving very destructively and has a suicidal life style, with drinking and adjustment problems. My daughter's son has had problems with his mother's death and his father is not helpful. I am raising my grandson."

This experience mirrors that of one of my friends whose daughter died of a heart attack. Her surviving son was behaving so erratically that she took him aside one day and said, "Just take me out in the driveway and run over me with your car. I can't bear to lose another child, and the way you are acting, you are going to get killed. Let's just get it over with!"

Mother of a murdered daughter: "My surviving daughter and I have a better relationship now, but at first it was strained for many reasons. Things are OK with my grandchildren." A follow-up letter indicates that this mother had to wait for her surviving daughter to come to terms with a bad father-daughter relationship before she could reconcile with the bereaved mother. Meantime, the mother suffered added grief. Perhaps it is as my friend Lydia says, "The unfinished business gets in the way of closure."

The mother of a son who died of drug and alcohol overdose: "The relationship with my son's widow is greatly strained. My husband and daughter want nothing to do with her. I, on the other hand, feel she is as troubled as my son was; co-dependent. I am working on this, though it is tough."

Mother of a daughter who died of Hodgkins Disease: " I still have a good relationship with her husband. She was an only child and he is too. They were married for fifteen years and had no children. Although he has not remarried, I would not object to his remarriage and he knows this, for we have talked about it."

Mother of a son who died of a heart attack: "My son's survivors do not seem to be grieving. It is impossible to talk with them about the death of my son." This woman goes on to say that her husband is rude and insensitive, spending his time at home out in the garage drinking. Unfortunately, that is a recognized method of coping with grief.

The mother of a son who was a suicide: "My husband never came back to himself after our son's death. He was overcome with guilt, cried constantly, and felt hurt and cheated. He died of cancer two years afterwards. During his illness, I lost my job because my co-workers were insensitive to my problems. I now have a good relationship with my three surviving children and also with my son's friends and former girlfriend."

Mother of a woman who died of scleroderma: "My daughter's husband remarried one year and two weeks after her death. I see two of the three stepsons fairly often but relations are somewhat strained." This mother confided that she felt her daughter was overburdened with family matters while she was ill.

Mother of a murdered son: "Although I was divorced from my son's father, we have since become good friends."

Parents of two sons and a daughter-in-law killed by a drag-racer: "Our surviving daughter-in-law remarried to a friend of our son's and is estranged. We have not seen our two grandsons for several years."

Mother of a young doctor who committed suicide: "Our marriage was very good before our son's death but now my husband and I don't communicate at all."

Mother of a daughter who died of lupus after a long illness. "Our two grandchildren are very close to us. However, we feel very uncomfortable about their father, who had a girlfriend four months after our daughter's death, and he brings her home."

Mother of a man who died of cancer: " There is no tension between me and my surviving daughter, though my relationship with my older son is strained."

Mother of a daughter who died of drug-related sepsis: "In addition to my husband and me, she left a brother and sister. They do not talk about her. If I mention her, they are very uncomfortable. It is almost as though she never even existed."

Mother of a son, the cause of whose death was never satisfactorily explained: "My son was married twice and had one child by his first wife and two by his second. My relationship with my daughter-in-law was strained at first, not about anything in particular, just the usual 'I should have done this and you should have done that,' but slowly we are making inroads in repairing our relationship. My relationship with my grandchildren is very good."

Mother of a son who committed suicide: " My surviving son is bitter and angry. My daughter went through a rough period of hurt, but she is very strong and has grown a lot through this experience."

Father of a daughter who died in an auto accident: "There was strain between me and my surviving daughter and we did not speak to each other for several months."

Mother of a daughter who died in an auto accident: "My husband and I had a strained relationship at first, as did my son. Now it is great."

Mother of a son killed in an auto accident: "I am divorced and my son lived with his father. Although our son's death was devastating for both of us, my former husband and I have continued a mutually supportive relationship. I have a wonderful relationship with our other son as well. I correspond with the girlfriend of my deceased son."

Mother of a daughter and granddaughter, who were aunt and niece and who perished in an auto-truck accident: "Family relationships are not strained, just difficult. The separate grieving, family to family, makes us unable to connect. My husband and I grieve for our daughter and granddaughter; our other daughter grieves for her child and for her sister."

Mother of a son killed by a car while he was walking on the Interstate: "Even though my son's girlfriend is now married, we still have a good relationship with her."

Mother whose daughter was killed in an auto accident: "Our relationship with our son-in-law is excellent."

Mother of a daughter who died of a drug overdose: "My daughter left a teen-age daughter who has had a lot of anguish over her mother's death. She has been in a psychiatric hospital. As for me, other survivors seem unable to handle my grief."

Mother of a daughter who died of cancer: "Our son seems more open, but there is strain between us and our surviving daughter. For some time, our deceased daughter's boyfriend corresponded with us, sent flowers on her birthday and death date and came to visit us. Then he married one of her good friends. We are no longer in contact with him."

Mother of a woman who died of an insect-borne disease: "My daughter left a three-year-old little girl and a one-year-old son. Their father never remarried and raised the children by himself. He took very good care of them, yet he was always estranged from my husband and me. Over the many years since then, I have sent airplane tickets so the children could visit me; otherwise I would never have seen them. On a recent visit, my adult granddaughter cut me off when I spoke of her mother. 'Oh Grandma, we don't talk about Mommy any more,' she said. You can imagine what a cruel remark that was for me to hear."

A mother whose son was twenty-three at the time he was electrocuted on the job: "My aunt Mary, age eighty, lost her fifty-six-year-old son to cancer on Christmas Day 1991. He lived in Texas. At his funeral she was overlooked completely. Her daughter-in-law did not do this, but everybody else did, from the funeral director to the priest. She had no say in anything that went on. Her daughter-in-law was so distraught that she didn't even notice this omission. All sympathy and compassion went to the widow and children. My aunt felt completely alone. I felt sympathy for her at the time, but after my son Dave died, I knew what she had gone through."

From the above recital, it would appear that complications with survivors of adult children are the norm rather than the exception. What can be done about it or how to forestall or correct it, is perhaps something for professionals to deal with. When relationships are strained, those whose presence should be sustaining may cause further anguish instead of comfort.

We bereaved parents find solace in the knowledge that we share physical and emotional responses to our children's death. It makes us feel normal when we know others also act crazy or forgetful, can't prepare meals, and/or get sick or depressed.

What comfort can we find in the knowledge that most of us lose not only our child but also the tender relationships we knew when that child was still living? That yet another loss is a part of our grieving, too, because our child was an adult?

The aforementioned complications with survivors represent instances in which there is slight comfort for us when we identify with each other. They seem glaringly to confirm our secret assessment of ourselves: because as parents we were supposed to protect our children, but did not prevent their deaths, we are failures. This subconscious assumption of guilt tempts us to chastise ourselves for being bad parents and worthless human beings.

It might help if we could look clearly and rationally at the other adult survivors of our child to evaluate the way they are reacting. Clarity and rationality are in short supply when we lose a child, however, so that may be asking too much. But if we could see clearly, we would have to admit that those other survivors are adults too, solely responsible for their own behavior. If they choose to cut us out of their lives, to break all ties with the deceased in order to start anew, it may be a valid solution for them. But it is not necessarily our fault. We are not guilty of causing their behavior.

If they indeed choose to sever relations with us, a break with our dead child's other adult survivors becomes a fact, explainable only in the light of irreconcilable needs, of conflicting agendas.

We, as surviving parents, need to keep our child's memory alive. We try at all times and at all costs to remind everyone of our dead child. From the very day of our child's death, we have been searching for ways to talk about him or her, to bring up stories about our child, to cling to every shred of memory, and to make sure people don't forget. Each of us makes an effort to prepare an appropriate memorial, which is one concrete way of keeping our child alive in our hearts and in the lives of others. The need to do this is compelling, almost all-encompassing. For some bereaved parents, it is the last vestige of hope that their child will not be forgotten.

On the other hand, some of the other adult survivors, in order to get on with their lives, need to forget the dead, to put their grief behind them.

When those other survivors are in our presence, they experience painful reminders of the death of their loved one so they avoid us. Our efforts at reinforcing the memory of the deceased are countered by their equally forceful efforts at forgetting. Double hurts are automatic in such cases.

From my present vantage point, I recognize that some of these breaks are indeed irreparable. You can probably deal with the disappearance from your life of your daughter's fiance, your angry daughter-in-law, or your remarried son-in-law.

The fact is, however, that you need to be in close contact with your grandchildren and your surviving children. That need is biological and will never disappear. To lose such a precious link with your dead child is to heighten the tragedy of your loss.

Sooner or later, the rifts must somehow be mended to the point where you can once again be a part of their lives.

How do we reconcile those two conflicting agendas for living after the death of our adult children? Each of the two approaches represents a valid choice for survivors. Making the choice, whichever it may be, then picking up the pieces and going on with life, is a positive response to loss.

There should be a resolution satisfactory to both factions. The bereaved parents must find a way to keep alive the memory of their child; the others must be respected and accommodated if they need to forget the deceased.

How these irreconcilable needs can be resolved without hurt feelings, without either party being judgmental, without alienation, is the big challenge. Recognizing it as a challenge is the first step toward resolution. This is the time to seek professional help, if possible. In some states, the laws specify rights of grandparents to be involved with their grandchildren. Recourse to legal action may be called for in extreme cases.

CHAPTER 13

Birthdays and
Death Anniversaries

In the fall and again in the spring, if we are out in the open, we are apt to hear an occasional faint, familiar call which turns our attention skyward to note the passage of migrating fowl. The V-shaped formations of ducks and geese pierce the airways as these wild creatures wend their long way to their seasonal homes. As winter approaches, the V will point southward. Half a year later, as winter ends, the birds return north to their summer abodes.

People have conjectured for countless centuries about this phenomenon. How, they ask, do these creatures know where to go? How to they know when and where to gather together to depart for their seasonal habitats? Fascinating studies by naturalists attempt to answer these questions.

Is there, perhaps, not only a physical response but also a biological response in all living creatures, not just in migratory birds, to the changing seasons? To the annual voyage of the earth around the sun? Is there something within which helps a person chart his or her life as it passes by, annually referring to personal events in the individual's past? Does this help us measure our days on earth?

Civilization has all but neutralized the differences between the hot and cold seasons of the year in the temperate zones, blurring the physical responses human beings once had to winter and summer. When the fierce, chilling winds blow outside, we can now come in out of the cold to the warmth of a house heated by a furnace, hardly noticing the threat winter formerly posed for survival. In summer, an air conditioner or a whirring fan can keep us cool.

Desensitized as human beings are in this modern, artificial, civilized world to the vast differences in temperature extremes of the out-of-doors, we still carry with us something of our past responses to the seasons. Even though our senses are dulled by our present safety from the elements, we still mark the seasons as our primitive ancestors did. A certain feel in the air in early March; the appearance of a crocus blossom peeking through the late snow; listening for the returning robin's song will remind us of former springtimes. The scent of the first rose of June will herald summer. The sight of fall's apples turned red, the orange leaf fallen to the sidewalk after a strong wind will tell us that autumn is at hand. And before the first white flakes of snow begin to flutter through the air, we remind ourselves to put away the lawn furniture in preparation for winter's blasts.

If we do in fact subconsciously number our days with the turning of the earth, then it is not hard to understand that, as our child's birthday or the anniversary of death approaches, a tremendous buildup of emotion will undoubtedly occur. Our child's death is a traumatic event which has seared itself on our subconscious as well as our conscious minds.

There is no way to avoid this; it just seems to happen. Apprehension and a sense of dread will also increase before other special days: Mother's Day, Father's Day, Christmas, and Thanksgiving; but it is different, somehow, for the birthday and death anniversary. The emphasis on the latter two occasions is on the dead child alone, not on the family, religious observance, or national holiday, so grief is also concentrated. For whatever reason, it is a bad time which looms long before the actual date.

Some parents experience the pre-anniversary pain without knowing the basis for their distress. In an attempt to understand what is aggravating their feelings of grief, they may ask another parent who has been bereaved for a longer time. The latter parent will undoubtedly ask, "Is the date of a birthday or death anniversary approaching? If so, you have found the explanation for your problem." And that parent will remind you how important it is to plan for those birthday or anniversary dates, to be ready to defuse the pain. Or, as we bereaved parents sometimes say, so you don't crash.

If you are a cemetery-goer, you will probably plan a special gift for your child's grave. In addition to that, I find it helps me to be out of the house during those days, doing something special to remember my child rather than allowing depression and sadness to take over.

On the first anniversary of Cathy's death, July 12, 1988, my husband and I decided to make an excursion to Glens Falls, about forty miles north of Albany, to visit the Hyde Collection in a wonderful small museum. Built on the plan of the Isabella Stuart Gardner museum in Boston, the Hyde Collection has many choice works of art:

a Rembrandt, some fine Medieval, Renaissance, Impressionist and modern works, sculpture and period furniture, as well as paintings.

My husband Bob and I shared a love for and appreciation of art with Cathy, who was a serious artist. A museum visit appeared to be a good way for us to get through that very sad day.

Her father and I visited Cathy's grave early that July morning with a special gift of flowers and then set out to drive to Glens Falls. It was a beautiful, sunny day; the countryside was lush and green.

The museum was quiet, cool, and deserted except for ourselves. We looked at each painting with a special feeling for Cathy.

At the end of our tour of the various rooms, I stopped in the museum shop. Because we were scheduled to attend a dinner at our Unitarian Church that evening, I decided on the spur of the moment, to commemorate Cathy's death anniversary by buying some beautiful, artistic paper napkins for the church dinner.

That night when I opened each napkin to put it into the wine glass at every place setting, I discovered that there was a picture of a gorgeous butterfly in the center of the napkin. The butterfly had not been visible when the napkin was folded and I had no way of knowing it was there. A butterfly, a symbol of hope for bereaved parents!

If you can't get away on an excursion on the birthday or anniversary, it might help to promise yourself a treat: buy something special in honor of having survived for another year. At one particularly low, low point for me, I went to Filene's department store and bought an exquisite Chinese bowl, a planter. I am careful of my money so it was a real extravagance.

As the years go by, I look at that Chinese bowl often, remembering the difficult time I was having when I bought it. Looking at it now, I am reminded how hard I am trying to stay afloat; how much better I am. It gives me courage.

We can use all the help we can get, even with little things.

The season of the year complicates the observance of Cathy's birthday. She was born March 3, 1948 . . . during an ice storm, incidentally. The year we observed her forty-sixth birthday was 1994. On March 3 of that year we were in the middle of a particularly fierce winter. When we drove to the cemetery on the morning of her birthday to bring her a rose, we couldn't even find her grave. The stone was buried beneath great heaps of snow and there was no way to get near it unless we had snowshoes, which we didn't. The fact of her being dead was emphasized and my grief compounded.

I have had trouble with snow since her death. Those first few winters without her found me weeping uncontrollably whenever it started to snow. Something about the jolly winters in my happy Wisconsin childhood triggers that feeling and I don't understand it.

This is all by way of background to explain my desperate reaction to finding her grave obliterated by a heavy snow cover on her forty-sixth birthday. I gazed through my tears at the white scene and said beneath my breath, "Oh, Cathy, if you could only give me a sign that you are still alive somewhere. . . ."

On our way home from the cemetery, we stopped at the supermarket. The weather was so wretched that at first I planned to wait in the car while Bob went into the store to pick up some groceries. But suddenly I was moved to open the car door. I stepped down into the slush. There, at my feet, was a pile of pennies. Not just one penny: twenty-one of them shining through the snow!

We give special attention to the needs of those in our bereaved parents' group who are approaching a birthday or death anniversary, helping them plan for the day. Our local *Compassionate Friends* chapter was founded by a couple whose daughter, Elaine, was killed in an auto accident, just before Christmas, at the age of nineteen. Lois Mitchell, the widow of our former leader, said she and Harold used to drive on Elaine's birthday to the Pennsylvania Dutch country, where they had adopted her. It comforted them to be in the part of the country where she was born when her birthday came around.

Olivia Merryman's daughter, Rose, died two years and nine months after she was diagnosed with scleroderma. Rose was thirty, with a husband and three stepchildren. Each year about the time of the anniversary of Rose's death in July, as many of her siblings as can get together join Olivia to go out to eat together. Then they visit the cemetery with flowers, have a prayer, and talk about Rose and what she meant to them. Olivia said she was weeping as she wrote about their observance of Rose's anniversary. She also described Rose's illness, the shock of her death, and the emotional pain and physical distress she herself has experienced since then.

Every year on the date of his death, the Crizers, parents of a son who was electrocuted, go to the utility pole where the accident happened. There they have a private ceremony of love and remembrance.

Some bereaved parents plan to give memorial gifts or contribute flowers to their church on those personal, special days. Our friends and Cathy's friends send flowers or call us on both her birthday and death anniversary. We are comforted to know they remember, although the number who do so decreases every year. That is an expected phenomenon. It makes us sad, but we understand. Losing an adult child means that the parents must expect other adult survivors to abandon thoughts of the deceased in order to get on with their lives.

For them, there will be other associates, other loves, and other friends to replace Cathy.

We, as her parents, can never forget, nor do we want to. We use the occasion of her birthday and death anniversary to commemorate her life in some especially meaningful way. And to remind ourselves once again how precious she was . . . and is . . . to us.

CHAPTER 14

Happy Holidays

Someone we know sees us across the street or in the supermarket. A cheery greeting rings in our ears: "Happy (fill in the appropriate words) "Birthday," "New Year," "Easter," "Passover," "Mother's Day," "Father's Day," "Thanksgiving," or "Merry Christmas." Each of these greetings can be heard annually.

Rather than happiness, every time these special dates come around, they bring pain for the bereaved parent, not just the first year, but for many subsequent years.

Two days after Thanksgiving, my husband and I were walking in the mall when we encountered Mary and Harry Minassian, neighbors whose son, a prominent young doctor, died a month after our daughter Cathy's death, leaving a widow and three-year-old son. "The season starts again!" said Mary, "How can we stand it? Everybody is full of good cheer and we are trying to face another Christmas without our son." They lamented the fact that their grandson is now twelve years old and never had the benefit of knowing his father during his childhood.

Bereaved parents are forced to change the verb which formerly described their response to all those joyous holidays mentioned above. They no longer celebrate; they honor, commemorate, observe, endure, or just get through them. Celebration is no longer an appropriate word.

Caregivers are alert to this phenomenon and usually suggest that the bereaved make a plan to deal with the anticipated holiday well before it arrives. Planning sometimes helps minimize the pain. The plan must be specific, not "Maybe I'll go out to lunch," but "I will get up on the morning of the holiday and do this, then that, then go here, and then go there. Everything will be focused. No sitting at home wondering how to handle my sorrow."

Even with a definite plan, there is no way to entirely eliminate the exaggerated feelings of sadness when a holiday comes around and your child is no longer alive.

You may be on your way to the cemetery on Thanksgiving morning, as I was, and look up to see a plane coming in for a landing. Your imagination transports you to the airport nearby where a family is awaiting the arrival of loved ones, home for the holiday. The fact that your loved one is not coming home for Thanksgiving, or any other holiday, is poignantly reinforced.

On the ninth Thanksgiving without my daughter Cathy, our family had worked out our plan. Because our son and his wife live in California, we do not share holidays with them. But our daughter Laurel and her son Paul live only a few miles away. After we all talked it over together, they decided to invite a few friends to their house rather than join us at church, where there was to be a potluck dinner.

Very early on that Thanksgiving morning, I began preparing a huge turkey to put into the oven. It was the first time I had done so since Cathy died. Beginning to stuff the holiday bird brought flashes of memories of past Thanksgiving days when our house was filled with relatives and friends, when we wondered if there would be enough chairs or dishes to accommodate them all for the big feast. These memories started the tears flowing.

But it was to get better as the day progressed, for I was among others at church and my sadness was muted, part of the plan to observe the holiday differently than we used to. It was the best we could expect, considering the emotional baggage we were carrying.

Mother's Day, and Father's Day—for bereaved parents—are occasions for stress and weeping, calling special attention to our loss, year after year. As with every other potentially painful holiday, the days which honor our status as parents must be planned for too. Your child probably made some loving gesture on those days prior to his or her death: a card, a gift, a phone call, and/or a visit on your special day. The absence of any possibility that there will be such a gesture, even as simple as a card, becomes a particularly glaring reminder that he or she is dead. This might be an occasion to consider purchasing a gift for yourself in honor of being your child's mother or father. Little rituals, and small indulgences sometimes serve to soften grief, although it may be hard for the non-bereaved to understand how something so simple can be helpful. "See this ring?" a bereaved mother said, encountering me on the street. "I bought it for myself on Mother's Day—from my son."

For bereaved parents who celebrate Christmas as part of their family tradition, it is probably the most painful and difficult of all holidays. The anguish experienced on the holidays mentioned previously lasts for only a few days at the most (including the buildup); Christmas is not only a day, it is a whole season building up, with elaborate preparations over several weeks. It is therefore important for parents whose children have died to come to an understanding of why Christmas is particularly sad for them, and to devote some time and thought to making it as endurable as possible.

In this chapter I will attempt to explore why this holiday may be more painful for those whose child was an adult at the time of death. It is my feeling that Christmas, with its focus on the family, made up of layer upon layer of accumulated memories, carries an overwhelming impact because of the sheer volume of such memories for those whose adult child died. To illustrate my point, I will take the reader on a long voyage into my past, hoping as I do so, that the bereaved parent who is reading this will gradually unearth his or her own package of Christmas Past memories, revealing at the same time the basis for Christmas Pain.

I am well aware that the Christmas memories of many adults are not necessarily happy. Those whose childhoods were scarred were nevertheless aware of the fact that Christmas was supposed to be happy. Those sad children were surely hoping and wishing to build future joys and often did so when their children arrived. Expectations are often not met and disappointment results. The very idea of happiness at Christmas may in fact be a myth. Memories of Christmas, whether happy or sad, are nevertheless vivid and enduring, influencing the present.

My own experience tells me that I will more readily accept a premise as true when I have convinced myself, not just listened to what someone else tells me. At the end of this painful unearthing, I hope you will be kind enough to yourself to say, "Yes, I now understand I have a valid reason to be sad about Christmas. I am not just being difficult or perverse. From now on, I will do my best to change the way I respond to the recurrence of that season in order to lessen my sadness."

In addition, this chapter deals with some ways in which bereaved families try to cope with the difficulties of the holiday season.

The Christmas holiday was once almost exclusively religious. Now, however, in our more secular society, it has become a time when the emphasis is primarily on the family: family reunions and exchange of gifts among family members. In fact, for many Americans, whatever their religious faith, the holiday might be described thus: "Christmas, which started out as a Christian celebration of the birth of Jesus, has become an annual secular festival celebrating the importance of the family." I nearly said "worship of the family," for that is almost what it has become.

Religious leaders, sociologists, and politicians toss around the term "family values" without any clear reference to its exact meaning. Perhaps it has become such a cliche that it means whatever anyone wants it to mean: something good, surely, but what? Is it the glue that binds us strongly or loosely to those who gave us life? Is a family value something that gives you a sense of your roots or your place in the world, therefore making you more comfortable? Perhaps, if you have strong family values, you have an abiding connection with the people who love you no matter what. Or is a set of family values what you learn and believe about life as taught to you by your nuclear family? Or it is what makes you a good person? Or are family values, as some of our leaders imply, the foundation of ideas and ideals on which our nation and our civilization are built?

Whatever "family values" may mean, most people agree that they represent something desirable, a veritable cement binding us Americans together as a people and as a nation. And whatever the meaning, it is not difficult to understand that most families, no matter how tenuous the ties to individual members may be, will feel some tugs of closeness, some identification with the concept of "family values" if they have ever celebrated a happy Christmas together.

Unlike any other time of year, the Christmas holiday season, although it may be subscribed to by the society in general and shared with others outside the nuclear family, is primarily a private celebration, steeped in traditions which have built up over the generations in that family alone, shared more or less equally by the birth family of the father and the mother.

During an annual relaxation of inhibitions against emotional outpourings, Christmas allows us to be slightly more sentimental, extravagant, impulsive, and generous in our purchases, more willing and ready to express our love and affection for those dear to us, even though we may pay scant attention to such matters during the rest of the year. And because it is so closely identified with love, it means the loss of loved ones will be felt more acutely at Christmas.

Christmas Day itself is packed with memories and stories of Christmas Past and Christmas Long Past: tales and rituals of parents, their parents, and grandparents. The ghosts of beloved ancestors long dead are called up in memory to link them to the present, to enhance the pleasures of the living. This year's joys (as well as catastrophes) are added to the list of memorable Christmas days of long ago, reinforcing what we know about our own family which makes it unique and cherished.

Family customs, once established, cry out to be followed. Everyone knows that stockings must be hung from the fireplace mantle, but when I was a small child, there was no fireplace in our house. We used to get a large cardboard packing box, cut it in the shape of a fireplace and cover it with crepe paper printed with a brick pattern. There! We had a fireplace!

A dish of cookies, a glass of milk for Santa, and a carrot for Santa's reindeer had to be placed near the fireplace. And nobody in our house decorated the tree before Christmas Eve. It just wasn't done!

As a little girl, my maternal grandmother wanted a doll. Her father woke her early one Christmas morning to tell her she had a doll. Not a toy, but a real baby had arrived during the night. That baby, little Maggie, died at the age of three months. When I was a child, my grandmother used to tell and retell that story, always with a hint of sadness in her voice.

I remember my mother telling me about how, when she was a child, she got up while it was still dark on Christmas morning and had to walk across the mound of snow which had sifted into her bedroom during the night. When I was tiny, and before I learned to play the piano, my mother taught me how to pick out with one finger the Christmas carol which had been her father's favorite, "Away in a Manger." Her father died the summer before I was born.

I recall that my younger brother Jerry, now dead, loved the Christmas tree so much he once prevailed upon my indulgent parents to keep it up until Easter. A few years earlier, there was Santa's gift to my other brother, Philip, of his "autom-beel," the toy car he could sit in.

One year there was a surprise visit from my soldier husband, home from the war for Christmas. The year of our first baby's first Christmas, her cries suddenly ceased when we placed her bassinet under the Christmas tree and she saw the multi-colored lights. I have a photograph of Cathy, aged nine months, on her first Christmas, sitting beneath the Christmas tree, reaching for a shiny bauble hanging from a low branch.

Then there was the year Santa brought our children the black and white kitten, placed in the stocking which Grandma Webster had knitted, hanging on the mantle among the other stockings. Mama had had to sing her lullabies louder to conceal the kitten's mewing when baby woke in the night and had to be rocked back to sleep. Then there was the year the tiny Fox Terrier puppy, "Buttons," kept at the neighbors' house to conceal its barking, arrived at the front door shortly after dawn. And the baby doll with real hair; the shiny new bicycles hidden in the foyer.

One year there was a frantic pre-Christmas search to locate the mermaid Cathy requested. When she kept insisting, with a three-year-old's great confidence in Santa's ability, that he could surely find a mermaid for her, we persisted. Someone told us he had once seen a lurid mermaid fishing lure for sale in a sporting goods store. I phoned all over the county and drove several miles until I found it. With some difficulty, I removed the fishhook from the mermaid's navel and filled the incision with red fingernail polish. Santa had found Cathy her mermaid.

Once the kids chipped in all their allowance money to buy Mom a blender, but she was too sick with the flu to open the parcel. I have never stopped feeling regretful that I did not respond more appropriately to their generosity.

In our family, the memories and rituals did not begin on Christmas Day. Besides a frenzy of shopping, early December used to bring a flurry of activity in our household. There was the baking and frosting of hundreds of cookies, preparing plum puddings and fruitcake, decorating the house, selecting the "just right" tree, sending and receiving invitations, cards and parcels, and long distance phone calls from long silent friends.

Just before Christmas Day arrived, when our children were little, the grandparents, laden with brightly wrapped packages, would come from Wisconsin on the train. In later years, our grown children, some with spouses, would arrive from college or their distant homes. It was sometimes the only time of year they were all home together. Because they enjoyed each other's company, the house was filled with hilarity, banter, and laughter. Just having them home was part of the joy of Christmas.

On Christmas Eve, decorating the tree, we would carefully lift the fragile ornaments out of their packing boxes. Each had its tale to tell, its special reference to Christmas Past. A few had graced my parents' Christmas tree during my childhood and had somehow magically survived the intervening years. An exotic decoration was brought from Pakistan as a gift by a former neighbor. Two others were sent to us by the Chinese friend we have known since 1949. Another came from overseas friends in Venice. We purchased the newest decoration , a smiling angel, to top our first tree in the new house in Albany. Every year the three glass birds were pulled from the box, each of which had belonged to one of our children. One of the tiny birds has no tail; it was pulled off by our baby son in 1951. The ceramic mouse and the dancing angel were sculpted and painted by Cathy.

Tossing the "icicles" onto the tree at the end of the decorating ritual often got out of hand, with most of them landing on the floor or in someone's hair. Piling gifts under the newly-decorated tree came next.

Next came the lighting of a candle in each window, Christmas carols, with Mom playing the piano and the others singing, then Bible readings of the Christmas story. Lastly, the hanging of the children's stockings on the mantle (even after those children became adults) completed the family ritual. And there was a lunch for Santa and his reindeer. Though we got to bed late, everyone was up before dawn to open the presents.

On and on, over the years, the memories accumulated in the family. Given the long-term relationship parents have established with their adult children, those memories are an almost physical presence in some families as the holiday approaches.

After thirty-nine years of celebrating family Christmas rituals with our daughter Cathy, those memories arrived on schedule after her death, each of them bringing a stabbing pain. What used to bring laughter in the recollection now prompts tears.

How are we to deal with Christmas without our child? I regret to say that the Blank family has never figured out a satisfactory answer to that question.

It is not that we haven't tried. We knew it would be too painful to handle each memory-filled ornament, so there was no tree after her death. Christmas carols made us cry, so the piano and record player were silent. Mom had no energy for baking and decorating cookies; she could scarcely force herself to go into the kitchen.

After the first Christmas of watching videotapes from morning until midnight, the approach of the second Christmas after Cathy's death loomed as a real problem for my husband and me. No more videotapes and moping around this year.

Someone suggested it might ease my pain if I did something to help others. Yes, the poor; I would help the poor. I volunteered to work in the kitchen of a local Catholic church preparing meals for the needy on Christmas Day. The kitchen was staffed by generous volunteers from a Jewish group, since they were not celebrating Christmas, anyway.

I put on my bright red apron and pitched in. Turkey and all the trimmings; lots of turkey and lots of trimmings; lots of volunteers, who outnumbered the poor about five to one. What a letdown! They didn't need me, and seeing the five or six forlorn men sitting at the tables was a real downer. Friends called the next day to say they had seen me on TV helping at the community dinner. Community dinner, indeed; I had been so depressed by it all that I hadn't even watched the replay on TV.

The third Christmas approached. No videotapes; no volunteering; this year Bob and I would escape the holiday altogether. Our son lived far away, so we wouldn't see him. We would let our surviving daughter and grandson who lived near us fend for themselves. We parents would escape from Christmas by leaving town.

How about going to Montreal, a strange city where we knew no one? Canada is a foreign country with no holiday customs familiar to us. And no memories.

This plan alarmed our more sensible friends, who cautioned us about the roads and the unpredictability of the weather at that time of year. Realizing that we were not to be deterred, they insisted that we stock up on food, take along their CB radio and blankets in case we slid off the road or were marooned during a storm.

The trip began well enough early on the morning of December 23rd. The scenery was beautiful along the Northway as we drove through the snow-covered Adirondack Mountains. We had the roads to ourselves. They had been cleared of snow and were only a little slippery.

As we drove into Montreal, fresh snow was falling gently, blanketing the dingy streets of that vast city with a sparkling white cover. After checking into a dismal and shabby hotel, whose name included some reference to Napoleon in deference to the French-loving Quebecois, we set out to do some sightseeing. This included visiting a museum almost empty of anyone but ourselves, touring the buildings constructed for the recent Olympic Games, then eating a dinner of indifferent quality at an overpriced restaurant.

Next day, a Sunday, was devoted to attending church, walking through the crowded underground shopping malls, and exploring China Town, where we bought a charming teapot as a souvenir and stopped for lunch at a lively Chinese restaurant. The streets were teeming with last minute shoppers.

It had been snowing intermittently since our arrival in Montreal, and soon after lunch on Sunday, it began again. We drove then to the Old Town, supposedly the most quaint and charming part of Montreal, a mecca for tourists. Parking our car in a deserted parking lot, we went exploring on foot.

Businesses had closed early in honor of Christmas Eve. It was getting dark. The Old Town was desolate and empty, its reputed picture-postcard loveliness completely eclipsed by winter gloom. Wandering the dark streets, we eventually realized we were lost because we could not locate our car. There was no one on the streets except ourselves.

Getting more and more disheartened, we stood at a bus stop, shivering and stamping our feet to keep warm, until a bus appeared. A woebegone pair, old and lost, we must have been a pitiable sight. The bus driver was puzzled by our request for information, but when Bob spoke to him in French, he finally understood our problem. Inviting us to get into his bus, he waved us away from the farebox and drove us to our car, going well off his route to do so.

We had already checked the location of the cathedral for Midnight Mass that was within comfortable walking distance of our hotel even in a snowstorm. The plan to Escape Christmas, though somewhat disappointing so far, was on schedule.

While waiting for the hour to go to church, the two of us dropped into a dreary Chinese restaurant a block or so from our hotel. We shared the place with one other customer, a tattered and forlorn street person who had been staked to a Christmas Eve meal by the restaurant owners. Supper was dismal; the food barely edible.

My husband and I were at the end of our resources. Without even speaking about it, both of us realized we could not face the pageantry and the music of the church service. The snow was now more than ankle deep and coming down harder.

Opposite the restaurant, we spied a cinema marquee, *Dances With Wolves* was playing. Instead of going to Midnight Mass, we stumbled across the street to the movie. The theater was huge, the audience sparse; probably as lonely and sad and out of place as we. Christmas is for happy people, celebrating their private rituals at home with those they love.

The cinema saved us once again. We could have stayed home and watched a film on video tape. Distraction was what we needed. After the show, sleep was all we craved.

Before dawn next morning, Christmas Day, we shoveled our car out of a snowbank and headed for home: Albany, New York. After stopping at the United States-Canadian border to buy gifts to carry to our neighbors' open houses later in the day, we drove for miles through an enchanted landscape.

During the night, while it was snowing in Montreal, the Adirondack Mountains had had freezing rain. Each branch, pine needle, and blade of roadside grass was coated with glistening, dazzling, sparkling ice. The sun turned the landscape into a crystal fairyland, flashes of light darting back and forth as the wind moved the trees; Nature's Christmas Show.

On that trip to Montreal we had learned a lesson. We discovered that, if you can't escape Christmas, you have to look for some way to defuse the sadness. Lately we have spent a part of each Christmas Day with our daughter Laurel and our grandson Paul. We don't stay at their house very long; just to touch base and exchange gifts but not long enough for the tears to start. We arrange to speak to our son and daughter-in-law in California the day before Christmas, not Christmas Day.

In the afternoon we attend first one, and then a second, and a third Open House of three kind neighbor families who live on either side of us, mingling with their relatives and friends, trying to ignore the void we feel in our lives without Cathy.

For us, no more Christmas trees; the ornaments and lights have lain in the attic, packed in their several boxes, since 1986. Seeing each decoration, even remembering them, brings tears. Our annual traditions are now too stressful to contemplate, let alone try to repeat.

A few years ago, for the first time since Cathy's death, I returned to my custom of baking on a moderate scale. I made a small batch of Christmas cookies and a few plum puddings, enough to send to our son Paul and his wife Annette, her mother, and sisters in northern California and for our local family, friends, and neighbors. And I placed a small artificial tree, decorated with miniature ornaments and fresh flowers, on our coffee table. Besides flowers, there was a little tree on Cathy's grave adorned with tiny angels.

Will I ever again feel like having a gigantic Christmas tree, so big it has to be cut off to get it into the living room? And will I hear my grandson say, "Grandma, remember the time we were just beginning to open our gifts on Christmas morning and the Christmas tree tipped over with a big crash?"

Shall we try to build new memories? For families who have lost young children, it is probably important to try to do that. As one grieving mother of a young child who died put it, "I don't want my kids to go through life hating Christmas because it is so sad."

For those of us whose adult child died, who now have no young children at home, it might seem easier to ignore Christmas. Our friends Mary Lou and Ed Clark have done just that since the death of their daughter Angela, though they take gifts to their son and his wife and the three little grandchildren. And I realize that my great-grandmother Susan also canceled her traditional Christmas celebrations after her daughter Jo and granddaughter Joey died early in this century.

Yet for me there is something unsatisfactory in ignoring Christmas. The need to feel closer to my dead child forces me to make some concessions to the season. I find it comforting to attend the annual memorial candle-lighting service at our bereaved parents group the third Tuesday in December. For the past few years I have accompanied violinist Albert Deresienski on the piano during the ritual readings and candle lighting. Planning the program and our hours of rehearsals provide yet another opportunity to concentrate on Cathy.

What follows are some suggestions for coping with Christmas; the first being a reiteration that we do things differently than before our child's death, in order to ease the pain of familiar traditions. Even if you try to follow these instructions, you may fail, as we did when we went to Montreal and even more spectacularly in a subsequent attempt to "do something different," which you will read about below.

To be attuned to your emotions means knowing what you can endure. It is important not to subject yourself to any more pain than necessary. Being surrounded by all the trappings of the holiday, the decorations, carols, Santa ringing his bell on a street corner, and smells of baking may accentuate your grief. Each one is a trigger to provoke tears.

At the first meeting in the fall of a bereaved parents' group, someone will suggest that those present finish their Christmas shopping immediately, before the Christmas decorations and the sounds of carols appear in the stores. If going to the stores is too difficult, an easier way to shop is to utilize the many catalogues which choke the mailbox.

A mother whose son died buys a gift for each of his siblings "from him." Setting a special place at the table for the absent child seems too sad for me, but some bereaved parents do it. Lighting a memorial candle or hanging a stocking for the missing child, filling it with notes of love, then burning the messages in the fireplace, might help those who find it difficult to talk about the deceased. If a family can manage it, asking each of them to write a reminiscence of the child who died, then reading the notes during the meal or while decorating the tree, could help them start to talk. There is healing in talking, in sharing memories.

Outside the nuclear family, among the extended family, there are often conflicting needs regarding Christmas. The adult siblings or other relatives, hoping to celebrate Christmas as it used to be before the loss, may make preparations for the traditional meal or get-together. They expect the bereaved parents to attend, to be cheery and "not spoil Christmas."

The mother and father, on the other hand, may be finding this the hardest season of the year. Just accepting the invitation to the family dinner becomes a big decision. They want to include memories of their dead child during the occasion in some way; the others feel any reference to the deceased does not belong at a "happy" occasion. The attitudes of the non-bereaved at a holiday dinner table often exacerbate an already tense relationship.

One year some of our local friends gave up in despair at trying to deal with their extended family. They dined on take-out pizza rather than attend a family dinner, with all the relatives present, on Christmas Day. Parents whose child died may feel more comfortable sharing part of Christmas Day with other bereaved parents rather than extended family. They don't have to explain their sadness or cause a scene when they cry. They are welcome to speak of their hurt, which does not ruin Christmas.

We have been told often enough, and therefore must believe it, that there is healing each year we face this most precious and difficult family holiday and survive.

Each year, Christmas baking in my house gets closer to normal, including my grandson's help with cut-out cookies. The Christmas tree ornaments have now made it down from the attic as far as the dining room, where they lie in their boxes during the Christmas holidays, still packed away under a table. But that is progress.

Some people are slow learners. Even though I should know by now that you can't escape Christmas, I can't stop trying. Christmas, 1996, our son and daughter-in-law were planning to go to China and Hong Kong on a combination business and pleasure trip over the holidays. We too, on the other side of the continent, decided we must make plans.

Again my husband and I opted for escape. It seemed such a logical thing to do. Our Venetian friends had suffered the loss of people close to them and to us during the past year. Why didn't we fill their empty places at the holiday table in Italy?

We invited our daughter Laurel and her fourteen-year-old son to go with us on what was to be a two-week vacation in Venice to visit our Italian friends.

The trip was a series of disasters. It began in an ice storm, with missed plane connections, lost luggage, and late arrival in Venice, where there was also bad weather. Immediately upon our arrival, I got sick and spent the better part of a week in bed, missing all the dinner parties, concerts, and festivities. While the others attended a party at the home of our friend Giorgio, I spent a solitary Christmas dinner sipping chicken soup in the flickering light of the memorial candle I had brought from the United States.

After recovering from the flu, I was barely out of bed (two days) when I was walking along a canalside and caught my heel in a hole in the pavement, tripped and fell, breaking my left hip. Hospitalization and surgery for a hip replacement followed.

I spent a nightmarish three weeks in the Venetian hospital, a series of complications making me wonder whether I would survive. After my husband and an Italian friend untangled the red tape attendant upon my release from the hospital, I was brought home on a twenty-four-hour journey on two planes and four ambulances (on a stretcher), then spent two more weeks in a local hospital. Spring arrived and was well advanced before I was able to walk without a cane. So much for doing things differently! Perhaps planning must be done more intelligently.

So if the occasion arises when I might be tempted to say to you, "Merry Christmas," you and I will know it is an inappropriate greeting. Your Christmas may never again be really merry, as it was in the years before your child's death, nor will the other holidays which return every year. Nor will mine. But some day, they may be more nearly endurable than they are now.

Mending Christmas in particular will mean mending our family; not just the nuclear family, but the extended family, all of whom are hurting in a special way at holiday time after the death of a loved one. Christmas, when family values whatever they may be are most painfully stressed (in the sense of being emphasized as well as being stressful), represents a monumental challenge to the bereaved.

Next year, I am staying home rather than trying yet another disastrous escape. As my friends at the local self-help group say, "Don't you know by now that you can't escape from Christmas?"

Perhaps I have learned that getting through Christmas is similar to getting through one of those phases of grief all bereaved parents must endure in order to heal. No detours, no escapes! Just grit your teeth, straighten your shoulders and do it!

If it appeals to you, you might try instituting a private ritual with family. The memorial service below is similar to that we observe at The *Compassionate Friends*.

SUGGESTED
CHRISTMAS MEMORIAL RITUAL

The leader of the bereaved parents' group or one of the family members will begin by lighting candles, probably a candelabra on a table at the front of the assemblage. In a basket to one side, there will be a memorial candle for each person, to be lighted at the end of the ceremony.

First candle: "I light this candle in memory of our children who have died."

Second candle: "I light this candle to represent the sorrow we feel because of our children's death and to honor and acknowledge the intensity of our grief during this holiday season."

Third candle: "This candle is the light of love, the love we feel for our dead children, which will live forever."

RESPONSIVE READING

All: We gather at this holiday season to remember in a special way our children who have died. It is helpful to do this in the company of other bereaved parents, grandparents, and siblings because it is difficult to do so anywhere else. At this time of year, when families get together to celebrate, we find ourselves out of step with most people. They are happier than usual; we are sadder than usual. At holiday season we have a greater need to talk about and include our absent children. Others would rather we did not do so.

Mothers: Tonight each of us remembers with sorrow a special person who is no longer with us. We recognize an end to one of life's most significant relationships, that of parent and child.

Fathers: We also acknowledge the grief of all the grandparents who lost their beloved grandchildren, of all the brothers and sisters who have lost their siblings. When our children died, those siblings suffered because their parents were unable to be the strong caregivers they had once been. They were changed by their grief.

Siblings: Death cannot end the feeling that the absent one is close to us. Although not physically present, our sisters or brothers are still with us in spirit and in our hearts.

Mothers: Thoughts of our children who died are with us constantly on our journey through life. As we share our memories of them, however difficult that may be, we are helped to affirm their lives.

Fathers: Although our children's lives were cut short, destroying our own hopes and dreams for them, we know their lives are not meaningless. We hope to carry out acts of kindness in their names.

Siblings: We cherish our memories of the days of childhood we shared with our siblings who died.

All: As we light candles in remembrance of our sons and daughters, our grandchildren, our brothers and sisters, we share and divide our pain. Let us bow our heads in loving memory.

At the conclusion of this reading, the leader will light one of the memorial candles from the basket, saying, "I light this candle in memory of _____." Then he or she will light the candle of another person sitting next to him or her, who says, "In memory of _____" and lights the next person's candle until all have been lighted.

At several points in this ritual, appropriate music, either live or taped, may be played.

CHAPTER 15

Your Health During Bereavement

Phyllis Long, a respondent from Virginia, writes: "My husband became extremely withdrawn and depressed after our son's suicide. He cried constantly and couldn't get interested in anything but the death and his grief. He never came back to himself. He felt hurt and cheated. He died from cancer two years after our son's death."

Mr. Long's is not an isolated case. In fact, serious illness is common among parents whose children have died. They frequently find themselves in need of professional care, calling upon psychologists, psychiatrists, and general practitioners to treat them. A recital of some of the conditions which prompt them to consult doctors will follow. It is common knowledge that bereaved parents do indeed, fall prey to more physical and emotional ailments than non-grievers.

Everyone expects copious tears, but few are prepared for the more subtle and insidious bodily reactions bereaved parents experience when their children die, including the parents themselves. Those parents were, until their child's death, members of the general public, which has a poor understanding of the grief process. This is also true of many members of the medical profession, psychological counselors, and psychiatrists.

Although recent trends in the education of physicians are beginning to correct this omission, medical schools have traditionally paid scant attention to training their students in this important and possibly unique area of health care. When doctors are called upon to treat grieving parents who show signs of illness or stress, those practitioners may be dealing with a condition about which they may have neither training nor understanding. The obvious result is that doctors often prescribe treatment or medication inappropriate for the patient.

Giving sleeping pills, with a strong component of depressants, to an already depressed person who cannot sleep is just one example. Another counterproductive response is urging the grieving patient to get on with his or her life. "Come, come, it's already a year (two years, five years). Shape up!" is possibly the worst thing a physician can say to a bereaved parent who already may be concerned about not being able to shape up. This only compounds the parent's feelings of inadequacy and despair.

The hidden component in the bereaved parent's stress-related illness is time. Some parents immediately get sick. With others, however, elapsed time from the death of the child to the emergence of the illness may be so great that the physician does not connect the parents' symptoms with their traumatic loss. For the older parent whose child was an adult at the time of death, the diagnosis of illness might be clouded by an assumption that it is age-connected rather than loss-connected.

The pain of dealing with grief can lead bereaved parents to ignore or as we often say, to stuff the grief inside themselves, where it festers to become depression and illness. Physical problems can be compounded by an overwhelming sense of hopelessness, during which time the bereaved parent does not really care whether he or she lives or dies. In fact, the urge to join their child in death contributes to the worsening of any condition of ill health as well as to the danger of suicide.

How can we explain illness as a common response to the death of a child? Bereaved parents desperately need an explanation, for they may blame their illness on some psychosomatic acting out of their grief or on an inability to deal with difficulties, or perhaps they are just imagining it. They need to be assured that there is a medical basis for their symptoms.

Since prehistoric times, the human body has been equipped with various mechanisms for survival in emergencies. One of these bodily mechanisms has been handily labeled "the fight or flight syndrome." A natural reaction which takes place when our security is threatened, a sudden rush of adrenalin and other hormones provides the extra strength needed to run fast or to stand and confront the danger at hand. This automatic reaction in an emergency enabled our primitive ancestors to fight off or flee from predators and is an evolutionary relic unsuited, except on rare occasions, to modern life.

When we are plunged into grief because our child died, our bodies respond as though we were assailed by an external enemy and ready us to defend ourselves. Every part of the human body reacts when the person perceives danger. Part of the trauma occasioned by the death of a child involves a feeling of fear and dread, of being out of control, with the world becoming suddenly unsafe.

Although the bereaved parent needs neither to fight nor to flee in such a circumstance, the body has no other way to deal with tremendous stress. Thus the mechanism operates in a primitive fashion, with an excess of hormonal activity. These hormones, normally dissipated during a fight or flight, stay trapped in the body to do their mischief, causing a host of problems. The blood rushes away from our gastrointestinal system, destroying our appetite and sometimes causing nausea. Blood pressure, heart rate, and chemical composition of the blood, change. Agitated and restless, bereaved parents are often unable to sleep, which leaves them in a constant state of exhaustion. Lack of sleep is known to be a factor in lowering the immune system, which puts them at considerable risk of illness or even death because of the imbalance their bodies experience during grief.

Self-help books put out to guide the general public in assessing medical problems describe the effect of severe stress on various parts of the body. Either caused by or aggravated by stress, the digestive tract will react with gastritis, stomach and duodenal ulcers, ulcerative colitis, and irritable colon. Attacks of angina and disturbances of the heart rate and rhythm often occur at the same time as, or shortly after, a period of stress. The bladder may become irritable. Mental and emotional problems, including anxiety and depression, may be triggered by stress. Baldness may develop. The skin may break out with eczema and psoriasis. Mouth ulcers and oral lichen planus crop up. Asthmatics find their condition worsening. Muscles twitch and the tremors of Parkinson's disease are more marked. Reproductive organs exhibit stress-related problems. One of the stressors listed by these books is the death of a close relative.

A recent bulletin published by the National Institutes of Health, "Understanding the Immune System," by Lydia Woods Schindler, explains how stress can deplete immune resources. A new field of research, known as psycho-neuroimmunology, is exploring how the immune system and the brain may interact to influence health. For years stress has been suspected of increasing susceptibility to various infectious diseases or cancer. Now evidence is mounting that the immune system and the nervous system may be inextricably interconnected. Research has shown that a wide range of stresses, from losing a spouse to facing a tough examination, can deplete immune resources, causing levels of B and T cells (antibodies which recognize antigens) to drop, natural killer cells to become less responsive, and fewer IgA antibodies (which protect the digestive tract) to be secreted in the saliva.

"Biological links between the immune system and the central nervous system exist at several levels. One well-known pathway involves the adrenal glands, which, in response to stress messages from the brain, release corticosteroid hormones into the blood. In addition to helping a person respond to emergencies by mobilizing the body's energy reserves, these 'stress hormones' decrease antibodies and reduce lymphocytes (small white blood cells produced in the lymphoid organs and paramount in the immune defenses) in both number and strength."

Research reported in the *New York Times* on Tuesday, January 23, 1996, lays some of the blame for intestinal upsets, chronic abdominal pain, and a host of other problems on the so-called "gut brain." In a report by Dr. Michael Gershon at Columbia-Presbyterian Hospital in New York, the existence and functions of such a brain are the subjects of a new study. "The human gut has long been seen as a repository of good and bad feelings. Perhaps emotional states from the head's brain are mirrored in the gut's brain, where they are felt by those who pay attention to them," the article concludes.

Bereaved parents will be reassured when they hear that there are actual physical changes which take place in their bodies as a result of the stress of losing their child. The breakdown of the immune system which causes illness to flare up among the bereaved now sounds logical and expected. Spelled out in detail, as in information from the National Institutes of Health, research indicates that the parents are neither defective in character nor mentally incompetent, but just plain sick.

As the pattern of bodily response to bereavement continues to be revealed in this chapter, it is important to note that the parent of an adult child who dies is particularly vulnerable to illness occasioned by stress. That parent is undoubtedly older than the parent of a young child who dies. Older people are generally more susceptible to illness, included as members of the two categories of the population thought to be most at risk for disease: the very young and the elderly. With the onset of old age, these parents will fall prey to disease at an accelerated rate.

At the same time, given their approach to the end of life, they are susceptible to hopelessness as well. Recent research reveals that hopelessness too, can cause illness and death. An added insight might be derived from an article in *Science News,* a weekly news magazine of Science, Volume 149, Number 15, dated April 13, 1996.

" 'Bleak expectations about oneself and the future bode ill for physical health, a new study finds. Men who cite an abiding sense of such hopelessness die at higher than average rates from heart disease, cancer, and other causes,' assert Susan A. Everson, an epidemiologist at the Western Consortium for Public Health in Berkeley, California, and her colleagues. Hopelessness also exhibits a strong statistical link to the emergence of new cases of heart disease and cancer. Moreover, the link holds up regardless of the presence of other major risk factors for disease and death, including depression, cigarette smoking, high blood pressure, frequent alcohol use, and lack of social support.

" 'We were astonished by these findings,' remarks epidemiologist George A. Kaplan of the California Department of Health Services in Berkeley, a coauthor of the report. 'It looks like people who experience a pervasive sense of hopelessness are at increased risk for a variety of serious health problems and require careful medical surveillance.'

" 'The findings contradict the widespread notion that hopelessness represents an extreme form of depression,' writes C. David Jenkins, a psychologist at the University of North Carolina at Chapel Hill School of Medicine, in an accompanying comment. In the new study, hopelessness incurred different, more serious types of damage than depression did,' he states."

The above research was done in Finland over a period of from four to ten years. "Physiological effects of prolonged hopelessness that contribute to physical disease remain poorly understood," the report continues. "Hopeless men may experience surges of stress hormones, which can undermine the heart or other internal organs, or they may undergo immune changes leading to cancer," the Berkeley researcher theorizes. (Quoted with permission from "Science News," the weekly news magazine of science, copyright 1996 by Science Service, Inc.)

Some specific examples of bodily responses to the death of their adult children may serve to illustrate the validity of the assumption that bereaved parents suffer physical and emotional illness as a result of their loss. Question 20 on my survey reads as follows: Did you experience mental and physical problems after the death of your child? Please check items which apply to you.

    a. Memory loss
    b. Inability to concentrate
    c. Sleep problems (too much? too little?)
    d. Eating/weight problems (gain? loss?)
    e. Thoughts of suicide
    f. Depression (needed medication?)
    g. Illness (tell us what illness)
    h. Accidents (tell us what accidents)
    i. Feeling that you are going crazy
    j. Other

The following responses to question 20 are culled from the survey. Because each of the questionnaires was filled out by one or two grieving parents, whose attention and concentration may be temporarily flawed, several questions were misinterpreted, left out, or only partially answered. Some neglected to give ages, dates, names, marital status, or other important data. But those who did not leave out question 20 answered as follows:

1. Mother, sixty, whose daughter committed suicide at age forty experienced memory loss, inability to concentrate, depression, and illness (breathing problems; panic attacks).

2. Mother, forty-five, and father (divorced): their son, twenty-five, committed suicide and killed his girlfriend. Mother checked inability to sleep, overeating, depression, bipolar mood disorder (psychiatric hospital), and manic state.

3. Mother, sixty plus, and father: their son, twenty-two, was killed in a car accident/suspected homicide. Suffered memory loss, sleep problems, depression, and illness.

4. Mother and father: son, thirty-five, was killed in military service (mysterious chemical accident). Mother checked memory loss, inability to concentrate, thoughts of suicide, depression, illness, and other: didn't want to be near anyone and felt she was losing her mind.

5. Mother and divorced father lost their son by murder. She is in the care of a psychiatrist and takes medication for clinical depression and suffers from post-traumatic stress syndrome. Has night terrors and dreams of executing her son's murderer.

6. Mother, forty-nine, and father, fifty-three, lost their son, twenty-three, who was electrocuted in a work-connected accident. Mother checked memory loss, inability to concentrate, sleep problems, weight and appetite loss, thoughts of suicide, depression, and had a car accident; breast cancer developed since son's death.

7. Mother, forty-eight, and father lost their daughter, twenty-six, to leukemia. Father had to have open heart surgery.

8. Mother, sixty-six, and father. Their son, a forty-year-old volunteer fireman, died of smoke inhalation. Mother checked memory loss, inability to concentrate, inability to sleep, depression, and illness.

9. Mother, forty-nine, whose son was murdered while in the army, was so despondent that her husband, not the son's father, threatened to leave and take their other children with him if she couldn't "shape up." The couple are now divorced.

10. Father and mother whose thirty-three-year-old son was killed in a mountain climbing accident suffered from depression.

11. Mother, forty-five, lost her son, twenty-four, from drug and alcohol abuse. Checked memory loss, inability to concentrate, sleep

problems, eating/weight problems, depression, thoughts of suicide, illness, and other: constantly exhausted.

12. Mother, thirty-five (divorced and remarried) and father (divorced) lost their eighteen-year-old son, who was stabbed to death. Checked memory loss, inability to concentrate, sleep problems, loss of appetite, depression, and illness.

13. Mother, fifty-six, and father (died soon after son's death; mother said it was grief which caused his death). Their twenty-two-year-old son died of suicide at college. Mother checked memory loss, inability to concentrate, and loss of job due to family problems.

14. Mother, fifty-two, and father, fifty-five, lost their son, twenty-four, to leukemia. Suffered both gain and loss of weight, thought of suicide often, had extreme depression.

15. Father, fifty-two, and mother lost their eighteen-year-old daughter to short-term viral pneumonia. Father checked memory loss, inability to concentrate, thoughts of suicide, and depression.

16. Mother, forty-four, and father lost their twenty-two-year-old son in an auto accident just after he graduated from college and was starting a new job. Mother suffered memory loss, inability to concentrate, and sleep problems. She lost thirty pounds in three weeks. She considered committing suicide, was depressed, and had her gallbladder removed.

17. Mother, fifty-five, and father lost thirty-year-old daughter to a long-term illness, scleroderma. Mother had sleep problems and developed fever blisters.

18. Mother and divorced father lost two children within a year: twenty-four-year-old son, hit by a van running a stop sign; twenty-year-old daughter, kidnapped and murdered. Mother developed diabetes, hypertension, depression, and overeating.

19. Mother, fifty-six, and father, fifty-nine, both answered. Their two sons (29 and 26) and new daughter-in-law (21) were killed by a hit-and-run driver en route to their wedding reception. Mother checked memory loss, inability to concentrate, sleeping all the time, and eating problems (gained 40 pounds); she developed lupus. Father had several heart attacks, one of which nearly killed him.

20. Mother, fifty-one, (divorced from father and remarried) and father lost their son, twenty-three, from a rare type of cancer. Mother suffered from weight loss, emotional instability, and fits of anger.

21. Mother, sixty-three, and father, sixty-seven, lost their only child, a daughter of thirty-eight, to lupus. Mother feels she is going crazy. Has too little sleep, weight gain, memory loss, inability to concentrate, depression, and a feeling she can't go on.

22. Mother and father of a thirty-one-year-old daughter who died of drug-related sepsis. Mother checked memory loss, inability to concentrate, overeating, a feeling that she is going crazy, and other: compulsive shopping; being busy-busy-busy all the time.

23. Mother (father dead for 12 years) lost forty-two-year-old daughter to long-term (7 years) Hodgkins disease. Suffers from inability to concentrate and loneliness.

24. Mother (41) and father, whose daughter, twenty, died in an auto accident, checked memory loss, inability to concentrate, sleep problems, eating problems, thoughts of suicide, depression, illness, accidents, and a feeling that she was going crazy.

25. Mother (60 plus) and father. Their twenty-nine-year-old son died of AIDS. Mother had memory loss, inability to concentrate, sleep problems, feeling she was going crazy, anxiety attacks, and panic attacks.

26. Mother (42) and Father (46). Their twenty-one-year-old son lived at home and died of suicide. Mother checked sleep problems, eating problems (lost 14 pounds), car accident, and loss of her job. She lost her father, mother-in-law, and son within a year.

27. Mother (58) and father lost their son, twenty, in an auto accident. Mother lost her job.

28. Father, sixty-one, and mother, who was sixty at the time of thirty-four-year-old daughter's death but she died eight years later. Their daughter was killed in a car accident. Father checked eating problems (weight gain), and depression.

29. Mother, forty-five, and father, lost their son, age nineteen, in an auto accident. Mother mentioned a terrible depression.

30. Mother, fifty-three, and father lost their daughter, twenty-four, and granddaughter, six, in an auto-truck accident. Mother checked memory loss, inability to concentrate, sleep problems, eating problems, thoughts of suicide, depression, illness, and a feeling she was going crazy.

31. Mother, forty-three, and father had a twenty-two-year-old son who was killed when he was hit by a bus while walking on the Interstate. Mother checked memory loss, inability to concentrate, sleep problems, eating problems, depression, illness, and a feeling she was going crazy.

32. Mother, fifty, and father, fifty-one, lost their daughter, age twenty-five, to a sudden heart attack. Mother checked too little sleep as well as illness: allergies, dermatitis, and bronchitis.

33. Mother, sixty-eight, and father, lost their thirty-six-year-old daughter in an auto accident. Mother developed diabetes caused by stress; father got colon cancer.

34. Mother, sixty-seven, and father, seventy-one, lost their thirty-nine-year-old daughter to breast cancer. Mother checked memory loss, inability to concentrate, sleep problems (too much), eating problems (gained 15 pounds), thoughts of suicide, depression, illness: had surgery for rare form of cancer; irritable bowel syndrome; digestive problems; lower back pain; pneumonia; accidents (fell and broke right foot and sprained ankle; was in a cast up to her knee for six weeks; fell at the cemetery and was again on crutches), feeling she was going crazy; constant exhaustion. Had a slight stroke.

If you felt, after reading the last entry, that that mother surely needed help, you were right. It is my story, and I did need help. My ability to cope with life after Cathy's death deteriorated rapidly. I consulted four physicians and one psychological counselor, all of whom failed to understand my problems.

Fortunately, I was then put in touch with a counselor specially trained in grief. My husband and I, as well as our surviving daughter, continued seeing her for some time. She operates a small counseling service in Greenfield Center, near Saratoga, New York, called "New Insights." Her name is Eileen Leary.

Because she is not authorized to prescribe medication, Ms. Leary has a working relationship with a sympathetic physician, Doctor Paul Okosky. We soon switched to him as our family practitioner. Knowing our wariness of doctors in view of the poor treatment our deceased daughter had received, he has been extremely careful to perform biopsies on my various suspicious lesions, referring me to the proper specialists and prescribing an antidepressant when I needed it. My husband and I sense that he is always fully aware of the precarious emotional state we are in, never neglecting to get to the bottom of a problem as soon as it surfaces, never denigrating or ignoring the smallest symptoms or concerns.

He has been a continuing source of comfort and strength to our family. When our surviving daughter was waiting for the outcome of a biopsy after a mammogram revealed a suspicious spot on her breast, our doctor knew her father and I were frantic with worry. He went out of his way to phone the laboratory for an immediate report on the result. To our great relief, it was not malignant. We were waiting in his office and burst into tears on hearing the news. "Nice to see tears of joy," he responded.

I wonder at his flexibility, at his realization that in spite of being an excellent doctor, he doesn't know it all. He is not ashamed to consult with our grief counselor when confronted with a despondent patient he doesn't know how to handle. My visit to her was once interrupted by an urgent call from the doctor, a grieving parent in his office having fallen apart during a consultation.

Although I was not privy to their conversation, I know from my own experience that Ms. Leary probably said, "Send her right over!" It might have been enough to calm that grieving mother to know that she now had an appointment with a specialist in the field of grief, that she would have some help in dealing with her grief, and that she was no longer alone. Her desperation would have been defused at least temporarily.

I knew too, that the mother would cry a lot during her sessions with Ms. Leary and the counselor would urge her to describe one and then another aspect of her sadness in order to bring her jumbled emotions into focus. Soon the counselor would probably begin giving that mother little assignments each week. To the non-bereaved these assignments might seem ridiculously simple; to the grieving mother, they would be important to her sense of her own worth. "Write a little note to Cathy to tell her how you feel," she would say to me. Or "This week I want you to make a list telling me all the difficult things you accomplished. Just getting up in the morning or going to the store, if that's all you could do." And to help defuse the anger against the doctors who treated Cathy, "Write them a letter telling them how angry you are. Get it all out! But don't send it."

Later, while chatting with some of her other patients, I learned that many of us bereaved parents forgot to do our assignments in the early days, but the counselor kept giving them to us until we complied with her requests. Gradually, when I could accomplish them, I realized that just focusing on those tiny jobs stopped the wild, whirling, destructive thoughts for a time, giving me a moment of calm during the storm which was raging within me.

The counselor would not be able to take away all the anguish of that woman who fell apart in Dr. Okosky's office, but she could guide her, little by little, along her grief journey. She could make certain that bereaved mother did not stumble and fall into despair when the way became darker and more difficult, when at times she felt like giving up. She would anticipate the road blocks facing that mother ahead: the dates of her child's death anniversary or birthday, helping her plan a specific activity to ease the pain and stress.

I sometimes think of my grief counselor as similar to one of St. Paul's companions who guided him after he was struck blind along the road to Damascus. Those companions took him to the house of Ananais, where he rested until he regained his sight. My counselor knew she could not take away all my pain, but she led me, she sat by my side, talked, encouraged, and listened until I "recovered my sight" and could walk by myself.

Because the trip to Dr. Okosky's office took an hour each way, we decided to switch to an Albany doctor when winter came. We have been fortunate in finding another caring, sympathetic physician, Dr. Jose David, just five minutes from our house. Those insightful doctors and counselors are out there! Don't settle for an unperceptive or insensitive one!

It is important for caregivers, both lay and professional, to realize that the bereaved parent's complaints are serious, perhaps life-threatening, and that their symptoms are probably connected to their loss, even if a long time may have elapsed since the death of their child. In addition, it is important that those caregivers understand that the extreme physical and emotional responses experienced by those whose child died are not aberrational but normal. Treating them as pathological, as tiresome character defects, is not only cruel, it is based on ignorance. Not treating them as serious may compound the patient's problems and interfere with his or her progress toward wholeness again. Or it may even reinforce the patient's urge to end it all.

The focus of this chapter has been twofold: the primary focus for the bereaved parents of an adult child; another for the caregivers who may read it. The final paragraph reemphasizes the message for both parents and caregivers.

Bereaved parents need to realize that their ailments, no matter what they may be, are genuine, physical, not imaginary. Those ailments are probably due to stress caused by their grief. Bereaved parents are not weak; they are just plain sick. Professional caregivers need to realize the same thing, and they need to listen sympathetically and treat their patients' symptoms with the seriousness they deserve. This may be a matter of life and death.

CHAPTER 16

Seeking Justice

When a child dies, a parent experiences not only a dreadful emptiness and sadness but in addition, a whole reordering of his or her ideas
about life takes place. This reordering often comes in the form of disillusionment. Almost every chapter in this book involves some aspect of
the loss of illusions, a complication which bereaved parents have to
deal with in addition to their grief.

As noted previously, the first illusion which disappears has to do
with one's attitude toward life. At the beginning of our lives as marriage partners, when we husbands and wives committed ourselves to
another human being and built a family with that person, we had a
certain degree of optimism about life in general. Most of us subconsciously assumed that if we lived a good life we would be rewarded by
happiness. It was only fair, and life was, of course, fair, another subconscious assumption.

Surely we must have been aware somewhere along the line, that
bad things happen to good people, but our optimism buoyed us up. We
never quite believed anything as bad as the death of our child could
happen to us. Maybe to somebody else, but not to us.

When our child dies, we discover that life is not fair. Along with the
realization that life is not fair comes the loss of optimism and hope.
But if we no longer believe in the fairness of life, that is not by any
means the only optimistic illusion which falls victim to our tragedy.

If doctors' errors caused your child's death, you will find yourself
disillusioned with the medical profession that you had formerly
trusted.

If military blunders caused the death, you may focus your cynicism
and distrust on the government and whatever branch your child was
serving in.

If the death was caused by criminal behavior, you may be involved with the police and with the courts, thus making yourself vulnerable to maltreatment by the judicial system.

Questions 8, 9, and 10 on my survey asked if the respondents had dealt with the medical, military, or justice systems when their children died. A follow-up question asked if they had been well-served by these systems. Of the thirty-six who had been involved with one or more of these systems, seven responded that they had positive experiences; twenty-nine had negative experiences.

A particularly flagrant abuse by "The System" involved the church, as reported by one of my respondents. Her local priest sent his aide, a verger, to comfort the young son of her deceased daughter. It soon became apparent that the aide was sexually abusing the boy. When it was brought to the attention of the presiding bishop, every effort was made to hush up the matter. No changes in personnel were made. There was no punishment for the offender.

Didn't most of us, in fact, build our attitudes toward society on the assumptions that doctors would follow accepted medical procedure; that our religious leaders would honor their vows to help rather than hurt?; that our military establishment would do its best to protect our soldiers?; that the justice system of our nation would bring us recourse through the courts?

We were naive to hold those assumptions, trusting so completely in the structural underpinnings of our modern society. It is particularly difficult for those whose child was an adult at the time of death to realize we could have lived so long with such blissful trust, with such delusions. For we had not taken into consideration something we should have observed from early childhood: every wrongdoer immediately runs for cover, refuses to take responsibility, and pay the price. Why shouldn't this ugly truth obtain in medical malpractice, misbehavior of clergy, vehicular homicide, murder, and military blunders?

Although justice should belong to the citizen who has been killed and to his survivors as much as to the killer, we have to come down to a hard, disillusioning, disappointing fact: we are not primarily a nation of justice; we are a nation of law. If the law can find a way for the criminal to escape payment for his crime, then justice may be poorly served. Loopholes, lying, technicalities, sloppy jurisprudence, lawyerly games, institutional cover-ups, military stonewalling may well win out over justice.

If doctors make mistakes, their peers close ranks to protect them from retribution. In our malpractice case, this was our experience. We still find it hard to deal with our residual anger regarding our treatment by the medical and legal systems.

If your child died while in military service, there is no guarantee you will get any satisfaction other than an impressive funeral. Janice and Harold Collins were ready to go out with friends one New Year's Eve when the doorbell rang. A soldier in uniform informed them that their son, Jeffrey, had been killed. The Collins' have learned that the United States Government will not tell you anything more than they want to tell you about a soldier's death. "A chemical accident," was all they were told. They will never know the truth about their son's death. For a long time, their anger at the military, at life, at the whole world, ruled their lives.

When parents confront the loss of a child and the loss of a sense of life's fairness, it is particularly ironic when they find out that there is no justice either.

Some of those who responded to my survey regarding legal, medical, and military involvement had positive experiences. They said: "The police were very kind; they called to tell us of the accident," or "The prosecutor was very understanding."

Those with negative experiences were particularly bitter, saying such things as "Not the justice system; the INjustice system," or "Justice system STANK," or "You wouldn't believe it! My son was killed and the driver was fined $15 for failure to yield the right of way."

Most offensive to those treated badly by the legal system were instances when the police destroyed letters and papers of a daughter after her suicide; when authorities refused to conduct proper investigations after a shooting death and called it suicide, while the parents are convinced it was murder; when technicalities got a confessed murderer off the hook; when parents brought charges against the driver in an accident that killed their son and then the charges were dropped without an explanation. (The unofficial explanation: the father of the car's driver had political influence.)

Elaine Christopher, whose son Tom died of leukemia at the age of twenty-four, says she has a nagging sense that Tom's death was hastened by an injection of pain killer. "I also experienced misunderstanding and callousness from many hospital staff members, especially in the Special Care Unit. I was prohibited by the unit rules from spending precious time with my son, and permitted only minutes at his side in the last days."

Bob and Eleanor Vought, parents of thirty-six-year-old Marci Fulweiler, waged a tireless and vain battle to bring an indictment against the man whose erratic driving caused their daughter's death. They solicited the aid of victims' organizations and friends to write letters to the New Hampshire authorities to get this killer driver off the roads. All to no avail; the charges were dropped. Eleanor says:

"There is something very wrong with the justice system if the victim has no rights and all compassion is for the person responsible for the death. Our beloved daughter's cruel and untimely death has left heartbroken parents, a devastated young husband, a community bereft of an active, valuable, and compassionate contributor, and hundreds of friends unable to comprehend why that community should not at least let a Grand Jury decide about an indictment. In our justice system isn't that the way it should be done?"

The above examples are only a few of many you can read about in greater detail, at least thirty-six, in Appendix 2 which deal with encounters bereaved parents have had with medical, legal, and military systems.

In our own case, our daughter Cathy's two doctors failed to follow proper medical procedure. She returned several times to the doctor's office over the course of a year with pain and a thickening in her right breast. Her primary care physician dutifully measured the increasing size of the thickened area over several months, then took a needle biopsy of the tumor. No fluid was present, which should have alerted the physician that it was not a benign cyst. But the doctor did nothing to check for cancer. After the office visit in October 1986, she sent Cathy to a specialist. There was no communication between the two physicians. The specialist said not to worry, but not to wait a year to get a mammogram. The doctor didn't order one, however. Precious time was lost in diagnosing cancer, time which might have saved her life.

Cathy got seriously ill in April 1987; the primary care doctor began treating her for a food allergy. After a turn for the worse, she was hospitalized in June, the cancer by that time having metastasized to the liver and bone. One of the hospital personnel told us he had never seen a cancer so far advanced prior to a diagnosis. The woman physician who took over from the primary care doctor at the same clinic in Boston was furious. Why hadn't they discovered the cancer earlier, while there was still a chance to save her? It was a case of shoddy medical procedure. Cathy died less than three weeks after the diagnosis of breast cancer.

An official State of Massachusetts medical review committee studied the records and decided that our case was not frivolous, that we had enough evidence to sue for malpractice. We initiated a law suit and the case was heard four years later in November 1991.

Our attempt to find a medical doctor who would testify against one of his peers was almost impossible. One of the two defendants in our case is a prominent Boston doctor trained at Harvard Medical School and a medical partner of the author of the definitive book on Breast

Cancer. When they read her impressive resume, none of the physicians who had originally agreed to testify would do so. But we did find one (retired) who was very good and a second who was a disaster, allowing the defense attorney to confuse him and destroy his credibility. Never mind; we had to pay his $5,000 fee anyway.

During jury selection the judge permitted a physician to sit on the jury, over our attorney's objection. This physician was employed in the same hospital where the defense's expert witness was on the staff. That defense witness almost admitted on the stand that the two doctors being sued were at fault. Fortunately for the defense, a weekend intervened before court resumed, time for the defense team to coach this doctor so that his honest testimony was not heard. This and several aberrations of the judge were the basis of an appeal after we lost the case.

We also lost our appeal. The Appeals Court didn't see anything wrong with having that physician on the jury because he "thought he could be fair."

Many pertinent facts were disallowed during the trial, including the clinic doctor's expressions of rage over the treatment Cathy had had from her primary care physician.

We had entered into the court case reluctantly, knowing it would be painful and expensive. But we felt we not only owed it to Cathy to validate her suffering, we also wanted to make sure those doctors would never again be as careless as they had been with her. Their guilt was so glaring that the judge at one point asked our attorney if we would accept an apology and call it quits. Our attorney had worked for four years on the case and was not about to go away unrewarded by a cash settlement.

Those doctors had nothing to worry about, however. They had a champion on the jury, a colleague who was not going to (a) jeopardize his standing at the hospital where the defense's expert witness held a prestigious position, (b) run up his insurance premiums by allowing a cash award to us, and (c) fail to exert his professional prestige as a physician among those lay people on the jury.

Our family feels we were cheated and a sleight-of-hand legal system allowed the guilty to go free. There was no justice for us or for Cathy.

One thing I feel quite certain about: those two physicians will never again watch and measure a lump growing in a patient's breast and not order a mammogram and other diagnostic measures. That fact alone has made it worthwhile to have pursued the case. Some unknown persons have been saved from Cathy's fate in the future by our having brought that court action.

My surviving daughter, Laurel, said that one of the attorneys for the defense came up to her after the deposition and before the trial. "Yours is about the finest family I've ever met," he said. Laurel said the translation is: "We'll screw you in court but don't take it personally."

I saw tears in his eyes while I was testifying about Cathy's death.

Why do bereaved parents put themselves through the agony of a trial? Some observers automatically assume that revenge is the motive. Although revenge may indeed be the reason some parents sue, it is not the primary one. In my own case, I did a great amount of soul-searching in the four years prior to the court action we initiated. Was I motivated by revenge?

Instead of revenge, there is a more important reason, mentioned above: an almost overpowering need on the part of parents to testify for their dead children, who were wronged and who are now powerless to cry out for justice on their own.

Before the verdict was rendered in our case, one of the two doctors who was a defendant came up to me and said, "I'm sorry your daughter died, Mrs. Blank." I was taken aback, knowing how difficult it must have been for her to approach me. "I know you are," I replied, "And I thank you for this gesture."

Perhaps she was seeking forgiveness, which I was not prepared to give. I am still unclear about the nature of forgiveness, even after thinking about it for years. If it means "It's all right that you killed my daughter by not following recommended medical procedure," then I cannot say that. It will never be all right. But if it means that I do not seek her pain, the destruction of her career, her punishment, then yes, I do forgive her.

All the partially buried anguish of our 1991 court case came up again when a dramatic murder trial was held in 1995 in Los Angeles. My attention was focused on the parents of the young man and woman who were stabbed to death, not on the defendant, a rich and famous athlete. Those parents had to sit in the courtroom in the glare of television and hear a "not guilty" verdict when it seemed obvious to nearly everyone except the jury that the athlete had committed the murders.

I was surprised at the ferocity of my own reaction to that verdict. Plunged again into the despair I experienced in November 1991, I once more confronted the anger, the frustration, the cynicism which became a part of our family's daily lives after our malpractice trial ended in the acquittal of the doctors who caused Cathy's death.

After the courtroom drama in Los Angeles, I found myself reliving our Boston trial. Once again I was reminded of my outrage at the distortions and lies, the deviousness of the defense team, the petulance of the presiding judge, the glaring unfairness of allowing that physician to sit on the jury, the jury's almost immediate decision after the judge's charge to them, indicating that they had already made up their minds without reviewing the evidence.

I found myself weeping for those Los Angeles parents and adult siblings of the two murder victims. It was not right, not fair for them; the Boston trial was not right, not fair for us. Injustice prevailed.

What do we say about injustice, which is what we get when there is a miscarriage of justice? We may say a lot, but what can we do? The law has spoken; that is the end. We have no further recourse.

We are left, then, with our destructive feelings and the problem of how to deal with those feelings. Cynicism, anger, and bitterness are the immediate responses. For me, it represented a further loss of faith in my fellow human beings as well as in the legal system. In addition, I felt a personal betrayal of the trust I had in my country as a just and fair nation, naive as that trust may have been.

How can we shore up the justice system, which seems from my vantage point to be eroding? How do we guarantee an impartial, intelligent, fair-minded jury, if in fact we continue to use the jury system? Such a jury can hardly ever be found under the present circumstances. I sense that cynicism is creeping into the public's concept of today's court system. Some modicum of trust in justice has to be restored. Money and fame; clever, devious lawyers; ignorant jurors: all weigh too heavily against impartial justice in judicial decisions.

Bereaved parents who have been treated shabbily by the medical, military, and legal systems will probably join me in shedding fresh tears for the two families in Los Angeles as they deal with the wretched feelings we understand too well. Perhaps the civil suit they have brought against their children's murderer will bring them some satisfaction, some measure of justice.

I hope those bereaved parents in Los Angeles can come to terms with their sense of betrayal by the justice system. If not, they will be plagued over the years by the inability to reach closure.

Closure is a word I have shied away from in this book until now. It means different things to different people; in the field of grief work it suggests that bereaved parents have finished grieving, have put their child's death behind them: closure, as in "the book is closed."

A better way to describe closure might be to say, "This chapter is closed, not this book," as the bereaved parent progresses from one phase of grief to another.

The fine distinction I wish to draw between closure and healing, or, to say it differently, between closing the chapter and closing the book on grief, may be hard for anyone who is not a bereaved parent to understand because of the intensity of the emotions involved.

To complete the healing process, the parents must have checked off the steps leading them toward a reinvestment in life. Each phase of grief must have been experienced and lived through: shock, denial, anger, guilt, acute sadness, and the final realization that the child's death is real and permanent. If some fragment of guilt, some shred of anger lingers even after many years have passed, then the parents find it almost impossible to complete their grief work.

The above stories about disillusionment with the medical, religious, military, and justice systems may lead to a clearer understanding of how difficult it is for bereaved parents to reach real closure. In these cases, it means closing the chapter on it, putting it to rest, swallowing the fact we can do nothing further about it.

Using respondent Carol Marshall's analogy of the death of our child as a wound which heals over, with a scab which can be disturbed and will bleed from time to time all the rest of our lives, then we can imagine in the case of injustice a portion of that wound never healed enough even to produce a scab. It is still open; still draining; still causing an irritation after the rest of the wound has stopped hurting so much. But it would be easier if the wound could be covered over with at least a scab, if not a permanent scar. That would happen with closure.

I think often of the survivors of those who perished when Pan Am flight 103 exploded over Lockerbie, Scotland, on December 21, 1988. Many of the dead were college students. I know several of their parents. After the crash, those survivors banded together to seek the truth about the terrorist act which took the lives of their loved ones, petitioning the United States government for action, agitating until they got satisfaction. After painstaking detective work, the exact cause of the explosion was determined. The identity of the perpetrators of that crime is known. They now hide from justice in Libya, under the stonewalling protection of a cruel dictator.

Will the parents of those students who died be able to find closure so long as those guilty of murdering their children evade punishment?

During the Civil Rights Movement, the battle cry of the African Americans was "No Justice, No Peace!" They were announcing to the world that they would practice civil disobedience until their goal of justice for all people, no matter what their race, was achieved.

But for bereaved parents who have experienced injustice, there will never be justice: their case is closed. Does that mean there will be no peace, no cessation of agitation and anger and bitterness for those parents? Bringing closure means we have done our grief work: we understand our feelings and reactions and we have dispelled our anger; we are no longer dwelling on some "unfinished business."

Bereaved parents may still feel great sadness and have a long way to go toward reinvesting in life. But if we can find closure, it will be easier to reinvest; yes, even to find some small measure of inner peace without the justice we have sought for so long.

For bereaved parents, it may have to be: "No justice; but peace anyhow."

CHAPTER 17

I'll Never Forget You

If you are like me, one of the most terrifying sensations after your child's death will be your inability to remember him or her. Friends, trying to be comforting, remind you how many wonderful memories you have, but try as you will, you can't find any. "You'll never forget her," they say, but it seems you have already forgotten. You can't remember the sound of her voice, the way she laughed or sang or turned her head. You cannot summon up an image of her face or her smile. What has happened to you? You have not only lost your child, you seem to have no clue that she ever lived. Wiped out; gone forever. You have lost your child and lost your mind as well!

This sensation may persist for quite some time. It is a symptom of grief. You are in shock, in denial, and when others tell you about all those wonderful memories, they are only compounding the agony you feel. You accuse yourself of being a wretched parent, for you can't even remember that child you loved so much.

One of the first desperate protestations of a newly bereaved parent is: "I don't want to forget," or "I'm afraid I'll forget her/him." According to the reasoning of these wounded parents, they are sad because they once had a child and that child is dead. They are upset because, during the early stages of mourning, they cannot remember the child. Therefore, it seems that they will be unable to keep the child in their memory unless they cling to their grief. Feeling the pain is the only way they can keep alive the presence of their child. Letting go of the pain means letting go of the child. They can't bear to do that.

Those who feel this way must be assured that this memory block is only temporary and they will soon regain a complete concept of their child, even if they relinquish their severe mourning.

Those who try to comfort us may say: "You are so fortunate to have pictures." In the long run this is true, and some parents may find it comforting, but looking at pictures may seem to others like being stabbed with a sharp instrument. There is almost no identification; only pain. For them, much time must pass before they can look at pictures of their dead child. Seeing those photos may serve to remind them that they have indeed forgotten their child, since the only time they can remember him or her is when they look at a picture.

Little by little, flashes of recognition will begin to intrude. At a certain point, I suddenly recalled hearing Cathy's voice as she used to respond when I answered the phone. (She usually called on a Friday night.) Not "Hello, Mom," but "Mom? Hi!" That was the beginning of the recall of the physical reality of my daughter, the Cathy who was healthy and vivacious in the days before her illness. I forced myself to reconstruct that greeting, over and over. Then I would say, "Yes, I remember her. I remember her voice." And I was momentarily comforted.

It was not as if I had not recently been in direct contact with Cathy. I was with her constantly from June 9th until her death on July 12th. We talked. We laughed. We cried together. But until I mentally reconstructed that weekly-telephone call several weeks after her death, I couldn't remember her. Her aspect, her body, her voice melted into a blur of anxiety, worry, agony, and terror.

Then, from time to time, a fresh memory crept in. At first the memories always focused on the period leading to her death, a part of that mental video which played incessantly in my head. I could see the scar resulting from the biopsy. I could remember feeding her bits of ice from a spoon. There was the silent reaching for my hand to place it under hers on her heart; the request that I rub her back, that I sing to her, songs from her early childhood. I had tried to sing, but I was so stressed that I could remember only some of the words. At that time, she was thirty-nine years old and it had been a long time since I had sung goodnight songs: "The Muffin Man," "Came Three Jolly Huntsmen, Dressed in Green and Gold," "There Was an Old Owl Who Lived in an Oak," all the nursery rhymes, the popular songs of the forties, and folk songs. We are a musical family and there were always lots of songs.

I managed to find all the words to "Sweet and Low" but haven't been able to sing it since. I was singing the old lullaby, this time not to help her sleep, but to help her die.

Those memories allowed me to reconstruct my daughter's physical presence in my mind, though they were painful. They are painful even now. But they also remind me how much she and I loved each other. And they reassure me that I will never forget her.

I was already an old woman when my daughter died. Memory plays many tricks on the elderly. My husband and I say we now practice

Memory By Committee: if one of us can't remember, perhaps the other can. Recollections of my dead child will necessarily fade, but that is not the same as forgetting her.

Remembering your child is one thing; it is personal and for yourself alone. Memorializing your child is something else. Most of us bereaved parents have an overwhelming need to keep the memory alive. It gives us a sense that our child's life had some significance for others as well as ourselves.

To memorialize our dead child gives us the assurance that his or her life means something in the larger context of the world. Perhaps memorializing is a way of continuing the good work our child did or would have done.

Cathy was socially conscious, much more so than I, having made contributions of time and effort, some actually sacrificial, to worthy causes. After her death, letters of appreciation came from several charities she had supported as well as from those in a reading program for deprived children and adults in which she had participated in Boston. In the earlier years, when she lived and worked in New York City, she had volunteered in a Women's Prison on Riker's Island. She belonged to several charitable organizations. We sent money to them after her death; and of course to the American Cancer Society.

But for ourselves, there was a need for a personal memorial. During the few short weeks when she lay dying, Cathy asked at one point what we were going to do with that big yard, nothing but grass at the time, surrounding our new home in Albany. "Why don't you check at the University and see if they would like to plan a garden for you as a project?" she suggested.

After she died, the idea of a memorial garden began to grow. I called the University to inquire if they wanted to use our property for a class project but they said they had no program that could make use of such an offer. One of the civil engineers in our surviving daughter's office made a drawing of a tentative plan. But we did nothing about it.

In October 1987, three months after Cathy's death, we attended a regional conference of *The Compassionate Friends* on Cape Cod. One of Cathy's best friends lives on Cape Cod, so I contacted Michele and asked if we could get together.

The meeting was arranged and we had breakfast with her one morning. She brought along wonderful photos of Cathy and her boyfriend, the two of them laughing and eating cake at Michele's wedding a few years earlier.

Michele is a landscape architect. I told her we were thinking of making a garden in memory of Cathy, and she leaped at the opportunity to plan it for us.

Early the next spring, I took several photos of our property, which consists of a house on a third of an acre of grassy lawn. I sent the packet of photos to Michele. Letters with drawings went back and forth between us.

The planting was arranged for the first weekend in June 1988, with relatives and Cathy's friends invited to attend. Cousins Ted and Ann brought their rototiller from New Hampshire to prepare the ground. Ann's sister Laurel and her husband Ronnie Schliftmann, cousins from Bedford, New York, brought their three children to help. Several of Cathy's friends from the Boston area came. Michele directed the activities and went with us to the nursery to purchase the plants which went into the garden. Everybody helped. The garden was beautiful. Money for the purchase of a bird bath came from Cathy's friend Anna Larson in Boston.

Cathy had illustrated a children's book, and we prepared reproductions of those illustrations for all the workers as a gift. We presented a packet of the reproductions to each of them during the dedication ceremony after the outdoor luncheon.

The first planting was a time for reminiscing and thinking of Cathy and her life among us, a profoundly meaningful occasion.

Each subsequent year we have had a special weekend for further plantings, of remembering Cathy together. But the number of people attending has dwindled. Only the closest loved ones come now. In 1996, Cousin Ann, aged 49, succumbed to the breast cancer which was discovered shortly after Cathy's death, bringing fresh sadness as we approached yet another gardening season.

Even though the annual gathering finds fewer friends and relatives, the garden goes on, grows and expands in size and beauty because many of the plants are perennials.

I am getting too old to spend much time working in the garden. In the early years, it was good to get down on my knees, to plunge my hands into the soil, to transplant the flowers, to clip, to weed, and to pick a bouquet every day. Today I must be content to watch the blooms as they change with the seasons.

I learned a lot while working in that memorial garden. I thought of Cathy more intensely than at any other time. I noted that my sense of the precious quality of life extended even to the tiny plants which volunteered from seeds dropped by parent plants the year before. It was almost impossible for me to weed out those minuscule plants. Discarding any which had started to grow made me remember that Cathy's life had been cut short before it had a chance to be fulfilled. How could I decide which plant should live or die? Philosophical ruminations of that kind do not make for good gardening.

The garden was, for our family, a personal memorial. One of the problems most bereaved parents encounter is deciding on a public memorial, which may be uppermost in our minds at a certain point. When we find a satisfactory solution it puts us in a better place as we walk through our grief. In this matter, bereaved parents of adult children may find themselves in conflict with other adult survivors, whose ideas of a suitable memorial may differ.

Recently I have read in my local newspaper that scholarships have been started for the children of the deceased as a memorial. This is an attractive and practical option for those mourning the death of a young parent who was a wage earner and support for the family. It ensures that there will be money when the surviving children need it for their education in years to come.

Trees, gardens, plaques, scholarships, donations to a charity, some needed object for a church or school or park, a commitment to some project our child would have approved of: these are all suggestions which might appeal to bereaved parents.

Eventually the appropriate memorial will present itself. There is no hurry. Some memorials seem good at first but serve, in the long run, to make the parents feel even more sad. In the beginning, the scholarship in your child's memory will go to someone who knew him or her. But in the ensuing years it will go to someone to whom your child is only a name, not a memory.

Perhaps it is just my own predilection for hands-on things, but I think the best memorial is something you can see, feel, touch, visit, and participate in in some ritualistic fashion.

Memorials, both personal and public, however you wish to establish them, are comforting. Some parents have unusual ways of remembering their child. My friend Sally Van Schaick says she always watches the concert calendar so that she can attend any performance which includes music her daughter Holly sang when she was in high school. She feels a special closeness to Holly during the performance.

A friend in California who works at the "Save the Redwoods League" (P.O. Box 44614, San Francisco, CA 94144-0001) tells of her contact with a bereaved father whose adult daughter died many years ago. He appears every year on the anniversary of his daughter's death and makes a memorial contribution in her memory. We too, have contributed money for a plaque in Cathy's name in a redwood forest.

Another similar memorial is sponsored jointly by the Penny Pines Program and the United States Department of Agriculture's Forest Service. Under a conservation agreement you or your organization can contribute $68 toward the cost of planting seedlings on about one acre of National Forest land. Using your donation together with Federal

funds, the Sequoia Forest will do the planting. For memorial planta-
tions, you will receive a special memorial certificate with the deceased
person's name. That name will be placed on the sign at the plantation
site: "Friends of___;" "Family of ___;" "Relatives of ___." Total donations since the start of the Penny Pines Program in 1941 have come to
more that $1,224,406. Using these donations combined with regular
Forest planting funds, more than twenty-seven million pine, fir, redwood, and giant sequoia seedlings have been planted on 88,000 acres
of National Forest land in California. To contact this organization,
call 209-784-1500 or write Sequoia National Forest, 900 West Grand
Avenue, Porterville, CA 93257-2035.

Nearly every worthwhile charity has a specific plan for memorial
gifts. The above suggestions are among many that could be made. The
idea of having a child's name affixed to a sign at the base of a memorial
tree may be especially appealing as a living, growing manifestation
of his or her life's importance. Redwoods and sequoias seem to live
forever.

There is also another avenue to not forgetting: many parents have
found comfort in after-death contacts with their child. A phenomenon
which lends itself to reactions ranging from complete acceptance to
total disbelief, it nevertheless must be dealt with non-judgmentally
because it is so common among bereaved parents.

If there is indeed a place for the paranormal, it will surely be found
among those whose lives have been so profoundly touched by grief,
those whose sensibilities have been heightened by the wrenching
experience of losing what was most precious in their lives. For a long
time after the death of their child, bereaved parents may be so
traumatized that they are reluctant to remain in the land of the living.
They seem to linger with their child at the edge of the realm of the
dead, which colors all their experiences.

The last page of my questionnaire asks matter-of-factly whether
the bereaved parents have had any after-death contacts with their
dead child. Many answered in the affirmative and have described their
experiences. You may read about them in greater detail in their individual stories in Appendix II. Some hesitated to reveal these stories,
fearing ridicule, not quite believing what happened to them, yet clinging to the comfort those contacts gave them.

The general public pays scant attention to stories of after-death
contacts, but studies harking back more than a century have recorded
such phenomena. I was present at a lecture on after-death contact
in which the two presenters, who have since published a book on
the subject, gave instances to verify its existence. In their research
they had recorded nearly two thousand examples of deceased children

contacting parents. Several bereaved parents in the audience stood up to tell of their own contacts with their dead child.

Workshops dealing with after-death communications bring overflow registration. Those who share stories of their after-death contacts with their children are the envy of bereaved parents who wish fervently for such contacts and have not had them.

Laile E. Bartlett, who has a Ph.D. in sociology and taught at the University of California at Berkeley, has written a book about psychic phenomena: *Psi Trek*. (McGraw-Hill Book Company, NY, 1981, quoted with permission.) Psi, pronounced "sigh," refers to the first letter of the Greek word "psyche," shorthand for psychic phenomena. (The scientific study of psychic phenomena is called parapsychology.)

At the beginning of a lecture given by Dr. Bartlett at Lake George, New York, she said, "People don't believe in it until it happens to them. For the average person, parapsychologists included, no number of statistics or experiments is as convincing as having it happen to YOU!"

Dr. Bartlett began her research on psychic phenomena after attending a conference on the subject as a reporter for an international magazine. "The world of psychic phenomena is wildly controversial, and sometimes frightening," she said. "It is beyond existing knowledge; it defies all explanations; it challenges scientific principles and laws. When I got the idea for this book, I thought it time for someone with academic sympathies and training, but outside the field, with no grants to seek, no ax to grind, to take a fresh look. Slowly I learned that my research gave me a point of view. In its barest, boiled down essence, it is this: There IS something to psychic phenomena. We don't know what it is, how it works, why it works, but we know it exists."

Of the many aspects of psychic phenomena discussed by Dr. Bartlett in her book, I have selected for this chapter only a few illustrations which impinge on the experiences of bereaved parents who answered my questionnaire: premonition, near-death experiences, crisis apparitions, and after death communication. In addition, some experiences involve the phenomenon known as psychokinesis, in which objects may alter their positions due to some unexplained force.

When Dr. Bartlett speaks of apparitions, she mentions four types: apparitions of the living; crisis apparitions at the time of death or an accident; apparitions of the dead; and continuing apparitions, which appear and reappear regularly. For those who answered my questionnaire, both crisis apparitions and continuing apparitions were experienced.

Cheryl Gentile told of after-death visits from her son, Sammy. "It comforted me when Sammy came to me a couple of days after his death and hugged me and said it was an accident. Recently he came and hugged me again but seemed lonely. He visited my husband once around his six-month anniversary. I hope he continues to visit as it helps me to cope better. I just wish he could stay longer."

Evelyn Guiliani, whose daughter was murdered, say, "It sounds crazy but I really felt my daughter has talked to me after she died, through dreams and whatever. I have wakened, thinking she's standing at the foot of my bed calling me."

Peg Wallace's daughter Winnie died after a long and painful struggle with a back injury caused by a snowmobiling accident. "One night I awoke," she says, "to feel Winnie in the house. I called to her; she didn't speak, but I saw her. A shadow moved in the hall and stood by the bedroom door."

An anonymous respondent from Pennsylvania lost two of her adult children, a son and a daughter. Her daughter Lilly was kidnapped and murdered. "I saw Lilly in a window in the sky," she wrote. "I believe God in his loving mercy allowed me a glimpse of her. She appeared whole, beautiful, and in complete peace."

Frances Phillips is the mother of two sons and a new daughter-in-law who were killed by a dragracer as they drove to their wedding reception. She has had several after-death contacts with her sons and her daughter-in-law. One occurred while her husband lingered near death after a heart attack. "I walked into the room and they were standing behind his chair, as if waiting for him," she said. "I shooed them away, telling them that I need their father longer. They went. I was sorry I sent them away."

Some parents seek out psychics who say they can contact the dead, or the discarnate, as they refer to those who have died. These meetings are extremely expensive and reactions to them are varied. Many bereaved parents I have spoken with felt bitterly disappointed and cheated after the encounters, branding the practitioners charlatans. Others say they are convinced that the "readings" from the dead are authentic.

No matter whether they sound authentic or not, however, it is important for the bereaved to realize that the pain of loss is not assuaged by discovering that their child is happy in an after-life. Although the parent may be momentarily comforted, grief work goes on, as difficult as before. Living with the void created by the child's death, loneliness, and despair must be dealt with.

As mentioned above, I have had several experiences which I attribute to contacts with my daughter Cathy, which you may read about in my answers to the questionnaire, "The Last Word." They are comforting, albeit unexpected and infrequent. On two occasions, the contact I had with Cathy involved the china-handled cake knife which had belonged to her. After I had used it and inserted it once again into its place, a large pitcher behind the faucets in the kitchen, it jumped out into the sink some twelve inches away, breaking the handle. This happened at two separate times; no other knife in that holder ever did this. This experience falls into the category of psychokinesis.

My daughter visited me after her death and conveyed messages through signs. Cathy also had at least one premonitory dream and two near-death experiences. Dr. Bartlett discusses these phenomena in separate chapters of her book. If we bereaved parents have had some psychic experience linked to our dead child, it is one more assurance that the child is not forgotten and has not, in fact, forgotten us.

In addition to after-death contacts, many parents cherish and cling to the memorabilia left after their children died. Many of us have inherited household objects from our deceased child. I have pots and pans, dishes, rugs, pillowcases, lamps, furniture, clothing, and shoes which belonged to Cathy which I have incorporated into my daily life. Her paintings and drawings hang on our walls. Her sculpture stands atop the piano. Other memorabilia are stored in the attic.

One of the mothers who requested my questionnaire wrote on her card that she was plagued by the problem of what to do with her daughter's belongings. She never returned her questionnaire, even though I wrote once again to ask why. She sounded bitter because her surviving children appeared to have no interest in the memorabilia of their dead sister, a woman who had brought honor to the family during her lifetime.

It seems doubly sad to think that those things which belonged to Cathy and are so precious to me might be tossed out after my death. Some of them will be incorporated into the lives of her siblings and their children, but not all. They will be the flotsam and jetsam of a life, floating away to oblivion as the generations rise and fall.

It is important that bereaved parents take steps to ensure that memories of their child are secure. If we cannot remember our children at first, we will soon recover our memories. It helps to understand the process of grief so that despair does not take over in the early days after their deaths. When the first few wretched months have passed, bereaved parents can be assured that they will again recall how their children looked and sounded. As the pain begins to ease, they will find comfort in their memories. That may take longer than they had expected, but it will come. Even the photographs will at some point begin to bring comfort rather than pain.

The memorials bereaved parents plan will continue to remind them that the person who died was significant and important in the larger scheme of things.

The private memories they will keep close to their hearts, assuring them those beloved children will never be forgotten, even when old age saps the parents' ability to remember.

Shortly before my mother slipped into the coma which preceded her death, I was at her bedside. She hadn't been able to speak for several days, but suddenly she looked intently at me and said, haltingly and with obvious effort, trying to put a sentence together, "You . . . mean . . . everything . . . to . . . me."

I read a true story some years ago about a man who went to a nursing home to visit his aged mother. Time and illness had taken a heavy toll; she was only dimly aware of who or where she was. As her son sat in a chair beside her bed, she took his hand and said, "I don't know who you are, but I know I love you very much."

After all the memories have receded, you will still retain love for your child. Love, the most precious of all, is the last memory to go.

CHAPTER 18

A Summing Up:
Special Problems of Parents
Whose Adult Children Died

Each of the preceding chapters has emphasized particular aspects of the grief experience and has highlighted troubling situations shared by many parents whose child was an adult at the time of death. This chapter will serve as a summation, almost in outline form, to reiterate and pull into focus the problems we face.

We have been told that grief is a process, that it is crucially important to forge through each phase of that process, however painful, before healing can be accomplished. Sometimes, especially early in our grief experience, when we are confused and overwhelmed by sadness, we cannot decipher our emotional responses. That is why a grief counselor will often begin his or her sessions by trying to bring our emotions into focus, to still the swirling chaos of early bereavement.

These characteristically chaotic emotions of the newly bereaved (meaning the first few years after their child's death) make it difficult to assess our position, to measure whether or not we may be mired in one place or another in our grief work.

First attempts at reentering the workaday world find us surprised at our strong resistance to going on with life without our child, unprepared for those reactions, surprised also at how radically our energy to deal with them has been reduced. When I phoned my cousin soon after her bereavement, she reported how exhausting she found it to grieve. "I'm tired all the time," she said.

Starting with the first stage of grief, that of shock and denial, the bereaved parents of older children are faced immediately with a formidable barrier to healing. Because the adult child may not have lived at home and physical surroundings have not changed as a result of their child's death, parents can pretend the death never occurred. This presents them with the temptation to continue denying the death and will thus delay the grief process. Parents whose child's body has never been found may fantasize that the child suffered a blow to the head, with subsequent amnesia, and is wandering around somewhere, in Europe perhaps, or in the Far East, alive and well.

When I moved to Mt. Vernon, New York, in the fall of 1946, I noticed that neighbors kept a flag flying, day and night, in all kinds of weather. This went on for years on end. Their son had been reported missing in action in World War II. They kept that flag visible not only in memory of their son; I was told they never gave up hope that he would be found alive. That tattered flag hung there for more than twenty years, until the soldier's parents died.

Others, even those whose adult child lived at home, can pretend their child is on a trip or still at college; it eases the pain for awhile. But pain deferred will wait, and it will not decrease in the interim. It may, in fact, cause depression or illness if not dealt with.

If bereaved parents do not have young children living at home and the father and mother are alone together, their pain is almost unbearable. The death of their child changed them; it changed their marriage. Because their joint grief is a constant, unrelieved aggravation, they may opt for separation or divorce. This phenomenon is unique not just to parents of adult children; it is also applicable to those of only children who died, no matter what their age. Dependent children living at home often provide an anchor to keep parents together.

Bereaved parents of a young child sometimes have at least the biological possibility of having another child. Making an affirmation of life by having another baby is something older parents cannot do. For parents who are beyond the age of reproducing, the possibility of having another child is foreclosed by the passage of time. Their biological clocks have run out.

If they cannot have another child, bereaved parents may succumb to the urge to find a substitute, perhaps by adopting a child. The strange, driving impulse to search for the dead child may culminate in finding a counterproductive way to fill the void in their lives: a new sexual partner; blissful oblivion provided by alcohol or other drugs; or becoming a workaholic.

The grief work of parents whose children died of murder, suicide, AIDS, or involvement in criminal activity or military action is complicated by society's attitudes toward such deaths. This Disallowed Grief makes it even harder for these bereaved parents to relate to the general public than it is for those whose children died of accidents or illness—which is hard enough!

Those contending with Disallowed Grief may find themselves involved in a painful reexamination of their own pasts, their birth family, the bases for their values, their child-rearing skills. Their sense of existential guilt, from which most of us bereaved parents suffer to some extent, is often even stronger than that of parents whose children died from more conventional causes.

Another category of Disallowed Grief might include bereaved parents who were really old, not just middle-aged, when their child died. Ageism brings with it discrimination against the elderly whose grief is thereby discounted and devalued. As an aged parent, I have sometimes been made to feel that I am out of order to be grieving for a daughter who had already had a rich, full life before she died. Or an aged parent may be shunted aside and ignored by those who come to comfort the surviving spouse and children.

Aging parents may be emotionally as well as financially dependent on their mature son or daughter and thus have greater difficulty facing life after the death. As one of my respondents says, "Long before my son became ill, I used to tell myself, when I sometimes feared the possibility of my husband dying before me, that I could always count on my son. He was more responsible than the others. He could give me sensible advice. He knew about finances and household repairs and things like that."

Over the years, as a child is growing up, his or her parents are also maturing. While they are shaping their child, they are also shaping themselves to accommodate that child's needs, personality, talents, and intellectual endowment. Parents, aware of the importance of their input, are continually making decisions regarding the child's welfare based on their own ideals and values.

In a very real sense, mothers and fathers make a total commitment to the raising of their children. They make sacrifices, take on extra work, give up personal indulgences and luxuries to insure that their children have the best in health care, education, exposure to cultural activities and body-building sports. The children have always come first. They represent the parents' life project, clearly distinguished from their working careers by the added components of biological bonding and love.

Faced with the death of their adult child, the parents see their life enterprise in ruins. Having arrived at the place where their children were their friends and confidants, they felt the blessings of shared experiences, pride in their children's character and accomplishments, perhaps even the gift of grandchildren. What had been a mere projection into the future when those children were little, had become a reality. They were friends, companions, in frequent communication, asking and giving advice, and sharing good news and bad. When the child died, the parents lost the very essence of what gave meaning to their lives.

The reality of the finished product these older parents had so lovingly fashioned contrasts with the hope of parents whose little child died. What that small child might have been, might have done in the future is, alas, only a vision in the mind of his or her parents.

Many people devote themselves to an ideal to give their lives meaning. Some ideals fail. Their devotees feel betrayed. Their psyches are wounded. They become cynical, concluding that they fought the wrong battles for the right reasons. They lose all incentives to persevere. They are disenchanted with life.

For parents, their children's lives are the ideal to which they gave primary devotion. They did not wage the wrong battles, but they are far more tragically wounded by the deaths of their adult children than those who were betrayed by the loss of an ideal. They too, are disappointed in life. They feel betrayed. Some of them must reexamine their religious beliefs and their philosophy in light of their loss. They have also lost a sense of meaning and purpose. Because they may feel they are too old to start over, to reinvest, the parents' grand project, their life work, died with their children. The sense of sadness and defeat is similar to the loss of faith in a great idea or a great ideal. Yet the parents' loss is infinitely more profound, more visceral.

One big difference exists, however, between the loss of a child and the loss of an ideal. Bereaved parents will never chastise themselves for having invested so much love, time, and effort in their child who died. They will not feel that their sacrifices were futile. If asked whether they would still want to have had that child, knowing the outcome, all of them would answer in the affirmative, or as one of my respondents did, "I would have missed the pain, but I would also have missed the dance."

Missing the dance would have meant missing all the cherished experiences the parents shared with the deceased, from babyhood and early childhood through adolescence and maturity.

Some occasions are harder for fathers and mothers who have lost young children. In the fall, the sight of pupils trudging back to school brings tears to the eyes of younger bereaved parents, who know their children's education will never be completed.

Hillary Rodham Clinton, in her first newspaper column after returning from the Women's Conference in China, said that she had regretted missing her daughter Chelsea's first day of school (Albany Times Union, September 17, 1995) "I couldn't help thinking about every 'first day' since kindergarten, and how her dad and I would make her pose for the ritual picture before driving her to school. No matter how hard I tried, I could never keep from crying after we dropped her off. There is something about the way the school year, more than any other part of the calendar, marks the passage of time in a child's life . . . and a parent's."

Each rite of passage involving education is painful for the bereaved parents of young children. The dead children's classmates graduate from elementary or high school, go off to college, and then graduate. Perhaps a few years will go by when the parents lose track of their children's classmates. Then wedding invitations and birth announcements arrive from these now-grown-up friends, reminding the bereaved parents of other precious joys of life which were denied their dead children.

The beginning of the school year holds no terrors for me, nor does the doorbell's ringing on Halloween, when little children dressed as goblins beg for treats. At the time of her death, my daughter Cathy was thirty-nine, with a Masters Degree from the University of Massachusetts. She was living in Boston, working as an artist at an architectural firm, taking courses at the Boston Museum of Fine Arts to expand her career into book illustration. The rites of passage which bring pangs of regret and sadness to parents of younger children have no affect on me.

However, there are other sorrowful occasions peculiar to the loss of an adult child. I remember how sad I felt when a letter arrived announcing the marriage of our daughter's boyfriend to one of her friends. Other grieving parents endure additional pain when their son's or daughter's surviving spouse remarries and has children. Even though the parents may have said they wanted that particular survivor to get on with his or her life, when it actually happens, it brings a feeling of sadness. At the same time they feel guilty about their reaction. Again, they sense that their dead child was cheated.

Sometimes older parents have impaired health and less energy to deal with their loss than younger parents. The very fact that their futures are severely truncated means that a recovery of hope, an affirmation about life, is more difficult for elderly parents.

Several among my survey respondents contend that it is harder to lose an adult child simply because that child's promise had already been fulfilled. All the emotional, financial, confrontational and disciplinary challenges that come with raising children were over; they had become responsible adult citizens. Yet with death, their professional careers were cut short. They could not raise and provide for their own offspring, could not contribute their fully developed talents to society, and could not be a comfort, an emotional—even perhaps a financial—support to their parents in their old age.

For some bereaved parents, caring for their children's survivors becomes a burden. My high school classmate lost his adult son from a viral infection of the heart. The widow and four young children were left without any financial support. My classmate, having already retired, had to go back to work in order to provide for his grandchildren.

Mary Cleckley, a *Compassionate Friends* member from Atlanta, has spoken eloquently about the importance of not getting bogged down in comparing intensity of grief. She concludes that there is no good time or way for children to die before their parents. All such deaths are cruel and hard. It is a reminder, rather, that all such deaths are indeed, devastating, even when the parents are old.

Lena Horne, the great jazz entertainer, has suffered many personal losses in her lifetime, including the death of her son from a kidney ailment. In the *New York Times* of Sunday, June 5, 1995, she was quoted as saying: "When they hear this album, I wonder if they'll say, 'Why would an old broad like that be singing with passion?' But of course, they don't know that people will ALWAYS have passion and romance inside them. We don't become empty shells just because we're older."

Love endures to the end. And it is love for our dead children which makes the hurt so great, no matter what their age or our age when they die.

The chapter on Conflicting Agendas deals exclusively with complications occasioned by the different needs of other adult survivors. These complications are not present for parents whose young child died. Older parents need to keep in mind the fact that we all have to make decisions in order to go on after the death of our loved one: not just the parents, but spouses, children, siblings, and lovers.

The decisions of some of these other survivors may conflict with the parents' need to remember, to keep thoughts of our dead child alive. For while we parents have a desperate need to make sure our child is not forgotten, spouses, children, lovers, even siblings, may feel an actual need to forget the dead. Because of this, those other survivors may take what seem to be inappropriate actions, cut us off from contact with our grandchildren, or say hurtful things, further wounding the bereaved parents.

The threat of depression and despair is probably greater for parents whose child was an adult at death. Older bereaved parents are more confirmed in their life-style and their belief structure than parents of a young child who died. Perhaps the longer you live with the illusion that life is fair, the greater the crash when you discover it is not true. The general sense of disappointment in life leads some aged parents to face their remaining years without anticipation of further satisfactions. They resemble the baseball team which has no possibility of winning the pennant: for the sake of personal integrity, the team must play out the string, but without any enthusiasm or hope of attaining their goal.

If the parents of deceased adult children can get beyond the pain of sorting through their memories and their children's memorabilia, they will discover they have many more of those memories and memorabilia than the parents of a young child. For my husband and me, there are hosts of letters, household items, photographs, gifts, writings, and wonderful art work to remind us of Cathy's contribution to our family's memory bank.

These are comforting to have. But, like all bereaved parents, what we really want, what would really comfort us, is to have Cathy with us again, alive and well. In that, we are exactly like parents who lost children of any age.

As our friend Mary Hennig said, when told she should stop grieving for her dead son and get on with her life, "What happened? Did he come back?"

Some day Mary may be able to say, "No, he didn't come back. He isn't coming back, but I am going on with my life without him."

In this book I have set as my primary goal a totally subjective description of the experiences which many parents go through after the death of their adult child. My purpose in describing them has been to show that these experiences, though frightening and unnerving, are normal and that we bereaved parents share many of the most devastating of them. My hope is that whatever feelings of unworthiness you may have about yourself will disappear when you realize that you are neither demented nor of defective character because of your reactions to your child's death; that you are not alone, but among thousands of others just like yourself who are wrestling with this most painful of all losses.

Some day, when we bereaved parents have learned how to cope with our day-to-day obligations, when we have dealt with our guilt, our anger, our sadness; when we have reordered our priorities to fit the new knowledge our child's death has forced on us, we will be ready to turn the corner toward investing in life once more.

Where that new road will lead, each of us must find the strength and the will to determine for ourselves. We will never be quite the people we were before our child died, but things will get better than they are now. Even though I am still grieving for my daughter, I know now that I am getting better. I am no longer thrashing about in that dark wood of early grief, where I had lost my way; so bitter that death itself seemed hardly more severe. I have emerged into a landscape where life seems worth living and the sun sometimes shines.

My only advice is to urge you to believe that you too, can get better, and to say "hang in there!"

APPENDIX I

Questionnaire:
Death of an Adult Child

The following is a copy of the questionnaire sent out several years ago to bereaved parents whose adult children died. This request for volunteers appeared nationally through the kind auspices of the *Compassionate Friends* in their newsletter.

My husband and I lost our 39-year-old daughter, Catherine, to breast cancer on July 12, 1987. At the time of her death, we were 71 and 67 years old respectively. The problems we have encountered trying to deal with our grief seem to differ from those of parents whose young child died.

Because there is not much literature about the death of an adult child, and at the suggestion of my grief counselor, I have initiated a study of people in our category.

If your adult child has died, will you fill out this questionnaire? Tell as much or as little as you wish, using the back of these pages or extra paper if you need to. If you are uncomfortable with some of the questions, just skip them. As you may suspect, all of them were devised from my own personal experience or the experiences of close associates in the *Compassionate Friends*.

The information you provide will be confidential; if there is an occasion to make some parts of it public, I will seek your permission to use it. Your name, address and telephone number on this paper would help me do this but is optional.

If you find a question not applicable to your situation, please respond with NA

1. Name of your deceased child.

   Date of birth_____ Date of death____ Age at time of death_____
   Did he/she live at home?____

2. Parents' name, address and telephone number.

   Age of parents at time of child's death: Mother_____ Father____

3. Cause of child's death: Please circle appropriate answer
   and elaborate if you wish:

   a. Accident: (tell what kind)

   b. Illness: (tell what kind; long or short term?)

   c. Military

   d. Murder

   e. Suicide

   f. Drug/Alcohol connected

   g. Other

4. Marital status of your deceased child: Please circle appropriate
   answer. Single Married Divorced Widowed Remarried
   Separated

5. Survivors of deceased child: Please circle appropriate answer.
   a. Mother b. Father c. Special friend d. Spouse e. Children
   (how many? Ages?) f. siblings (how many? Ages?)
   g. Grandparents h. other

6. Marital status of parents: Please circle appropriate answer.
   Married Divorced Widowed Remarried Other

7. Relationship with your spouse: Please circle answer and
   elaborate in space provided or on separate sheet.

   a. good

   b. stressed

   c. considered divorce or separation

    d. sexual problems since death of child (Please note: all refer-
ences to this most personal of questions will be omitted from
your story and dealt with anonymously in a separate chapter
if this report is made into a book.)

    e. difficulties in communicating

    f. differing grief styles

    g. other

8. Relationship with survivors: (for example, tensions during the
last illness; conflict over choice of cemetery or funeral arrangements; their inability to handle your grief; disapproval of the
way the survivors are behaving; how surviving children are
being raised; other.) Please circle appropriate answer and
elaborate in space provided or on a separate sheet.

    a. siblings

    b. special friend, fiance/e

    c. widow/er

    d. children of deceased

    e. other

9. What do you find difficult to bear? Please circle answer and
elaborate in the space provided or on a separate sheet of paper.

    a. how my child died

    b. being cheated out of my child's companionship

    c. not having grandchildren

    d. the unfairness of it all

    e. anger

    f. guilt

    g. a feeling that my child was cheated out of a full life

    h. other

10. Was the legal/justice system involved?_____ Did it serve you well?_____ Why or why not?

11. Was the medical system involved? ____ Did it serve you well?____ Why or why not?

12. Was the military involved?____ Did it serve you well?____ Why or why not?

13. In what way has your attitude toward life changed?

14. In what way has your attitude toward religion changed?

15. How has this experience changed your friendships?

16. Have you sought help from the following?

   a. The Compassionate Friends_____ Helpful?

   b. Professional counselors_____ Helpful?

   c. Clergy___ Helpful?

   d. Friends_____ Helpful?

17. Do you think a book about the experiences of other parents whose adult child has died would help guide parents through the grief process?_____ In what way?

18. Have your responses to grief changed?____ Can you break this down into phases?

19. Based on your experience and what you have heard from other bereaved parents, what do you think are the differences between loss of a young child and an adult child?

20. Did you experience mental and physical problems/changes after the death of your child? Please circle or check proper items and elaborate if you wish.

   a. Memory loss

   b. inability to concentrate

   c. sleep problems (too much?___ too little?_____)

    d. eating/weight problems (gain___ loss___)

    e. thoughts of suicide

    f. depression_____ Taken medication for depression?_____

    g. illness (tell us what illness)

    h. accidents (tell us what accidents)

    i. feeling that you are going crazy

    j. extreme fatigue and lack of energy

    k. other

21. Have the other survivors of your adult child suffered any physical, mental or job-related problems as a result of his/her death? Will you tell us about this?

22. Are you aware of a possible Near Death experience your child had prior to or at the moment of death?

23. Do you feel your child communicated with you or other survivors in some way after death?_____ If so, please tell us about these occasions.

24. Are there other insights about the death of an adult child you wish to share?

Thank you for answering this questionnaire. I know it has been painful and I salute your courage and generosity. I hope my report will help other bereaved parents deal with their grief.

APPENDIX II

Introduction to Appendix II

Reverend J. Robert Smudski was our minister at the Hastings, New York, Unitarian Church in the sixties and seventies, at a time when our young adult children were responding to the shock waves of a troubled society. He was infinitely wise and insightful, guiding my husband and me, as parents and as marriage partners, through those difficult years.

Reverend Smudski was the son of Polish immigrants who had come to Pennsylvania to work in the coal mines and steel mills. Before becoming a minister, he had been a steel worker and a business man (he and his father-in-law ran a restaurant for a time).

During his early ministry, Bob Smudski acted as chaplain in a large hospital. He was called one day to the bedside of a young man who had been horribly burned over his entire body in an industrial accident. Distraught and beyond reach of anyone in the hospital, the injured man had turned his head to the wall; he wanted nothing but to die. Who would ever love him, so disfigured? How could he pursue the career he had planned to pursue, a career dependent on his former handsome good looks? What was left which could give his life meaning?

At first the patient would not listen to Bob Smudski. What did he know, a minister, comfortable and whole?

Bob sat at his bedside and spoke quietly; the patient refused to recognize his presence. The minister sat for a few minutes in silence. Then he spoke gently. "I want you to look at my hands," he said. The young man turned toward the minister, his eyes barely visible in the swaths of bandages. "Look at my hands," Bob repeated. "Do you see these scars? My whole body is covered with scars like this. I, too, was in an industrial fire and burned almost as badly as you. I, too, wanted to die. But as I began to heal, I realized that life could go on. Not as before, exactly, but it could regain meaning and significance. It could be fair again. Your life can, too."

For the first time, the young patient was hearing from someone who had been in the same situation, with the same pain, the same despair, the same wish to die, the same anguish he was experiencing now. For the first time he listened, with trust in the wisdom of the speaker. There was no way to discount or argue with Bob Smudski. He had been there. He had felt it. And he had healed to the point where he could make an affirmation of life's worth. It was what that patient needed to hear.

When you read the responses to the Questionnaire which are recorded almost verbatim in Appendix II, you will be listening to people who have themselves been there. All are bereaved parents whose adult children died. By the very fact of making the effort to respond, each has made a choice to try to heal, to reinvest in life, though many of us still wonder whether or not we can do it.

If you are a bereaved parent, you will understand why some of the respondents misinterpreted certain questions or left out seemingly important data: the name of their dead child; the age of the parents at their child's death; the marital status, survivors, relations with friends. Bereaved parents are sometimes unfocused and can't see the questions through their tears. Reading these stories, no matter how sketchily recounted, no matter how their children died or how the parents reacted, you will know they ring true because they ARE true. They will assure you that you are not alone; that it is OK to feel the way you do, that there is hope as you forge a new future without your child.

That is also true.

ANONYMOUS 1: Illness

Anonymous Mother, 70, who filled out the questionnaire at the Regional Conference of The Compassionate Friends in Bethlehem, Pennsylvania, in March 1994.

"My daughter, who was 36, died of double pneumonia on May 22, 1990. She was single and lived at home. Her father also survives and our aloneness is one of each having no one else to survive with. We talk more about our loss and less of the mundane. Compassion can be found only when two or more share the same experience. Commonality and compassion walk hand in hand.

"I feel very sad about how my child died. It was so unfair. I feel she was cheated. I miss her so and will always feel sad being denied her companionship. I feel guilty, and angry, too. As time goes on, my anger has somewhat abated and I find myself more tolerant of others than I used to be, even those who don't understand.

"When you spoke of religion, I have to say that there is no religion; only opinions. Clergy were not supportive in my loss.

"Now all my friends are from The Compassionate Friends. I have not sought professional counseling. Research for your book and listening might help but only when it is done from the heart. I don't think there is any difference between the loss of a young child and an adult child. The pain and grief of each are the same.

"I have had no physical or mental problems."

ANONYMOUS 2: Murder

Anonymous mother who answered the questionnaire at the Regional Conference of The Compassionate Friends in Bethlehem, Pennsylvania, in March 1994.

"My daughter's name is Joyce Ann. She was 25 when she was murdered in September of 1985. Joyce Ann was single and had a boyfriend. I was 53 at the time. My husband and I have difficulty communicating. Besides Joyce's father and I, two brothers survive. The older one has trouble with my grief.

"I find it very difficult to deal with the fact that my daughter was murdered. She was cheated out of life and I feel that was terribly unfair. I miss her so much and will always regret being cheated out of her companionship.

"The legal system really failed us. In fact, I would say it stank!

"My attitude towards religion and towards friends has changed. I guess I would have to say I have learned what is really important in life. The Compassionate Friends, other parents who have lost children, and the clergy have been helpful. I had no professional counseling, though there have been many times I have considered suicide and I have suffered from not being able to sleep."

ANONYMOUS 3: Accident and Murder

Anonymous mother lost a son, Jimmy, and a daughter, Laurie.

"When my children were young, my husband abandoned us; I have been divorced for many years. In the early years I was destitute and worked very hard, studying to acquire skills to support my children while doing menial jobs.

"I lost two of my five children when they became adults. After making it through the awful teen years, we had become friends and then they were gone. I feel robbed. On June 8, 1982, my son Jimmy, who was 24, was hit and killed by a van that ran a stop sign. His killer was charged with vehicular homicide. Because he knew the right people, his charge was reduced to failure to yield right of way and he received a $15 fine. I feel that the justice system really stinks. Jimmy was married and had a daughter. I was 41 at the time of his death.

"The next year, on December 28, 1983, my daughter Laurie, who was 20, was kidnapped and murdered. She had a 3-year-old son and was separated from her husband. The authorities did everything they could; I was well served by the legal system in her case.

"There have been a lot of problems in the family which were brought on by their deaths. The sibling closest in age to the dead children is behaving very destructively. He has a suicidal life-style, with drinking and adjustment problems. Laurie's son has had problems with his mother's death. The boy's father is not helpful.

"My health has suffered. I am depressed, have developed hypertension and diabetes. I had private counseling 6 months after the 2nd death. My church, including my clergyman, has been very loving and supportive. I am bitter about how my children died and the fact that I am cheated out of their companionship. Most of my friends have dropped me and vice versa but I have made new friends. Many of them are in The Compassionate Friends. My grief is softer now: time, working at it, and my attitude have contributed to that. I would say the most important thing is to keep your 'I love yous' up to date; you may not have a tomorrow.

"I saw Laurie in a window in the sky. I believe God in His loving mercy allowed me a glimpse of her. She appeared whole, beautiful, and in complete peace."

BILLMIRE: Suicide

Eleanor Billmire was 60, the divorced mother of three adult children, when her middle child, her daughter Leslie, committed suicide at the age of 40.

Eleanor's request for my questionnaire was a large scrawl across a single page; I sent out the material immediately, but received no response from her.

One Saturday afternoon some weeks later, while I was out walking and my husband, Bob, was watching a football game on TV, she phoned from a large city near Washington. She told Bob she was having some trouble filling out the questionnaire and wanted to talk to me.

I have learned never to ignore a call from a bereaved parent, so I checked and found her address but no telephone number. A call to the information operator told me Eleanor had an unlisted number. I was concerned: was she having a bad time? Was she in danger of suicide? I sent off a hurried note, requesting her phone number.

She called a few days later and, to my great relief, I discovered her difficulty had not been emotional but physical. She had fallen and injured her arm. Could she answer the questions over the phone? Not now, but Tuesday morning at 9:30, when her nurse-helper would be able to set her up properly.

I initiated the phone call as instructed and we began our interview. I learned that Eleanor is partially paralyzed and finds writing painful and slow, particularly since her recent injury to her arm.

She told me her story. Some forty years ago, when Eleanor was the young mother of three little children, she contracted polio. She spent a year in the hospital, during which time her parents came to help Eleanor's husband care for the two girls and a boy. During that time, a great amount of tension grew up between the grandparents and the middle child, a 5-year-old girl named Leslie. Eleanor credits that terrible year as the beginning of Leslie's mental illness, which afflicted her on and off over the years.

Even though Eleanor was released from the hospital and sent home after a year, she was very seriously handicapped and needed nursing care. Her husband abandoned the family a year and a half after her return from the hospital, leaving her to raise their three children alone. He has been through several more marriages since then. It is hard to imagine what Eleanor has been through.

At 60 Eleanor became a bereaved parent when Leslie's mental illness culminated in her suicide by an overdose of medication in 1989, when Leslie was 40. Leslie had been married and divorced by that time and lived in an apartment upstairs from her mother with her 17-year-old son, who found his mother's body after her suicide.

Eleanor's surviving daughter, Karen, is a psychiatrist with a husband and two children; Eleanor's son, the oldest, is a responsible professional, also married, with a young daughter. They have been very supportive. The ex-son-in-law has behaved badly, both to Eleanor and to his son.

"Thanksgiving Day fell the day after Leslie's Memorial Service," Eleanor writes. "Two kind women who were my personal caregivers cooked the dinner and set the table. Of course no one was hungry but we went to the dining room to sit around the table. At that time my surviving daughter had only one son, who was then two. He had no idea of Leslie's death, so he kept asking 'Where's Leslie? Isn't she coming to the Thanksgiving party?' He adored Leslie; she was wonderful with him."

After his mother's death, Eleanor's grandson came to live with her. He suffers from a learning disability and was especially traumatized because he found his mother's body. "Although he never talks about it, he believed it was his fault, that somehow he was responsible," Eleanor writes. "Suicides tend to make family members feel very guilty and responsible for the death. It makes those left behind think: if only I had done or said this or that. It doesn't, of course, have any basis in reality, but try telling any guilt sufferer that. I know about guilt feelings and of course No One can tell me I'm not guilty. We can all be wonderfully objective with others, I've found."

In addition to the severe physical handicaps Eleanor has endured, the death of her daughter brought a host of other ills: memory loss, an inability to concentrate, depression, accentuated breathing problems.

When I began writing about her, I asked that Eleanor describe her physical condition so that I could be accurate. Her answering letter follows:

"A working computer! How good it is! Until October 1992, when I rented a computer from a group which rents rebuilt computers at a tiny fee to the disabled, I had no idea what an asset a computer could be. A few months ago I was given a two-year-old computer, with more memory, by a friend of Leslie's.

"You asked about my physical condition. Waist up, some very limited and rather weak movement in fingers and hands. Small movement in trunk. That's it for my upper body. Waist down: legs and feet move, not 100%, but they are good enough to stand. I use my toes for typing, remote controls and dialing my special telephone. I do not have pain, but have lost my ability to rise from a chair unaided. As I told you in our telephone conversation, as a result of that loss, I am now using a wheelchair. Also, the other result of the loss was my falling on attempting to stand up. After the third fall, when I broke my arm, the doctor advised me to use the wheelchair all the time when out of bed. I use a breathing machine . . . a respirator . . . fourteen hours daily; also use a long body brace and arm braces. The arm braces enable me to use my fingers and hands to hold a toothbrush, lightweight finger foods, hold a long pencil to turn the pages of a book (with the eraser) and keep my arms from being dislocated. I am on a city health program which pays the salary of a personal care aide. The program is designed to keep people out of nursing homes.

"When we spoke on the phone, I talked with you about being unable to read for three and a half years after Leslie died. My difficulty was not in comprehension, but an actual aversion, amounting to panic, complete with panic symptoms: shortness of breath, dizziness, etc. Having seen Leslie's many panic attacks, I was, sadly, all too familiar with the physical manifestations of panic disorder. It is now obvious to me that one of the ways I was able to handle the terrible fact of Leslie's death was by rejection of reading, an activity that had been an important part of my life since I first learned to read. My point about 'not being able to read' is that there must be many people who can deal only with a life that is no longer normal, by reacting most negatively to some everyday activity, something that was a regular part of their life before the death of their loved one.

"I've been thinking of you at Cathy's grave saying 'I can't do anything about it.' I agree that you have reached another stage of awareness, the kind of awareness we wish no one ever had to have. I well understand the feelings that envelop one when the birthday or the date of the death of one's child comes round, yet again. It seems that every breeze, raindrop, bird call points to the time of year it is. We are so attuned to the terrible date that even uncaring nature seems to take delight in adding to our misery. At a certain time of day one can think, 'that's how the sun was the day she died.' Or smell the scent of a flower garden, the whiff of pine and say to oneself, 'Oh yes, that was the scent in the air around the time she died.'

"Leslie and I shared a birthday. This year my daughter called, my son, granddaughter and daughter-in-law came with gifts and food, to spend the day. Noah gave me a gift. But no one mentioned Leslie's name. All of them have their own ways of dealing with Leslie's suicide and of course each one's perspective is very subjective. Why am I writing you about what you know so well, as regards reactions? I believe that Karen and Bo feel, justifiably, that they tried for years to help Leslie in whatever way they could, that most of my conversations with them consisted of or ended up with a discussion of Leslie's problems and that I didn't seem to think that they, Bo and Karen, were very important. I think they want to put that part of their lives to rest, to not have me still putting her and her problems first. I was so immersed in her constant threat of suicide, her excessive need to have all my attention, my belief that the newest prescription, therapy group or psychiatrist would be the ONE that would make her well, that of course my other children would think their lives weren't very important to me. I can never assuage their pain, nor erase my unconscious cruelty to them.

"Unfortunately, whenever I see either of my surviving children, I feel the loss of Leslie very acutely because their presence makes me aware of the missing one. I certainly have never told them, nor would I ever tell them of my feelings, as I know they would understand but I also know they would be troubled.

"I've been having large spells of bursting into tears with no provocation. This happens from time to time; part of the grieving condition. I picture my brain as a rounded receptacle filled three quarters up by gray cement; this is my depression and there it sits, always making its presence known. How right you are to object when your non-bereaved friend asks you to lighten up, that you should have a more cheerful ending when writing about our condition. There seems to be a fair number of people who think one may be allowed a certain period of mannerly grief and then, for THEIR comfort, behave in a 'proper' and optimistic way regarding OUR loss. I say Off With Their Heads!"

In December 1995, Eleanor's former husband died unexpectedly of congestive heart failure at the age of 67.

"His death was difficult for my children. In Karen's case, she felt anew the lack of attention from him, despite the concerted efforts she made over the years to connect with him. Bo, having been eight when his father and I divorced, had more childhood memories; he felt a loss wondering, now that he is a father himself, how his father could have left his children. I, too, had some very unhappy memories awakened. But they are all a part of the past, the ebb and flow of life."

BONK: Accident

Noreen Bonk, 55, mother of Deborah, 35, grandmother of Ashleigh, 8. Noreen and her husband lost them both when they were killed in a one-car accident March 2, 1989. Quoting from Noreen's letters:

"Yesterday (March 2, 1994) marked the 5th anniversary of Deborah's death. She was the first of our eight children and would have been 40 on February 7th of this year. She and her 8-year-old daughter Ashleigh were in a one-car accident. Deborah died immediately and Ashleigh 3 days later. They were buried on March 7, 1989.

"Deborah left a husband and two surviving children: Brandon, who was 6 years old and Jenee, who was 10. Jenee was born with Down's Syndrome. We have a good relationship with our son-in-law, Wayne, and grandchildren. He is doing a wonderful job of raising them. He has not remarried.

"Wayne had surgery this past summer and stayed with us for 3 weeks while recuperating. The children stayed with his parents in Philadelphia. We celebrate most holidays together and they get to see as many of their 14 cousins as are able to come.

"I had turned 55 just 2 weeks after Deb celebrated her 35th birthday. My husband Gary was 57. I don't believe our relationship has changed. It has stayed fairly constant over the years. Gary is easy to get along with and doesn't get angry very often. I think we grieve pretty much the same. Deborah seems to be in our thoughts at the same time. Gary is more apt to break down and cry with me. I cry more when I'm alone.

"Being denied Deb and Ashleigh's company seems to affect me most. They were both fun-loving and talented. Deb always looked on the bright side and was caring and helpful to everyone.

"The only problem I had with the 'system' was that an autopsy was not performed on Deb. On the night she died, when I went to identify her, I was told her body would be released after the autopsy. I was never asked to sign anything and didn't even think why not. We weren't aware that an autopsy was not done until the day before the wake. The death certificate just stated that she died of head and chest injuries. She had been treated twice for phlebitis and still was not able to go back to work. I keep wondering if she had a blood clot that went to her heart or brain. There were no witnesses to the accident; the weather and roads were clear. She just went off the road and down an embankment into a tree.

"My attitude towards life has changed somewhat. Many things important to me before such as my home and 'things' don't seem to matter as much. My religion or faith has not changed; it helped a great deal in my attitude. My friends and family were and are wonderfully supportive. I truly don't know what I would have done without them. My grief has diminished over the years. The horrible ache in my heart and arms is gone; I feel not only both of them, but all others who pass over are at peace and happy.

"As for the differences in losing an adult child and a young child, I can only imagine that the grief is the same and perhaps longer lasting for a young child. With an older child's death you have many memories to keep alive, while with a young child I suspect there would be many 'I wonder what's' and 'If only's . . .'

"I really can't say what would be helpful to me in a book. I did experience inability to concentrate and some memory loss. It seems to have taken care of itself for the most part.

"I definitely feel that Deb communicates in the form of a cardinal. After her death, every time I was really down, I would pray for a sign and a cardinal would show up and begin to sing. It always gives me a lift and has happened many times.

"I want to tell you about the visit to the psychic, George Anderson. We found the visit to be very helpful and comforting. Although he knew nothing about us, he told us many things and names that could only relate to Deb. He didn't tell us why the accident happened (blood clot, etc.) but did say there was a pressure in her head and told just how the accident happened. Also he told about Ashleigh being alive after the accident but our having to sign to remove life support.

"He does feel that those who have passed over like to receive prayer. Deb said they were like letters from home. It makes you feel that even if you don't get a sign from them, they know what you're doing for them.

"Many of the books on Near Death Experiences were not only fascinating but comforting to me. I do realize that one's religion or lack of it has a great deal to do with what one believes about that."

BUFFINGTON: Suicide

Buffington: mother Cynthia, 45, lost her son Mark Edwin Buffington. He died May 28, 1993.

"When Mark committed suicide, he also took the life of his girlfriend. Her little son witnessed the incident and has difficulty understanding why his rescue efforts did not save his mother. The child's classmates have been cruel. Mark was divorced, as were his parents. My ex-husband expects the younger, surviving son, to comfort him. I will miss Mark, this son I loved so much, until the day I die. A homicide/suicide is such a tragic, shocking end. The guilt is so very painful. When my son lost his job and asked for help I did 'tough love.'

"The investigating officer was informative and helpful; so was the coroner. I would like to have been called by the hospital at 3 A.M. when the incident occurred, rather than waiting for the police at 6 A.M. It was the funeral home people who disturbed me.

"I have difficulty wanting to go on living. I have questioned my belief, but I must believe my son's spirit lives on and I will be reunited with him. I have had help from The Compassionate Friends and from clergy as well as professional counseling. I was hospitalized in a psychiatric hospital. I suffer from bipolar mood disorder. My son's death sent me into a manic state, with lack of sleep, which was then followed by a depressive state and overeating. Although I was hospitalized after Mark's death, the Compassionate Friends support group has been far MORE HELPFUL than counselors.

"As for books, I found Iris Bolton's book 'My Son, My Son' most beneficial.

"At first I was numb; my mind did the funeral; my heart remained detached. For several months I was in denial. I was sure my son would call. Then the grieving, crying, wailing, yearning to hold him. Now the pain, the depression, the ache, the emptiness: what next?

"Mark always questioned the value of his life with respect to the universe. I wish I could feel his presence. It was difficult to get appropriate psychological help for him, particularly because he was an adult. When he had difficult times the law would not allow me to commit him because he was supposedly no threat to himself or others. We know NOW that he was a danger to himself and the young woman whose life he took.

My younger son (19) misses his brother but has accepted the suicide as a choice. Also he believes Mark was depressed.

BYRNE: Accident

Eileen Byrne lost her daughter, Eileen, in an auto accident in June, 1991.

"At the age of 30, my daughter Eileen was killed instantly in an auto accident in June, 1991. She had been married for 9 months. I was 52 years old at the time. Also killed in this accident was my ex-husband's girlfriend. My ex-husband was very badly injured, mostly head injuries that are permanent: he no longer can smell or taste anything, has double vision, plates in his head and jaws, etc. My son-in-law Dave was driving and he sustained minor injuries. Legally the accident was not his fault but I can't help feeling some resentment towards him because he should have been more alert. We don't communicate very often since the accident. He remarried in 1995.

"For the first eight months after Eileen's death, I had a weight over me, sometimes referred to in writings as a 'veil' or 'cloud.' This 'weight' was with me *constantly;* I never woke up in the middle of the night or in the morning that the reality of Eileen's death didn't hit me. It never left for a moment! This 'weight' lifted after 8 months, never to return, not even for a day.

"I did not get sick after Eileen's death, but I did lose 12 pounds and have just begun to put back a few of those pounds. I remember the exhaustion, the confusion, memory loss, the inability to recall many simple, often-used words. It seemed I was constantly losing things. It was like a never-ending nightmare.

"Eileen was my first-born; I also have three sons. She was petite, energetic, enthusiastic, and had a spontaneous face-brightening smile. Eileen was active in school, got excellent grades and was involved in many extracurricular activities. She graduated from the University of Delaware. After graduation, she worked for an airline for two years so she could travel. Part of this decision was so I could travel at a reduced rate also. We took full advantage of that.

"She then went on to school to become an air traffic controller, which she said was the hardest thing she had ever done. The only female in her class of 22, she graduated first in her class.

"At the age of 26, while still single, she bought a town house. Forgive me for touting her accomplishments, but I was so proud of her. You always knew where you stood with her. She demanded a lot from herself and lived life to the fullest. Thank God for that!

"I have been divorced from her father for 14 years. In all that time we communicated only when absolutely necessary. Since Eileen's death, we've been able to talk at length and be in each other's company without feeling stressed, something Eileen always wanted. It took her death . . .

"The aspects most difficult to bear are all you listed: how she died; being cheated out of her companionship; not having grandchildren; the unfairness of it all; guilt; a feeling that my child was cheated out of a full life. I am angry that I can't think about her without pain. In all my readings I am told that in time this will change, but it hasn't yet and it's already 4 years. In your letter, you mentioned closure; I don't think there is ever closure in the death of a child.

"Eileen's death has made me aware of the great amount of suffering that is all around me. And I am aware more than ever now of the reality of my own death, which has become much less frightening.

"When I talk to newcomers to The Compassionate Friends in my community, I leave feeling better if I have been able to encourage them in any way. Nothing that you can say or do will relieve the pain, but it's a place you can say anything and know that it's OK.

"Every book I've read on grief has brought some new understanding of the grief process. The fact that I have been inside a church only 3 times (a christening and two weddings) since Eileen's death indicates my attitude towards religion. As for old friends, I've totally detached from two and become closer to others.

"I've thought much about the difference in the loss of a young child as opposed to an adult child. It is my opinion that the actual pain is probably the same. The difference is that there are more losses in the death of an adult child. In my own case, my daughter was my best friend. Sometimes I think she felt my joys and pain more than I did. She was in my corner no matter what the situation. Her wedding night letter to me ended with 'You're like a part of my soul.' She was 'me' when I was young. We had many of the same likes and dislikes. We traveled; we confided in each other; we talked on the phone almost daily. She was the light of my life. These are some of my losses.

"I have yearned for a communication from Eileen, though I have not experienced any. I bought a Ouiji Board but had no success contacting her.

"Whenever I try to assess where I'm at in my grieving, or try to assess what it's done to me, I feel I don't belong in the world any more; I am an alien. I realize that you never 'get over' the death of a child— ever. The grief is yours till you die."

Eileen responded to a letter in which I wrote: "I don't initiate any activity but tend to let myself be dragged along." She said it reminded her of a favorite quote: "The joy that comes my way I savor, but the seeking, the aiming, the clutching is gone. Instead of rowing I just float."

"What you are writing has to be said," she wrote, "if not for the general public, then for bereaved parents. I had company when the mail came and I intended to just scan all the material you sent. But instead I just sat back and read it all. I had such a thirst to keep reading. There is a need to share our emotions with others."

CHRISTOPHER: Illness

Elaine Christopher, 53, a divorced mother of three children,
lost her son Tom from leukemia on March 29, 1990.

"My son Tom was 24 on March 9, 1990. He died of leukemia on March 29, 1990, two months after receiving a 2nd bone marrow transplant, donated a 2nd time by his brother, Philip. Tom relapsed three times since the first diagnosis of leukemia in January 1980. Besides his father and me, Tom is survived by a brother and a sister.

"Tom was in graduate school at Hofstra University. He was single but had a girlfriend he hoped to marry. He returned from college in December of 1988, a year before the transplant.

"I have a nagging sense that Tom's death occurred due to an injection of pain killer (morphine) given very shortly before he breathed his last breath. I also experienced a lot of misunderstanding and callousness from many hospital staff members, especially in the Special Care Unit of the hospital in New York City.

"I miss my son very much and have an increased feeling of deprivation because I was limited by the unit rules from being with my son. I was permitted only minutes at his side in the last days.

"Tom's father and I divorced in September, 1989. I think I used Tom's illness to cover up a lot of my own shortcomings that have become glaringly apparent now. I am aware of waves of depression, deep at times, coming and going, which can be frightening. I am also aware of my loss of mental agility, my aches and pains that doctors can't help. Unfortunately I am not able to read for pleasure and my attention span is minimal; I have little time to call my own.

"As for changes, I am more sober, sorrowful at times and very grateful to hear Tom's name mentioned by family and friends. My faith grows daily. I do wish I had more friends or social contacts. The Compassionate Friends helps me put death in perspective, especially a child's, by sharing my own and others' experiences; it is a joy to talk freely about my child. I am so grateful for the experience of raising my son to adulthood.

"I lost my six-year-old brother when I was eleven. I recall thinking about his returning to God, his creator, untouched by the world but leaving behind a feeling of incompleteness.

"I accept the lack of grandchildren from Tom. He received a lot of radiation and was sterile, I believe. I also accept God's divine plan for all of us and believe that Tom's earthly life was complete at 24.

"A few times I have experienced dreams that include Tom. I always feel closer to him following such a dream. My younger son admits having had an unpleasant dream or two about his brother. My daughter has had many dreams, some she feels are messages while others are comforting memories.

"Writing this has been quite a therapeutic exercise for me."

CLARK: Accident

Mary Lou and Ed Clark lost their daughter Angela when her car was hit by one driven by a man who was out of control, probably because he was ill. The Clarks went through a wrongful death trial which left them frustrated and bitterly disappointed at the turn justice took in their case.

Angela was born March 10, 1966 and died December 28, 1992. The Clarks are members of the Albany Compassionate Friends and Mary Lou asked if she might write a letter rather than answer the questionnaire. Although she does not dwell on any of the details of Angela's death and the publicity of the subsequent trial, Mary Lou shares her insights about the experiences she and Ed went through and are still going through as the result of this tragedy.

"I have tried many times to answer your questionnaire but it was just too painful for me to go through the questions line by line. I would like, instead, to send you a few of my thoughts in letter form.

"Ed and I cannot believe how our life has changed since Angela was killed. I never say Angela died, she did not: she was killed by a man who had no business being where he was at the time he was.

"I often sit and wonder what it would have been like to plan her wedding. She became engaged the evening before she was killed and she never even had time to call and tell us. Her long-time boyfriend had asked her not to tell anyone until she had the ring on her finger. After her death, while I was going through some of her things, I came across a small piece of paper, a really tiny piece of paper. I unfolded it and there it was, a picture cut from a book: the ring she wanted! I died again! I wanted to run right out and buy it. I don't know why I wanted it but I did. No, of course I didn't buy it; in fact I never went to a store to search for it. I folded the paper up again and put it back where I found it.

"Probably because Angela was about to be married, I hate going to weddings and most of our invitations are sent back with WILL NOT ATTEND. When we have to go to a wedding, I sit in the church and let my mind wander: I plan what I have to do next week; I read a hymn book; I look around at people's clothes and wonder where they got them, if they look nice, if the shoes match. Anything so I don't have to pay attention to the ceremony.

"Now I try to imagine her being married. Would she have children? Would I babysit a lot?

"Ed and I get headaches from forcing smiles. We don't sleep. We spend time in our garden, where we nurse the rose bush Angela gave her Dad on Father's Day, the peony she gave me for Mother's Day. We sit and stare at the huge maple tree she planted as a little girl two days before we moved into our house. 'Angela's tree,' we call it. I have tried planting a wildflower garden under that tree but because of the shade, not much grows, so last fall I planted hosta to fill in the area, nice and shady and cool.

"Ed is sometimes very quiet and I give him his space. We give each other space. Usually in the evenings he is in one room and I am in the other, most times on separate floors. When the weather permits, he takes his tape player and earphones and listens to his music out on the porch. Sometimes when he comes in he says he just listens and cries. One night he told me he was going out to listen to his music but this time he wasn't going to cry. When I see his pain, I cannot speak to him. Sometimes I sneak out of bed in the middle of the night and just sit at the kitchen table and cry.

"Ed loves to travel but I hate it. Don't want to be away. I was never one to go away unless we had the two kids with us. Then it was OK. We were all together and we could face anything. Now I don't want to leave my house for any period of time. There will be a family reunion this July which we are committed to go to; I don't even want to go, but we will. We will smile, see aunts, uncles and cousins and wish we were home.

"Ed came from a wealthy family but his mother was a cold woman without a loving relationship with her four children, none of whom was baptized. My family gives him the affection he never got from his own. Right after we were married, Ed was baptized and MY mother is HIS godmother. Strange but true.

"Many beautiful things were inherited from Ed's mother, some of which were supposed to go to Angela. Those items reserved for Angela were assigned last year to our son Chris's three children.

"Many of our dear friends are no longer around, but the ones who have stuck by us still do, like glue. My family is wonderful. Besides my mother, I have three brothers and a sister. They were so helpful handling details immediately after Angela's death. My sister gave me a silver locket with Angela's picture the first Mother's Day after she was killed, so I would always have Angela next to my heart. It is the last thing I take off, first thing I put on each day. People often ask us if going to The Compassionate Friends helps. I have a very hard time explaining. I tell them I cannot say it helps, but it does something to us. Maybe it is because we can say what we want and no one thinks we are off the wall. For example, there is really no other place I could talk about my feelings about people who never bothered to call us or offer any sympathy when Angela died. It may sound very sick, but I get satisfaction when someone we know has a death in the family and that particular person has avoided us, stayed away, never called. And then I go to the wake. I make sure I am seen; I usually shake their hand, I say 'sorry for your loss.' But I am thinking, 'How does it feel to see us after you have neglected us? How does it feel to lose someone YOU love and WE show up for the services?' Sometimes we don't go at all. I just take the attitude, the hell with them. When I see them, maybe I'll say I'm sorry.

"Another way to explain how I feel about the TCF meeting is it makes me see people in a different light and it has made me aware of other people's feelings. Sometimes I ask, 'Where else can a doctor, painter, housecleaner, broker, restaurant owner, nurse, carpenter, teacher, streetcleaner, housewife, dentist or bookkeeper go, tell each other things they would never tell anyone else, intimate things, become friends for life, and enjoy each other's company? We share nothing but having gone through the same deep black hole. We are trying to climb out, hanging onto each other, sometimes clawing at each other, each one helping the other inch their way out to the light. If we were all thrown together in one room at a political fund raiser, a party or other social event, without ever having met, we would probably all leave without meeting. The Compassionate Friends is a society of its own. No outsiders can join. We are a closed group. There is only one way you can join and no one in the world wants to be on our waiting list."

COHEN: Accident

Toba S. Cohen, 60+ mother of A. Meyer Cohen, age 22.

"My son died as a result of a car accident/suspected homicide, on March 24, 1985. He was single and did not live at home. My husband and I and our surviving son have a very good relationship and our son has become concerned about us and our well-being. He suffered a double-whammy because he has now lost two brothers. We lost our four-year-old son 34 years ago—both losses hurt equally. My husband is not as good at verbal expression as I am but we do not have difficulty communicating.

"It is hard for me to deal with the feeling that my child was cheated out of life. The authorities stonewalled the investigation and did not find the culprits who were responsible for his death.

"TCF have been helpful but clergy have not been very supportive. Mental and physical problems: inability to sleep; memory loss, illness and depression.

"There have been Near Death Experiences as well as after death communications but it is too time-consuming to enumerate here, pertaining to both sons."

COLLINS: Military

Janet Collins, 57, and her husband Harold, 57, lost their son, Jeffrey, 35, in military service on December 31, 1992.

"We are not sure what exactly caused our son Jeffrey's death. He died on active duty with the US Forces. They told us a chemical reaction poisoning; he worked with hazardous chemical waste. Jeffrey was divorced, with two surviving children, 12 and 11. Relations at first were quite strained with our ex-daughter-in-law because our son had had custody of his children. We, the grandparents, tried for custody but lost. With the grandchildren the relationship is just perfect; recently, relations with our ex-daughter-in-law have improved and are now much better.

"Our marriage at first was very strained. We had a lot of difficulty communicating. For awhile we feared that a marriage of 39 years was going to fall apart. Each one of us was grieving in our own way and not telling the other how we felt. It took a vacation away from everyone, except us, to take the time to talk, really talk to each other. The first time away was too soon, less than four months, but our next vacation was about 8 months after our son's death. This time it helped a lot. At that time we communicated with each other about our son who died and our living son, how our lives would go on without our oldest child. And I determined to get better. I was having the hardest time with it all, not so much my husband.

"It is most difficult to bear the fact that we don't know how he died, not knowing the truth, not ever being able to see him again, hear his voice, that happy smile, the hugs, and most of all: 'Mom, I love you!' We are very fortunate that we are not denied access to our grandchildren.

"The military system did not serve us well. Because we have learned if the US Government or the military does not want you to know, they do not tell you any more than they want you to know.

"There have been many changes in our life since then; we realize life can be very short. I don't know how anyone could handle something like this if they have no religious beliefs. Friends; they stay close for awhile and then nothing: no cards, phone calls, etc. The attitudes of close friends changed somewhat, especially if they were close to your child.

"I am so glad The Compassionate Friends were there when I so needed help. I have noticed changes. It took me over 8 months to decide I was going to get better, to go on without my son, to realize I would not see him again and to say he died.

"I experienced mental and physical problems after my son's death. I could not concentrate, had a lot of indigestion, headaches, I was depressed and really didn't care if I lived or died. I felt I was losing my mind and didn't want to be near or with anyone. I felt anger at the whole world! I don't believe it makes any difference if your child was young or an adult: it's still not fair that our children died before us. The hurt is just as great. I believe it is much harder for parents to accept and understand the death of a child when that child was not ill, but suffered a sudden, accidental or violent death, because it really makes no sense at all. When one knows that their child has a terminal illness, one can sort of prepare for their death, even though the hurt is just as great. I feel there is nothing worse than having someone, a stranger, ring your door bell or call on the phone to tell you your child has just died.

"I resent it, and I hope you will put it in your book, when someone tells me you had your child for such and such years and God wanted him or her. Parents should be helped to understand why we would lose a child when grandparents and parents are still alive. It is not a good idea to lean on the surviving adult child, for they are also hurting and grieving for the loss of their brother or sister, especially if they are the only child left.

"I had a dream, so real, in which Jeffrey spoke to me and told me that he was OK and not to ask questions because we would never find the truth and that he loved us and said he had to go now. Since that time I started to heal."

COOK: Murder

Gloria Cook's son was murdered.

"My son was married twice. I have been friendly with his former wife; his second wife and I are estranged and I don't see my grand-children. I have two daughters who are very close and supportive. My husband died of a massive heart attack 1 year to the day after our son's murder. We supported one another in every way during the year before he died; we were never closer.

"It is difficult to bear how my child died, being denied his company, the unfairness of it all and the justice system. The INjustice system, I call it, was very callous towards my son as a victim of a criminal act. We as survivors were treated with disdain. The murderer was given all of his first amendment rights in the court room; our son, as victim, was given none. The murderer, an ex-convict, confessed to robbing and murdering our son. He recanted his confession on the advice of an attorney paid for by contributions from the minority community. The jury brought in a 3rd degree murder verdict despite overwhelming evidence of robbery and murder (2nd degree). He was given 10-20 years, a travesty of justice.

"I'm no longer the person I was. I have new priorities in life. My faith in God goes back and forth between doubt and belief. Some old friends have drifted away. I'm trying to understand why they avoid me.

I believe some of them do not want to face the fact that it may happen to them; it's called denial.

"Initially The Compassionate Friends have been of help but most of my support has come from Parents of Murdered Children, POMC. As a group we have been successful in keeping murderers in jail. I believe I've read a book on the loss of an adult child. As I remember, it helped me to realize my loss was not unique.

"As time goes by I grow more angry and despairing at the complete disregard for human life exhibited by the culture of our day: murderers being released from prison after serving only a fraction of their sentence.

"Of course the loss of a child at any age is devastating. The young child will never experience life here and parents grieve over a gift of life being snatched away. An older adult child, one who has accomplished much, may have a wife and children, family who are dependent on them for love and support.

"As to my health, I have been in the care of a psychiatrist and take medication for clinical depression. I have experienced sleep problems and still do; night terrors, etc. My thoughts are called bizarre by my psychiatrist because they are of executing the murderer of my son, if and when he is released from prison.

"My son was a lover of music; music was very much a part of his life. He designed stereo systems. When he was 15 years old he put together a system and the first record he played on it was George Gershwin's "Rhapsody in Blue." Hearing it always reminded me of his great joy and achievement at that time. One day when I was grieving hysterically, I heard the strains of "Rhapsody in Blue" being played on the radio, the same recording as my son's. I believe he was telling me that he was at peace."

CRIZER: Accident

Phyllis Crizer, 49, and her husband Charles, 53, lost their son David John, 23, when he was electrocuted on a utility pole while on the job on May 18, 1992.

"I'm David's Mom. I was 49 years old when he was killed and his father was 53. He was the middle of three sons. He worked for the local Gas and Electric Company and was electrocuted. David was killed five days prior to the date he and his fiancee, Kim, were to have been married.

"Kim's parents thought of David as their son. They have a young daughter who was born after Dave and Kim started dating, and she never knew life without Dave. His death was very difficult for her; Dave was her big brother and they were very close.

"David's best friends were his co-workers. They cleaned out his locker and brought Kim his hard-hat, goggles, wallet, personal belongings. At the time that was OK for me; I felt as though she should have them. But I don't feel that way now. I want all his personal belongings and I can't get them back.

"I put Kim before my husband and two sons, even myself, when David was killed. I had to be there for her and neglected my own family. My youngest son had a hard time with this. This was my own doing, not Kim's. I felt she had the biggest loss; I was wrong.

"When David was killed, my husband and I had been married for nearly 25 years. It's very difficult communicating with each other about our son. David was very close to both of us. I know my husband is hurting as much as I am, but I can't help him because of my pain. When I talk to my husband about David, I just start to cry and he cries, too. It doesn't seem to get any easier as time goes by. My husband can't sleep at night. Dave was his buddy, best friend; they thought alike. I feel when our son was killed, so were we.

"Charles, my husband, has to be constantly busy, always working. Before David's death, they planned to construct an out-building together. Charles has built that building single-handed; I know Dave was there beside him every moment.

"I not only feel that it is difficult to face all the items you listed, I would underline them for emphasis: how my child died; being denied my child's companionship and having grandchildren from him; the unfairness of it all; anger and guilt; a feeling that my child was cheated out of life; other (explanation): David was killed by carelessness, neglect, and simple negligence on behalf of his crew leader. We are unable to do anything legally on his behalf. I feel the legal system has not served us well; in fact, my answer to that question is HELL NO!

"My attitude towards life has changed dramatically. I simply do not want to live any longer. I will; I know I have to, but all the joy is gone.

"As for religion, I don't blame God for David's death probably because I blame his crew leader. I do know now that if I don't live a decent life here, then I will not see David in Heaven, which is my ultimate goal.

"Friends? I have one special friend who stuck by me through my worst nightmare and we are still very close. With other friends, there is not much difference.

"We started going to The Compassionate Friends four weeks after David was killed. To say it helps may not be correct; nothing helps. But

I'm very grateful they are there for me. Professional psychiatrist? What a joke! David's company sent me to a psychiatrist who just sat and continued writing prescriptions for several anti-depressants and sedatives. Their purpose was to keep me quiet and control me and I fell for it. No, professionals did not help me at all; just the opposite.

"I got no support from clergy, either. I felt that since priests do not have any children of their own, how can they possibly understand my loss?

"If you wrote this kind of book, it might be a big help to me. All other books I've read thus far are about the death of very young children. My David was about to be married. I love Kim as much as I would love my own daughter. I also lost her and any grandchildren she and David might have given me. They were practically in the palm of my hand, living less than a mile away.

"I can't break down phases of my grief, because I am still in constant pain and agony over losing my Dave. It's been 22 months and the pain has not lessened at all. I will never get over losing David; I don't think I even want to.

"I believe there is a difference between losing an adult child versus a young child. It's difficult to put it into words. My aunt Mary, age 80, lost her 56-year-old son to cancer on Christmas Day, 1991. He lived in Texas. At his funeral she was overlooked completely. Her daughter-in-law did not do this, but everybody else did, from the funeral director to the priest. She had no say in anything that went on. Her daughter-in-law was so distraught that she didn't even notice this omission. All sympathy and compassion went to his wife and children. My aunt felt completely alone. I felt sympathy for her at the time but after my Dave died I knew what she had gone through. I somehow wanted to make it up to her, but there was no need to; she understood.

"I have to answer 'yes' to all 15 physical and mental problems you mentioned on the questionnaire except for over-eating. I lost all appetite. I still experience these physical and mental problems after 22 months. I think of suicide, but that's all; I don't plan it like I used to.

"Besides close family, David's friend, also a lineman, had a hard time dealing with this senseless tragedy. I am not aware if his fiancee is experiencing any problems or not. This could be simply because I have not been told. Many people believed I couldn't handle much after he died and maybe they were right.

"If a Near Death Experience means he had a choice to go towards the light or return to his body, he would have returned to his body. I know this.

"Dave communicated with his fiancee, Kim, twice after his death and before he was buried. He told her to continue on with her life, to do exactly what they had planned to do together: plant the trees in the yard, plant the green beans and cabbage; do everything they had planned. He said he couldn't stay with her but he would always be near. He told her life is always worth living and to find someone to love. She did.

"You asked if I have any other insights. Do not do what I did! When Dave died, I felt Kim had the greater loss. I felt that Dave would want us to protect her, be financially supportive of her, to simply be there for him since he couldn't be. Because they were not yet married, Charles and I were Dave's beneficiaries from his life insurance. At 23 Dave took life seriously and was covered quite adequately. I believed that Kim should have everything; my husband did not. In the end we gave Kim quite a lot of money, all of Dave's personal belongings, a new car, and a place to lie next to him when she died. I am not sorry for what we did, because when we see him again, we can look Dave in his eyes with our heads held high.

"The day David went for his first job interview he met a young man whom he liked immediately. He told us that if the company needed only one person, this other applicant would definitely get the job. As it turned out, they hired both. Dave and this other man soon became very good friends. He became Dave's replacement in Kim's life. Dave gave Kim not only permission to go on with her life, he selected the person who ultimately got everything that belonged to him. I have a very difficult time dealing with this. I am very sorry I gave Kim all of Dave's personal belongings, especially all the photos he took.

"Dave was very good at his job. The company started a career path for him that would eventually lead him to management, but in order to do so Dave had to go to night school and take some college courses. One of his courses was English composition. He had to write on certain aspects of his life. He would write them and I would print them on my computer. The morning after he died, I told my husband that Dave had written his own eulogy. Charles thought I had lost my mind. When I showed him Dave's writings he couldn't believe it. I told the priest that this was what he would say about my Dave. He did. It was perfect.

"Dave and Kim were to have been married in her church the day after what turned out to be the date of his funeral; it was reasonable for him to be buried from there as well and I asked our priest to be there. Dave was buried on a Friday. On Monday I had a Requiem Mass said for him at our church and it was just as crowded then as it was on Friday.

"I want to thank you for this opportunity to say what I had to. I would be interested in knowing the results of your survey.

"P.S. In 1988 I was diagnosed with breast cancer. They told me I was one of the lucky ones: I survived. They were wrong. I was not one of the lucky ones."

Phyllis sent follow-up letters telling of her progress through grief. One, dated January 7, 1996, answers some of the questions I had posed in my Christmas letter.

"I also wanted to get away for the holidays, as you did, but I realized the pain would only follow me wherever I went. This year wasn't as bad as I thought it would be. My new daughter-in-law decorated our Christmas tree in butterflies. It was so beautiful I hesitated to take it down. This Christmas was much better than the three previous ones, thanks to my two/three surviving children (two sons and one daughter-in-law). My husband has a lot to do with my new-found optimism as well. I owe a lot to the conferences I attended, too. At the time I didn't think they helped me, but gradually I absorbed what I heard and now I understand much of what I was told. I didn't believe them when they said I would laugh again, and some day look towards the future, but I do now.

"You mentioned in your letter that there were certain aspects of parental grief which were not covered in the original questionnaire. Yes, I would like to share my experiences and insights.

"In regard to memorials: when Dave died we set up a scholarship fund for children who wanted to attend the 4-H summer camp and could not afford to do so. It has been three summers now, and I heard from only one young girl who was kind enough to thank me—and Dave—for allowing her to go. Her thank-you letter is priceless to me.

"I planted a butterfly garden in our back yard in Dave's memory. I've received many plants from friends to put in that garden. A tree was planted in his memory at the gas and electric plant by his fellow linemen. It was dedicated to Dave and all the linemen. I was, and still am, very upset that they did not even have the courtesy to let us know about it. They have yet to apologize.

"Each year on May 18, his death date, we attend Mass. We then go to the cemetery, and at the exact time of his death we are at 'his pole' where he died. I read his memory books on his birthday and death day. They are quite large and took 10 months to complete. I also listen to his funeral, on his death date, from beginning to end, because I did not hear it then.

"His fiancee still has his personal belongings and the things we gave her. I did not give anyone else anything that belonged to him, except this past Christmas. Dave had a very good camera. I gave that to his brother Craig. It took me three and a half years to finally let go.

"You asked if the passage of time has lent a new perspective to my grief experience and I have to say 'yes' to that question. I laugh more and cry less, which is good. I will always miss and love my Dave, but I think he would be more proud of me if I lived my life as I had before he died. He loved life and would surely be disappointed in me if I lived a less full life than I could.

"I don't know if I told you this before. One day several months after he died, I was very depressed. More so than usual. I was looking for something in my cedar chest, when I found Dave's journals. I thought I had read them all, but apparently I missed one. A page fell out of his book, and as I picked it up the last line literally hit me in the face. I read, 'No matter what happens, life is always worth living.' The strangest thing is, this had nothing to do with the rest of his story. It was completely out of place, but not for me then!

"As for men's grief, I can't help you there. I know Charles will never get over losing Dave. They were exceptionally close. He not only lost a son, but his best friend and confidant. No one will be as close to him as Dave.

"You might find this interesting. One night at dinner I asked Charles if he had one wish, what would it be? His answer was to have a grandchild. I was surprised. I had wanted grandchildren when Dave was alive more than anything else. But since his death, I have no desire to have grandchildren. I never want to love another child as I have loved him; I couldn't endure the pain of losing another child. And though it's a small possibility, I don't want to take the chance, although my surviving children think differently.

"My answer took Charles by surprise, too. I told him I would like to be transported back in time to 1966, the year we got married, and to do everything all over, not to change a thing, just to have all my boys back home again.

"Charles said he could not endure the pain of losing Dave again; he couldn't live through it a second time.

"Two different answers, but both afraid of the PAIN."

In response to one of my letters to Phyllis, she wrote as follows:

"May is always a hard month for us. The 23rd would have been Dave's wedding day. I could quite possibly have been a grandmother twice. But I am not going to dwell on the 'could have beens' or the past.

"When you wrote that you had purchased some napkins on the first anniversary of Cathy's death, I had the feeling she sent you a message that day: the butterfly, which was inside the napkin and not visible until opened. She was telling you , 'Mom, I'm OK. I love you both.' See how we grasp for even the smallest bit of affirmation? Is this crazy thinking? I collect butterflies now; small consolation to what I have lost.

"I thought I was getting better. I was. I know it. Until today, when I started to buy two Mothers Day cards . . .

"My husband Charlie got out of the hospital yesterday. He was admitted last week for a bleeding ulcer. His ulcer began three years ago. See a pattern? I had a severe case of Shingles last February. The doctor said it comes from the chicken pox virus and it's stress-related.

"In the beginning of this letter I said some of my feelings and attitudes have changed. I'll try to explain. I no longer hate Dave's crew leader; I am trying not to blame him for what happened. I now believe it was David's time to go. If he hadn't been on the pole that day, it would have happened some other way. He was destined to 'go home'.

"When I think of my Dave now, I think of him in the present. Where he is now; what he's doing now. I imagine him being in a spirit form without a restricting body. I had said earlier, when I filled out your questionnaire, that if David had a choice to go towards the light or return to his body, he would have returned to his body. I don't believe this any more. He had every reason to live, this I know. But I imagine the instant his soul left his body, and he saw the brilliant white light filled with love, my Dave would have said, 'Awesome!' as he embraced the light."

DANKER: Murder

Sue Danker lost her son, Jeff.

"On June 7, 1992, when I was 11 days shy of my 49th birthday, my 27-year-old son, Jeff, was shot while he was in military service. His assailant was in a jealous rage, looking for Jeff's roommate. He shot Jeff instead and killed him instantly. Jeff is survived by 2 brothers, with whom I have a close and very good relationship. Jeff's father and I are divorced. Since then I have remarried. However, that marriage has now terminated because my present husband couldn't deal with my grief.

"I feel that Jeff's death is cruel and unfair and I grieve because I am now and forever denied my son's company.

"I realize now how fragile life is, how you can never take anything for granted. I've always been a very spiritual person and that hasn't changed. I found I can't depend on friends for support. I take my support from anyone I can receive it from. The Compassionate Friends have been helpful and I've needed grief therapy. Books help you to know that what you're feeling is normal, that you aren't losing your mind. Most books I've read have dealt with a child of no particular age.

"In the beginning you keep waiting for the nightmare to end. In time you realize it is not a dream, that it's real. Then you have to learn to deal with your loss. As time goes on, you find you have OK days. That makes you feel guilty because you feel you shouldn't have good days when your child is dead. But eventually you see if it weren't for the good days you couldn't survive the bad days. The pain would destroy you. Good isn't really a word to describe the OK days: tolerable is more the word. Add to the pain of losing a child the pain of losing a marriage and you've got a lot of sad, lonely, painful feelings.

"I think because we've had so much more time with our adult children and been through so many bad times when our kids were growing up, we've invested so much love, energy and emotion in our children to the point we lose them. Letting go of our kids seems close to impossible.

"I've had many wonderful dreams of Jeff that seemed too real to be dreams. Again, things move when they shouldn't and I've experienced smells that remind me of Jeff, so I would have to say yes, I have had communications from him since his death."

DE FORD: Murder/Suicide?

Beverly and Michael DeFord lost their son Doug on June 15, 1990.

Beverly says: "I'll try to answer the survey for Mike and me. Our beautiful 20-year-old son Doug was found shot to death in a remote area called Wildcat Creek on June 15, 1990. It was ruled suicide by the authorities but we, his parents, think it was murder and are continuing to press for justice. Because of the fact that the case is unfinished, there are many details which must be left out of this discussion.

"Five days after his death, I dreamed I saw him at a party in a crowd of people. I made him sit down on a chair and asked, 'What happened to you?' He held up two fingers and said, 'There were two of them.' He was found with the shotgun which had been given to him by his beloved grandfather, a highly-decorated veteran of WWII. The shotgun was Doug's prize possession and he had started carrying it when trouble began at the store where he worked. Doug had been close to his grandfather, who was killed in an accident in 1988.

"Doug left a girlfriend who is a troubled woman and she has given us a lot of grief, both in her erratic behavior and in being uncooperative in the ongoing investigation. At first we tried to help her as much as possible but had to let the relationship go because it was too much of a burden on us. We were in such bad shape that we felt we just had to concentrate on taking care of ourselves. As it is, Mike and I are feeling the death more as a physical thing now, a violent act on our bodies. I have a sinking feeling a lot and suffer from dizziness. My husband has been going to the doctor for stomach spasms for the past several months. We both feel it's the after-effects of trauma.

"We let Doug's name be used by the Chicago people in a mural of 148 gunshot victims. Many of the cases were uninvestigated, as was ours. The names are on the Cole-Taylor Bank Building on 47th Street and are meant to call attention to gang violence. Elected public officials were invited to speak at the dedication on Memorial Day but didn't show up and didn't even phone to apologize. I was a speaker at the event. What a coincidence: just down the street was a grocery store run by the same chain Doug worked for, and whose labor troubles may have been the cause of his death.

"We also participated in the Sea of Shoes: victims' shoes were presented before Congress in September with notes telling what happened to their loved ones. Afterwards the shoes were given to the needy.

"When Doug was a child, I took him to a department store to have his picture taken. As the camera lens closed, the thought came to me that this child would be shot by a gun. Both of us had watched the camera lens as it closed. Doug and I looked at each other; Doug was frozen, wide-eyed with fear. It was as if both our souls knew at that moment what lay ahead.

"Doug has communicated with me a lot in dreams, even to the extent of explaining some of the mysterious details of his death. He tells me it is the greedy, lazy nature of those who caused his death and I should forgive them if I could. When he appeared to me just before I went to sleep and then to his father in a dream, Mike and I compared notes and found that Doug was dressed in the same outfit. And I have felt his presence several times.

"At Christmas time, Doug visited in a dream again. We were shopping with his brother and my husband. Doug was all dressed up and picking out new clothes that he wanted for Christmas. He was very happy. Then he led us through a beautiful garden. He had me sit with him on a bench beneath a poinsettia tree. On top of the tree were two white doves. Doug asked his Dad to take a picture of us together and he was having fun.

"It's been three years since Doug's death. My anger has softened. I'm working now to touch people's hearts so they will learn not to hurt others. I now realize that forgiving is the most powerful thing you can do. I've redefined myself not only as a victim of violence but as someone who can learn to cope with a terrible experience by practicing forgiveness. I still have times when waves of anger wash over me. But I try to be gentle with myself and continue to work on forgiveness. I know when you resent someone, you're bound to them; when you forgive, you're free.

In September 1995, Mike DeFord had surgery for the removal of a cancerous tumor at the opening of a bile duct behind the stomach. Part of his stomach, pancreas and intestine had to be removed. Because of the rarity of his cancer and the nature of his operation, Mike has become famous among the medical profession, a fame he would not seek and does not particularly enjoy. His surgeon is very understanding because he, too, suffered the loss of a child: a 2-year-old son. Beverly was supported throughout the ordeal, surrounded by many kind people. Mike said finding out he had cancer was the most physically painful thing he has had to face in life, but the emotional pain is nothing compared to losing Doug.

Beverly has written at length about her late father, a highly-decorated veteran of World War II. This story may be read in the chapter entitled "Why?" It describes her search for an understanding of the violence of her father's wartime experiences as they impinged on her life and her son's life.

DERESIENSKI: Accident

Ingrid, 49, and Albert, 52, Deresienski: Mark, their 18-year-old son, was a passenger in a car when he was killed on March 9, 1989. His dates: 2/17/71-3/9/89.

"Our son Mark was killed in a one-car crash on March 9, 1989. I emphasize the word 'crash' because it was a violent end. We were assured that he died instantly. At least we think he didn't suffer; we desperately want to believe it.

"At the time of our son's death we had been married 27 years. During those years, I don't ever recall seeing my husband cry. When we came upon our son's accident scene, the police directed us to Albany Medical Center Hospital, where the ambulance was en route. On our arrival, we were ushered into a special waiting room located next to the Emergency area. This, I knew, was not a good sign. When the doctor walked in, I sensed the worst and said to him, 'He is dead, isn't he.' He simply answered 'Yes.' My husband put his head on folded arms and sobbed. I stood like a statue; I was numb. My flood of tears came when I had to make a long-distance call to my mother. I was barely able to speak and only managed to say, 'Mutti, Mark ist tot.' (Mummy, Mark is dead.) Hysteria enveloped me.

"As grief settled in over us, we have often—oh, so often—cried together. I know my husband also cried alone. His pain was a heart-rending and vocal release. It hurt to see him that way but it was also a relief for me to know that he could express his grief.

"Men's and women's grief expectations and actions have been conditioned by society. Al's emotional outbursts were like flash flood in the desert. I, on the other hand, cried for hours and days, and what seemed like weeks on end.

"Our relationship has always been a good one, though Mark's death has certainly stressed it at times. If we have had occasional difficulties in communication, they seem to be improving as time goes on.

"At the time of his death, Mark was still living at home with us and with his brother Paul, who was 20 at the time. In addition, he was survived by three grandparents, an uncle and an aunt. With one or two exceptions, these relatives were not at all supportive during our ordeal, which has been very hurtful. At one point the aunt said, 'The subject of your son's death is becoming tiresome.'

"Since my husband and I were so out of touch with reality and turned inward most of the time after Mark's death, it is difficult to remember how our surviving son, Paul, was coping with his brother's death. He had a girlfriend then who was absolutely wonderfully supportive, and she has our undying gratitude because she was there for him when he needed her.

"Looking back over the years since Mark died, we question what could have been done differently to help our son Paul in his grieving. He tended, then as now, not to bring up his brother's death. His concern shows when he sees his parents sad, depressed or teary-eyed. We want to appear up-beat to him. When sadness raises its unwanted head, we feel that an optimistic, full-of-life young man should not be dragged down.

"Friends were somewhat helpful after our son's death and then slowly drifted away. Sympathy of others who have lost children is very high; it is easier for me to talk to someone who is grieving because I have been there. This is particularly true of The Compassionate Friends, who have been very supportive. Ordinary friends who have not experienced such a loss have dropped by the wayside. They would rather see me go than come; eventually contact stopped. That was a great disappointment. A professional counselor was somewhat helpful.

"Mark's absence is an ever-present void. He is not in the house, not joining us at meals, not in the living room, his bedroom, in the garden or the yard. No 'Mother, I'm home!' No 'Mother, the pie is delicious!' No 'Mother, see, you later.' No 'Mother, I just met the most fantastic girl!' No conversations; no hugs; no nothing.

"I regret that Mark will never have the joy of falling in love and getting married. He will have no descendants; his gene line ended on March 9, 1989. It is so very unfair! Why should a healthy, strapping young man's life be snuffed out while the scum of the earth continue to live?

"My anger was huge; unbearable. The anger was at times directed at myself, my husband and surviving son. The anger was sometimes rational and sometimes irrational. I didn't seem to care whether it was appropriately directed or not; I was blind with anger.

"At the same time the guilt was haunting. I questioned myself thousands of times about what I could have done to prevent the tragedy, about my failure as a parent in not being able to protect my child. My guilt feelings took on absurdity when I began thinking we should not have moved upstate; I should not have married Al; should not have come to this country at age 15. See, it was really my parents' fault for having emigrated from Germany. This is how my guilt traveled.

"I feel Mark was cheated out of a full life. The 'could-have-beens' make an endless story.

"After Mark died, I suffered from memory loss and an inability to concentrate, from depression and thoughts of suicide. I was always tired and felt an extreme lack of energy. I developed a serious metabolic illness, diabetes. From time to time I was certain I was going crazy. I lost interest in cooking and avoided contact with people, distancing myself from them. Fantasizing and daydreaming occupied much of my waking hours.

"My attitude towards life changed. Now I see life as brutally indifferent. In a fraction of a second, my life changed forever. Now, I savor every day and pay more attention to nature. I am no longer afraid to die.

"In answer to the question about the difference between the loss of a young child and an adult child, I would say there are several differences. When parents lose a young child, they often have the option of having another baby, which bereaved parents of an adult child cannot do. The loss of an older child means there has been a larger depository of living and thus more memories for us to cherish. We have made a greater, long-time investment of love, work, etc. and finally set them on their own. This is a difficult question to answer. A book on the subject might address specific needs of different age groups, even though grief is grief.

"Our son's death was caused by negligence of the driver and there was a subsequent hearing in which we felt victimized over and over by the legal and judicial system. We feel a certain bitterness in realizing that the case was just not important enough to pursue, according to the authorities in charge.

"Insofar as the medical system was concerned, we were involved with the emergency room only, and they served us well. Looking back, I wish that the hospital had asked us about organ donations, which they did not do.

"My quest of asking where my son is has started. His body has gone but his essence and energy have to be somewhere. I am quite convinced of this. Items in or around the house keep turning up unexpectedly or are suddenly missing, which I interpret as contacts with him. I feel his energy near me when I talk to him or think of him. Where is God and what does He do in the scheme of things? These things are on my mind a great deal."

DONALD: Illness

Terry and Gregory Donald lost their daughter, Miriam Donald Carr. Terry says:

"My daughter Miriam died on November 25, 1988 of leukemia. She was 26 and I was 48 at the time of her death. She left a husband, two children and one sibling besides her father and me. Our relationship with them is good. My husband and I have difficulty communicating and can't talk about our deceased child. As her mother, I feel particularly cheated out of my relationship with my daughter as I grow older. I feel sad that she missed out on a full life, the way she died, and the fact that the medical professional did not serve her as well as I would have expected. We were given false hopes and little compassion.

"Since Miriam's death my attitude towards life has changed. I feel you must enjoy it as much as possible. My very early grief was emotionally overwhelming; as time passes death becomes accepted and the real chore becomes going on. My husband had open heart surgery and my son-in-law had hard times. I have had help from The Compassionate Friends and professional counseling.

"The circumstances of losing an adult child are quite different from losing a small child, especially when they are married and have children of their own. When you lose an adult child, you lose a friend, too.

DUNN: Accident

Dunn, Mary, 66, and Thomas, lost their son Tommy from smoke inhalation.

"My son Tommy died on January 4, 1994 at the age of 40. He was a volunteer fireman and suffered smoke inhalation while fighting a fire. He was married and the father of three children, aged 4, 3, and 1. We still have a very close relationship with his widow and our grandchildren.

"My husband and I have been married 46 years and would be lost without each other. He tends to grieve privately but encourages me in whatever I undertake. We have a daughter who lives in Seattle and she has been supportive but of course she is far away from our New Jersey home.

"After Tommy's death, I found it hard to accept how he died. It is sad to be denied his company. It seems so unfair. I wonder why it had to happen; so many unanswered questions. I was angry, wondering why it couldn't have been me; I've lived my life.

"The police and fire departments were extremely kind to our daughter-in-law and family.

"Since Tommy's death I have become much more tolerant, less judgmental of others, and my priorities have changed. I can only hope that with time will come acceptance.

"The Compassionate Friends have been very helpful, making books available. I read all materials and it is comforting to know others feel as I do. I am not alone!

"I have problems sleeping; thoughts just crowd in and the tears begin again. I experienced memory loss, inability to concentrate, depression and illness as a result of my bereavement. I just wish people would talk about my son. I am not comfortable talking about him when it seems to be the last thing on other peoples' minds. As The Compassionate Friends say, 'We get through it, not over it.'

"My religion (I am Catholic) has helped me enormously; I do think faith is the key. God has given me peace, a feeling of deep calm.

"Although I have had not communication from my son, my husband remembers the sensation of my son's hand on his shoulder, gently."

EVANS: Illness

John Evans, 8/30/59-3/24/92, was 32 at the time of his death from leukemia. His parents are David (61) and Alice (56) Evans.

"Our son John was diagnosed with leukemia on November 13, 1990. He had a bone marrow transplant in Seattle and died on March 24, 1992.

"John was married and had two little daughters, two and three and a half years old. Besides his widow and his parents, he also is survived by two brothers.

"Although my husband Dave and I have differing grief styles, our relationship is good now. I cry easily and this is upsetting to Dave, so I tend to save my tears until I am alone. Dave was in denial right up until John died; afterwards we talked about it for awhile.

"His younger brother misses John a lot and is trying to build up a stronger relationship with Douglas, the oldest. Doug, however, is resisting most efforts to get him together with remaining family members. His life is troubled at the moment.

"John's widow, Doris, tries to put up a good front but of course she misses him terribly. Dave and I have been close to her and continue to be. She is searching for a 'father' for her children and we are concerned about the young men—too young—she keeps bringing home.

"Little Janice, now six and a half, had a strong bond with her father. I held her soon after John died. Her mother, being a Born Again Christian, had told the children their Daddy was up in Heaven. Janice asked me if she could get up there if she held onto a big bunch of balloons. When I said no, she cried and cried, saying 'I want Daddy to come back down here right now!'

"Ellen was just two when John died; only 9 months old when he was diagnosed with leukemia. She never really knew him. It upsets me that she gets teased too much by her maternal grandfather and Doris' younger brothers.

"Dave is extremely important to the little granddaughters and to Doris, who counts on him for financial guidance and household repairs. Both girls are very loving towards us, as is Doris.

"I have never gotten over my grief over what John went through. He was a handsome, strong young man with an excellent job and a great marriage, two darling baby girls, plans to build their dream house. Then Bang! He is under a death sentence. Scared, wanting to take care of his family, going through the Hell of the bone marrow transplant, always caring about the others, always using his sense of humor to spare us. Then finding out the transplant had failed. It breaks my heart to realize that Janice and Ellen will not remember.

"I am not sure of my answer to your question about whether the medical system served him well. Apparently everything that could be done was done. Yet the doctors in Seattle are constantly rotated so he had no one he really knew there all the time throughout the frightening, painful procedures. Should John have had a second transplant? Jose Carreras, the great tenor, had the same leukemia and look at him now: recovered!

"Since John died, I feel much more cynical about life. I feel I need to live every minute to the hilt, knowing that at any moment I, Dave, or others I love may suddenly be taken away. I think about death frequently now, whereas I seldom did before.

"Regarding religion, I feel confused. When John was facing death and then the transplant, I could find no words of comfort for him. Meanwhile, Doris and the people in their fundamentalist church were very comforting and hopeful; this seemed to help him greatly.

"This experience has not noticeably changed my friendships. Like John, I try to be up-beat around people because no one wants to be around someone who is no fun. My friends were supportive when he died but I'm sure they don't want to keep hearing about it anymore.

"I have not sought help from a self-help group nor from professional counselors. My clergywoman was there at the hospital when John died, though the clergy of my denomination in Seattle who were contacted did not respond.

"I haven't read any books about the experiences of other parents whose adult child has died. I read a chapter in a book my clergywoman gave me. It was full of exercises for the bereaved but they seemed dumb and artificial to me.

"My grief itself has changed of course. Like 'they' say, time heals. And keeping busy. And spending time with the grandchildren. And TRYING not to constantly dwell on it.

"I lost a baby girl in my 6th month of pregnancy. Dave and I were heartbroken. But we never even saw her and we had two active young sons two and a half and four at the time.

"On the other hand, John was a grown man, our pride and joy. We had loved him for almost 33 years. There is no comparison.

"As to my physical and mental problems after John's death, I experienced memory loss, an inability to concentrate—especially at first—insomnia (exacerbated by thoughts of John's death), weight gain, depression. My completely irrational guilt was terrible: mothers are supposed to keep their children safe from harm, aren't they?

"Everyone involved in John's death is dealing with it by getting on with his or her life. In that sense, Doris suffers the most. She says, 'everybody has their life back again but me.'

"Even though I am not sure, I feel John sometimes puts his hand on my shoulder and says, 'Lighten up, Mom!'

"Because of the circumstances—the diagnosis followed by a year and a half of struggle to beat the odds—John was a wonderful role model. He was terrific at taking all the fear and pain while continuing to be uncomplaining and making little jokes to ease our tension. His mother-in-law remarked about going to see him in the hospital and John looking at her and saying 'You look nice in that dress, Ruth.'

"He arranged a family trip to Vermont to our ski place the winter after the diagnosis. He also arranged a day on Lake George for the whole immediate family on his boat late that Spring before he went to Seattle.

"He wrote in his will that he wanted the girls brought up in the Christian religion and that Dave and I should never be denied access to them. He even wrote out the instructions that if Doris were unwilling or unable to end his life, 'to pull the plug,' I was empowered to do so. I did.

"When we went to Seattle he rented a house for us with a lovely view and a safe play area for the children. He rented nice furniture for us to use and a van. He continued to take care of his family throughout his ordeal.

"Long before he became ill I used to tell myself, when I sometimes feared the possibility of my husband Dave dying before me, what I would do. I knew I could always count on John. John, the one in the middle, was bright, sensible, cheerful, thoughtful, capable, likeable, devoted to the entire family, fun to be around. Not perfect, of course, but pretty darned close!

"So now I try to be as much like him as possible. When he was ill he declined invitations to a cancer support group. 'I don't want to be around sick people,' he would say. 'I want to concentrate on being well.'

"If attitude counted, he would be well today!"

EIS: Accident

Lydia Eis and her husband lost their son, Scott, September 4, 1978, when he was 19. She was 47 at the time.

"Two of my four sons were mountain climbing when they were caught in a rockslide on a Colorado mountain peak. Randy, the elder, barely escaped alive, but Scott was killed. Although I was 2,000 miles away, I knew shortly after his death that something terrible had happened to him. That thought came into my head a few hours after the accident. I have always felt that was his last communication with me.

"Scott had such promise. He was optimistic, bright and cheerful, a really good comedian. He had just finished an Emergency Medical Training course and was planning to be a doctor. That is the hardest thing to deal with, the unfairness of his being cheated out of a wonderful life, and the missing him, the longing for him.

"Scott's brother Randy was divorced 2 years later and I'm sure Scott's death contributed to his ensuing marital problems. Both he and his ex-wife agree. It caused a great chasm between them. They have since bridged that gap and are good friends. Scott's younger brother, Mark, who was 14 when the accident happened, was much affected by the death of his closest brother. After he got over the shock, he gradually became very solicitous of his parents.

"There were times in the first 3 or 4 years after Scott's death that I seriously considered separation from my husband, but I slowly began to realize that our problems had more to do with my own depression, which gradually subsided after 5 years. My husband and I still cry over our son's death even though it has been almost 16 years. There are times we are each able to talk about our feelings and other times we avoid it. Somehow we have managed to survive this terrible ordeal and are still friends. Men like my husband seem to grieve alone and silently, especially in the beginning. This made me feel so alone in my grief.

"This experience has taught me to cherish my family and friends and to cherish each day more than ever. For sure, we have only today, the present. As far as religion goes, I think these tragedies happen not because of God's will, but by chance.

"Although The Compassionate Friends was not available at the time of Scott's death, I would recommend it to others. I think I would have been wise, perhaps would not have grieved so long, had I obtained some professional help or joined a bereaved parents group.

Close and very understanding, dear friends helped a lot. I read a book which was not particularly applicable but it did help a bit. I think a book about the death of an adult child would be very helpful.

"You asked whether there is a difference between the death of a young and an adult child. For the latter, the length of time is so much greater, there are more memories for parents, the personality of their child is fully developed and they are usually settled into a career. Perhaps the loss is more intense because of the time element and known lost potential of the adult child.

"I experienced all the problems circled in the questionnaire: memory loss, inability to sleep, inability to concentrate, depression. I did not think of suicide, but I found myself wishing over and over again that if one of the 6 of us had to die, why couldn't it have been me? I, as a mother, would have gladly gone instead. My poor husband felt that way, too.

"My responses to my loss over time have changed. Year one: shock and continual disbelief; Year two: gradual acknowledgement that he was dead and subsequent depression; Year three: deep underlying depression, although on the surface I coped. I should have sought help then, but I didn't. Year four: some of the pain in my heart and mind seemed to be diminishing; Year five: I think I finally believed that he was really dead.

"I now know that we, as parents, never 'get over' such a loss. We know life has to go on and we learn somehow to cope. If we are lucky, we are once again able to appreciate those family members who are also survivors. But the loss of a child changes us forever. The heartbreak never completely leaves us and we know we shall always miss that missing one. Family reunions will never again be quite the same."

FEINGOLD: Accident

Solomon Feingold, aged 65, and his wife lost their 33-year-old son Joel on August 1, 1987.

"My son, Joel Steven Feingold, was killed in a mountain climbing accident on August 1, 1987. He was 33 and was not living at home at the time of his death. He was single and had a girl friend. I was 65 when he died.

"My wife and I have experienced some stress in our marriage because of Joel's death and sometimes we have difficulty in communicating. We have an occasional flare-up, though there is really no significant difference in the way we grieve.

"We have one surviving child, a daughter, who has had a very hard time with her brother's death. She is younger and experienced extreme guilt about Joel's death. She blames herself in hastening his death but is gradually working out the guilt. She has trouble earning a living because of her emotional disability.

"My wife is burdened by a second career; her family society oversees cemetery arrangements. I feel a sense of anger and guilt about my son's death. Knowing how he died is very painful, as is the knowledge that we will never have grandchildren from Joel. I am sad that he was cheated out of life and I was cheated out of his companionship. I have experienced some depression.

"We instituted a suit of wrongful death against the tour operator involved in Joel's death. It was undermined by circumstantial technicalities.

"Since Joel's death, I find myself becoming impatient with trifling relationships. The Compassionate Friends have been helpful; clergy have been only somewhat helpful. I sense that my understanding of life and religion has been deepened by my loss.

"A book might help clarify the issues for grieving parents. There seems to be a generation gap in grief, yet some mutual appreciation can probably be derived. As time goes by, I have made some progress, though the sadness never goes away and is sometimes reinforced.

"Although I have not felt my child really communicated with me since his death, a symbolic continuation of our relationship remains.

"A child's loss will always be traumatic for the survivors, even though heedless critics will assume that surviving siblings should fill the void or that the relatively long life of the deceased child should pacify the bereaved parents. I feel that a loss is a loss. Parents of a young child who died may feel oppressed by a longer anticipated future dealing with their grief than the bereaved parent of an adult child."

FITZGERALD: Illness and Accident

Neil J. Fitzgerald, 70, a widower, lost two children within one year. His son Neil died at the age of 42 on July 30, 1993. Peggy, aged 37, was killed December 12, 1993.

"My son Neil died from AIDS which he acquired either from a blood transfusion several years ago or from a dirty needle when he was using drugs. He was a recovering alcoholic and drug user five to six years prior to his death. He was employed for five years in the Crisis Center for alcoholics and drug users. He left a wife and three children.

"My daughter Peggy was killed in an auto accident. The driver of the other car may have been trying to kill his wife, who was suing for divorce.

"Both of my deceased children were married and did not live at home. At the time of his death, Neil had been married, divorced, separated and remarried. I have one surviving daughter; every time the phone rings, I am afraid I'll be told she's dead.

"My wife Marilyn died in November, 1986. We had had an excellent marriage. I also have an very good relationship with Neil's widow. I seldom see Neil's children because one is in California, one in Maine and one in New York. We are friendly, though, and communicate occasionally.

"While I loved my wife of 37 years and my son for the 42 years of his life, both were incurably ill and I accepted the fact that they were better off dead. Because their illnesses were protracted and their suffering so great, I thought I was prepared for the final moment. I wasn't. It was still a crushing blow when each of them died. While I miss them, I take some consolation from the fact that they are not suffering any more. I have a sense of guilt that I didn't do enough for my son. I feel the medical system did all it could for him and for my wife.

"But with my daughter Peg it was different. Her death was so sudden, so unexpected, it has devastated me. I'm not fully recovered yet. I am angry; the person who killed her got off 'scot free' because of politics. It makes me feel the expression 'legal/justice system' is an oxymoron. She was snuffed out before her time. I feel deprived of her company and I really hate the person who killed her. I hate the fact that he's not being punished for taking my daughter away from me.

"Although I still hurt a lot and have found it difficult to concentrate, have experienced sleep problems, weight loss and some physical problems, I have not sought help from any source. I did not turn away from my religion and I attend church weekly.

"Peg's husband was badly injured in the accident and may have some brain damage. He hasn't worked since then and has stopped communicating with my surviving daughter. He has moved and changed his telephone number. Although he has called me four times when I wasn't home, he does not leave his phone number so that I can call him back.

"When you lose an adult child, you have not only lost one of your offspring, you have lost a friend. Children should bury their parents, not the other way around. Neither losing an adult child nor losing a young child can be easy.

"A few days after Peg was killed she appeared to my sister-in-law and said that she was all right and Neil was, too. She said Neil needed her. I've never seen either my son or daughter since their death, but I know they love me, as I always loved all my children."

GENTILE: Drugs

Cheryl Gentile, 45, mother of Sammy, 24, who died of drug and alcohol overdose on March 27, 1993.

"Thank you for letting me be of some help to myself in responding to you. The last week has been rather difficult for me. The closer I get to March 27, the date of Sammy's death, the sadder and more depressed I become. Last year at this time, before he died, I felt pretty content; what a difference a year can make! I've done a lot of reflecting over this last year and I am somewhat amazed that I function and have come this far. But I know I have so much farther to go and it will never end.

"Sammy was married for 10 months when he died of drug and alcohol overdose. The relationship with his widow is greatly strained and my husband and my daughter want nothing to do with her. But I feel she was as troubled as he was; co-dependent. I am working on this, though it is tough.

"Our son's death has put a tremendous strain on all aspects of our marriage. We have difficulty communicating and my husband feels a lot of guilt whereas I do not. I feel I did everything possible to help Sammy with his ongoing problem. We could only be there when he wanted to accept our help; only he could help himself.

"You gave me a list of the aspects of my loss which seem most difficult to bear: how my child died; being denied my child's company; being denied grandchildren; unfairness of it all; and I would have to answer 'all of the above.'

"I now live each day as if it were my last. Although I do not regularly attend Mass, I feel that I believe more in God and a life after death now than I ever did before. Some friends are no longer friends. With some I'm reestablishing relationships; others it's as if we have become closer. I have also made new friends through The Compassionate Friends who are supportive.

"In addition, I have found several women at my work place who have experienced the loss of a child. I've talked and had lunch occasionally with them, especially at the harder times: Christmas, holidays and this first anniversary of Sammy's death. And I find I am now able to laugh sometimes. I want to do something constructive with my life rather than destructive.

"No matter at what age your child dies, I feel the loss is just as devastating, although I at least feel I have raised and enjoyed my child and will not have to wait as long to see him again.

"Again, I experienced all the mental and physical problems you mentioned in your questionnaire: memory loss, inability to concentrate, thoughts of suicide, depression, illness and accidents. In addition, I am still exhausted most of the time due to the fact that grieving has been the hardest work I have ever encountered. There are days when I am so physically and mentally tired that I don't know how much longer I can push myself.

"It comforted me when Sammy came to me a couple of days after his death and hugged me and said it was an accident. Recently he came and hugged me again but seemed lonely. I dream of him often. His sister dreams of him frequently, too. He visited my husband once around his 6-month anniversary. I hope he continues to visit as it helps me to cope better. I just wish he could stay longer.

"Again, thank you and please let me know how your report goes."

Cheryl writes in answer to my date-of-death letter at the end of the second year:

"Well, we have managed to get through another year without our son. Since the anniversary date, my husband has been a little better, but he has had several bouts of severe depression. I have suggested that he see a doctor or try to get someone to talk to but he has refused. As you know, it is not easy to get the help you need. It seems at times he just wants to die; he's lost that will to live. I have felt that way one day or another; his is more constant. I try not to worry as I know we all grieve differently. For some it will never change.

"For one solid year my husband called the District Attorney daily, two and three times a day, to try and have the man who sold Sammy the drugs arrested. We felt he was a partner in murder. But they said they could do nothing.

"I now have days of peace and start to feel happy, but then I feel so guilty. I have heard this is normal. I find it a lot easier now to laugh and to recall the nice memories I have. I think of Sammy daily and hope I always will. Not that terrible, horrible day. Now I smile instead of crying all the time as I think of how happy he made me; not always, but most of his life. He was a good person and I miss him. I also know he is with me and pushing me to go on.

"One bit of good news: my daughter is expecting her third child on October 11, her father's birthday."

Cheryl writes again after the birth of her granddaughter:

"I was so glad to hear from you; I know you weren't feeling well but I thought of you often and wondered how things were going. I was glad to help in any small way that I could in writing your book, for you see it has helped me to express my feelings. So what you have done has been to help others as much as you helped yourself. The tears or the mending heart will never completely heal, but we find peace and joy in small ways.

"Our new granddaughter is just perfect! My daughter has named her Samantha, which is such a nice tribute to her brother, Sammy. We were able to stay with her in the delivery room and were there when Sammi came into this world. What a wonderful event!"

GUILIANI: Murder

Evelyn Guiliani, 35, lost her 18-year-old daughter, who was stabbed to death in 1984.

"Thank God, I had Joe, my second husband (I was divorced for quite some time before my daughter's murder). Otherwise many times I think I would have lost my mind. My surviving daughter and I have a better relationship now, but at first it was strained for many reasons. Because my daughter was stabbed to death, it seems terribly unfair, particularly because the communication with the justice system was very poor and her killer was never indicted. He will probably kill again.

"Since her death, so many things in life now seem trivial. I look at just about everything in life differently than I did before my bereavement. Some good; some questions. I finally have a more positive attitude. I welcome the sunrise of each day, and my positive attitude came about from the love of my husband. I lost touch with old friends and don't see any of them any more.

"If God doesn't have a master plan then there's not much sense to anything. Parents of Murdered Children have been very helpful and I read everything I can get my hands on. I find something that helps in each thing I read. I deal with it better. I cry when something triggers it; with each good thing, no matter what it is, I somehow think she's saying, 'Right on, Mom!' I have not been to a meeting, just contact with a chapter leader of The Compassionate Friends and I am a 'call friend.'

"People seem to think the younger the child, the harder it is to get over your grief initially. That's just not always true. My daughter was my daughter, 18 or a baby.

"Many people tried to be helpful and understanding, but unless you've been through it you just can't really understand. Getting through that first year was a milestone; I knew then somehow I would make it. But one person told me that for 2 weeks I didn't put a sentence together correctly. My husband said I didn't do anything 'crazy' I just didn't remember I said something, etc. I experienced memory loss, physical problems like loss of appetite and headaches.

"It sounds crazy but I really felt my daughter has talked to me after she died, through dreams and whatever. I have wakened, thinking she's standing at the foot of my bed calling me. I really can't explain it.

"A doctor friend painted a picture of my daughter for me and told me someday I'd only remember the good things."

HENNIG: Illness

Mary Hennig, 60, and her 59-year-old husband lost their son John on June 19, 1994 to a sudden and unexpected heart attack. John was 35 and did not live at home; he had a wife and two children. Mary's report follows.

"My son John died on June 19, 1994. He had had a congenital heart condition since childhood but the heart attack which killed him was unexpected. Besides his wife and children, he is survived by his father and me and our two daughters.

"My husband and I have differing grief styles and there is absolutely no communication between us. We live in the same house like strangers. I have seriously considered divorce. It is also impossible to talk with my two surviving daughters about the passing away of my son. They refuse to talk about it and seem to be mad at me. It seems to me that John's children don't seem to be grieving.

"The only person I can talk to about this is a special friend, a woman at work whose daughter died. I avoid everyone else. Friends have not really been at all helpful, though The Compassionate Friends have been supportive. I was told about them by a clergyman. I have also sought professional counseling, which has helped.

"My son was a good person and I can't understand why he died. I should have made him see a doctor, but he was a grown man. He worked too hard. I had trouble with the undertaker, who didn't do things right and we had to do a lot of it over.

"I can't read; I can't watch movies or TV; I can't eat—all I eat is crackers and look at me, I'm getting so fat. I feel there's something wrong with me. The only thing that will help me is to have my son come back, and he can't come back.

"My attitude towards life has changed drastically. I feel that nothing matters, and at the same time I know I can never hurt again like this. Sometimes I wonder if God cares.

"If there were a book about the experiences of other parents whose adult child has died, I think it would help guide parents through their grief process. Knowing I am not alone in this awful pain is a comfort. It must be the same for parents who lost young children, too.

"Almost all the choices you mentioned on the questionnaire were experienced by me: inability to concentrate, too much sleep, weight gain, attempted suicide, depression, vomiting and heart pain, a feeling I am going crazy. I am a nurse and I have had a hard time concentrating on my work. I had two car accidents and sometimes I feel like I can't live another hour.

"I don't think John's other survivors suffered any physical or mental problems as a result of his death. At least I have not heard about it.

"Since he died, John has not communicated with me and I am not aware of his communicating with the other survivors. I am left with just the awful, unbearable pain."

HENSON: Illness

Mildred Henson, 74, lost her only child, Jody Henson Santoro, 41, on March 20, 1991. Jody had Hodgkins Disease.

"This is about my daughter, Jody, who was a very beautiful person inside and out. She was born September 8, 1949, in Muscle Shoals, Alabama. She died March 20, 1991 of Hodgkins Disease. After the diagnosis, she survived for seven years. There were periods of remission when she was able to lead a rather normal life and work some. She was a Pharmacist with the V.A. Hospital in Birmingham, Alabama. She loved life and enjoyed both kinds of skiing, scuba diving as well as traveling with her husband. Jody was a fighter who wanted to live but not as an invalid. She would want her husband, Joe, and me to go on living and enjoying life.

"It's not been easy but with the help of the Lord and lots of friends we've made it so far.

"Now back to Hodgkins Disease. She had surgery, radium treatments and chemotherapy. After everything that could be done in Birmingham had been done for her, she and Joe went to the National Jewish Hospital in Denver, Colorado. She had surgery out there and the doctors said no Hodgkins Disease showed up but her lungs were like an orange being peeled. Radium did the damage; some people do well with radiation treatments and some do not and she was one of those who do not. The medical system let her down.

"At times I feel like she was in Denver for 40 days. Joe stayed with her and didn't come home until she died. I went out for several days but she wanted me to come back home. Joe and I were really mentally and physically exhausted when she died. And then came the red tape of getting her home. One of the doctors stayed with Joe until everything was taken care of in Denver. There were arrangements to be made here, too. It still seems like a bad dream. Some things I really don't remember and maybe that's good.

"Jody had planned most of her funeral before she left for Denver and picked out her clothes. Because her arms were in bad shape from the treatment, they couldn't use the short-sleeved dress she had chosen. So Joe picked out something really beautiful; he has very good taste.

"I still have a good relationship with Joe. He has not remarried and it has been a trying time for him. He is an only child and so was Jody and they had no children. His mother died 6 months before Jody and his father was already dead. My husband has been dead for 12 years.

"I do not object to Joe's remarrying and he knows this, for we've talked about it. He was good to Jody and stayed with her when she was sick and did everything to keep her with us. She had the best! Lack of love and attention didn't kill her!

"Joe sends me flowers on March 20. Jody and Joe had been married for 15 years, so he's been a part of the family for quite a long time. I had a good relationship with Joe's mother. She was a wonderful mother-in-law to Jody and they loved each other. Although we had different religious beliefs, it made no difference. I don't pick people for the church they attend but for the person they are.

"I have some wonderful memories of my Jody, for which I am so thankful. An adult child has been with you longer and you have more memories of them to treasure. Sometimes I feel she still communicates with me. I still miss her. Some days it seems only yesterday I kissed her goodbye to go to Denver and then again it seems like it's been forever. She was a person who had lots of friends and they are still good to me. They check to see if they can do something for me and they take me out to lunch often. I appreciate them very much.

"About five years ago I sold my home in Muscle Shoals, Alabama, and moved to Birmingham. I had a lot of adjusting to do, living in a bigger city, Jody being sick as well. I had to make new friends, although I had made a few as I visited Jody. I tried to make a place for myself in the community; the church as been wonderful to me.

"After Jody's death I had lots of trouble concentrating. I have prayed Jody's death would not make me bitter. I still have contact with old friends. I feel I need to get as much as possible out of the time I have left because Jody loved life so much she would want it that way."

JUSTAK: Accident

In 1981, my husband Bob and I met Martine and Ray Justak on a TWA Getaway Tour to Egypt, Jordan and Israel. In Egypt they shared some time with our son Paul; in Israel, with our daughter Cathy. After Cathy's death in 1987, Martine wrote to answer some of my questions regarding the way she and Ray had handled their grief when their son, Brown, a college student, was killed in an auto accident some years before.

"Yes, I do know what you are going through, and no, it is not a club I like to welcome new members to. One does survive, and having other family and little children does help. I always found the easiest thing was to talk about Brown with the people who had known him. The hardest thing was having people express their sympathy for me, because then I would begin feeling sorry for myself, and that would break me up.

"Activity helps; friends help; faith helps most of all. I had done a great deal of reading about reincarnation and life after death for some years before Brown died, and I had very strong feelings that it was not happenstance, but that his days were numbered. And I believed then, and still believe, that there will be some kind of reunion, a reunion with Brown in the physical garment he wore when he was with us. But I also feel that in certain aspects he is very much like our grandson, Brown, and that there is an identity of spirit between the two, you might say, part of the same spirit wearing a different suit of clothes. I have what I consider supporting evidence for both of these beliefs. But my point is, it helps to have a philosophical reference that satisfies. At least for me it was. Ray's approach was very different, but we respected each other's right to grieve and adjust in our own ways. What I do find hard to understand are the statistics which purport to show a 70% divorce rate in bereaved parents. Regardless of our different ways of handling our grief, we supported each other; and we both loved the same person. How awful to have a new spouse, one who didn't know the child you loved, and with whom you couldn't recall little details.

"This fall a gentleman called saying his name was Floyd Gregory, and could he stop by the house for a few minutes, he had something for us from Ruth. I said, of course, we'd love to see him again, but I couldn't place either the name or the reference to Ruth. He came about half an hour later, and I still didn't recognize him. But suddenly it came to me that he was talking about Ruth, Brown's girl friend at the time of his death, and Ruth had asked him to return Brown's fraternity pin, because it was a jeweled pin which had been handed down in the family.

"Then he showed us pictures of Ruth and her little girl: she got her nursing degree subsequent to Brown's death, and then did her practice in a hospital, and then married a doctor and moved to a small town in Missouri and had a baby.

"It was a bitter-sweet experience: sweet because we were very fond of Ruth; she looked blooming and happy; bitter because we thought of the years Brown had missed, and wondered, and asked the 'why' question once again. Why him? Why us?

Wish I could go on that trip to Egypt with your Paul. He must be a marvelous guide. I remember him, and yes, I do remember Cathy with her curly hair and wonderful smile."

KRAMER: Suicide

Carolyn Kramer, 52, lost her 25-year-old daughter to suicide in 1980.

"It has been 13 years since my daughter Lenore died at the age of 25 from suicide. She lived in Sioux Falls, South Dakota, and had never married. I was divorced from her father 20 years ago and have remarried. My current husband has been very supportive, though we grieve differently and have difficulty communicating. I feel it's important not to be afraid to talk about it. Lenore's father has had no contact with me.

"It is difficult for me to bear the fact that my child died of suicide, the unfairness of it all, and the guilt I feel.

"Relations with the police department in Sioux Falls have been frustrating. They refused to give me a copy of the police report. They also discarded letters she had written to her parents which they found in her room.

"I have suffered from depression and received help from being active in The Compassionate Friends. I found that writing a book about my daughter, using her own writings, was the most therapeutic thing I did after she died.

"Here is an example of her writings: 'Nothing, nothing at all but what other people see it as being: an endless emptiness. What is it like, trapped in a dark closet unable to get out, beating on the walls and screaming, ramming my head against the wall . . . and the wall is the shell of myself.' This quote from the book represents an actual documentation of a young person's mental illness, from age 15 to twenty-five, written in Lenore's own words 6 months before her suicide October 26, 1980.

"Critics have commented that there is music in Lenore's words that aroused emotions that made them weep; troubled but beautiful. They make a valuable contribution to the understanding of mental illness. The creativity, the beauty in her writings are truly amazing, yet the sadness is almost ever present."

LONG: Suicide

Phyllis Long's son, John, died at the age of 22 of suicide.
His dates are: 10/06/68-10/14-90.

"I was 56 when my son John committed suicide while he was away at school. The police called to inform us about John's death and instructed my husband to phone the police in the city where he killed himself. At first my husband told me it was an accident. He didn't want any burial hassle. It took me three weeks to find out it was a suicide. You see, my husband was trying to protect me.

"After my son died, I had an especially hard time at my job. If I had my wish I could only ask for more tolerance among co-workers and supervisors after a parent loses a child. Some people just can't understand why you're not functioning. They have no mercy as to whether you can keep your job or not. The very occasional person will think it's amusing that your child died, especially by suicide. Some may blame you for the death and want to vent their anger on you or slap your face. It was never expressed to me directly, but I believe a co-worker was referring to me as she talked about that on the phone to another person. Her behavior was very hurtful.

"I had to leave my job because of my husband's deterioration and on the last day of my employment, this person hugged me and said she was so surly because she is so sentimental about children. That particular co-worker seemed insensitive when someone in the area lost two children who walked on an icy lake and fell through and drowned. Their dog stayed on shore. Her response: 'I guess the dog was smarter than those girls.' Yet I understand that she mourned for a week when her dog died, even though she had no sympathy for me after I returned to work after my son's death.

"I would remind experts on suicide that they should avoid a preachy attitude and avoid blaming the parents.

"After our son's suicide, my husband became extremely withdrawn and depressed. He cried constantly and couldn't get interested in anything but the death and his grief. He never came back to himself; felt hurt and cheated. He died from cancer two years after our son died.

"I was able to go on with life and concentrate as usual, but I ultimately lost my job due to various problems with my husband. I have three surviving children, with whom I now have a good relationship. I also have a good relationship with John's friends and his previous girl-friend. But I miss him very much and feel sad that his life was cut short and that he will never give me any grand-children. "I know I must try to go on with and enjoy life. I would suggest that, if bereaved parents cannot get comfort from their religion, they should try another faith. I still hold onto my old friends. The Suicide Survivors group is good and The Compassionate Friends is helpful as long as they focus on the loss of their children instead of their pets, etc. It has helped me to read a lot on loss due to suicide.

"The severe ache has lessened and although I still have sadness at times, the inability to concentrate and the short-term memory loss I experienced at first have disappeared. If you lost a young child, so helpless and dependent, perhaps you would always wonder how the child would have turned out. That might be more difficult to bear than the death of an adult child.

"In regard to communication with my son after his death, my husband dreamed about the funeral and I saw John in a dream. I thought he was in a giant star trying to tell me he was OK in Heaven."

In a follow-up letter, Phyllis reported that her surviving daughter had attempted suicide and was hospitalized in critical condition. She is improving every day and her mother has every hope that she will recover. It has been extremely painful for Phyllis, who did not have the slightest inkling that she had a problem. Initially Phyllis has felt angry at not being forewarned of her mental condition and angry at her daughter for not thinking of other ways to solve her problems, although she is aware that her daughter was in a lot of pain and probably not able to think straight.

During Christmas vacation, 1996, Phyllis's son phoned to inform me that his mother died of cancer some months before.

LAWRENCE: Illness

Susan and Harry Lawrence lost their 24-year-old son, Earl, to Leukemia on 7/25/91

"Our son was 24 and had leukemia for a year before he died. My husband and I were 55 and 52 respectively. Earl, who was single, also left one sibling, a brother who has been most loving and supportive. Earl's medical treatment went as well as we could expect, I suppose.

"Although my husband and I have differing ways of grieving, our relationship is a good one. We feel anger, guilt, sadness that our child had such a painful illness and was cheated out of a long and wonderful life. Besides being very depressed, I have considered suicide and experienced a problem with weight gain.

"Earl's death has made me rearrange my priorities. I don't get upset over minor annoyances any more. Since his death, most things seem minor. It is an effort to attend Bar or Bat Mitzvahs, weddings and anniversary parties. I force myself to go to these so-called 'happy' occasions but they just make me feel more empty. I do hope I don't have to live to be old. That's my constant prayer.

"Although I have had help from professional counselors, the clergy and friends, it has been too painful to continue attending meetings of The Compassionate Friends.

"The longer you have loved and gone through the various stages of development and life with your child, the more memories you have. But if your child was very young, the intensity of your love is condensed into fewer memories. My son seemed to understand me better than anyone. His perception of me was incredibly accurate. Believe me, there were many times in his 24 years that he made me crazy, but the love was always there. The last words he said were: 'I love you, Mom. Goodnight.' I miss him so much, sometimes it's unbearable. I've tried to be grateful for having him for 24 years. I keep telling myself that I was more fortunate than mothers whose child died at a younger age. But I realize now that it doesn't make any difference. Mothers love their children with an intensity that continues from their birth to the parent's own death. The loss of your child is devastating, whether the child was an infant or 65 years old.

"There were two occasions when my son Earl communicated with me after he died. The first was 2 months after his death. It was during the memorial service of the Yom Kippur holiday. My husband and I were clinging to each other and crying when I felt this intense electrical feeling. Then I felt Earl sitting next to me with his arm around me. He was THERE! I didn't turn to look at him; I didn't feel the need to do so. I was comforted by the intensity of feeling him next to me. He was dressed in a suit appropriate to the occasion, the Jewish Day of Atonement. It was such a comfort and so reassuring to have him there. I felt him saying 'I'm OK, Mom, I'm OK.' As the electrical sound faded, the sense of Earl's presence also diminished.

"The second and last experience of this kind occurred after the first anniversary of his death. I was at the cemetery not long, maybe a month, after we had the inscribed stone put on his grave. I was standing by the headstone and crying. It was July and very hot, and all of a sudden a cool breeze came and then the electrical sound and then Earl was there. I didn't have to look at him as his presence was sufficient for me. He put his arm around me and I leaned against him. (I am 5'3" tall and Earl 6'1" and 300 pounds.) I felt so comforted and relieved. He kept assuring me that he was OK. Presently I asked him if he wanted to see my new car. He was delighted and we walked to the car and then the electrical sound abated, as did the coolness, and then Earl's presence faded away. I am very grateful for these two experiences. They have become my two bearable memories; they don't make me cry, they give me comfort.

"I wish I had some other insights about the death of an adult child. Maybe one day I'll have some insight into this horrible thing that happened to Earl. I feel that my family is not whole and that's hard to accept.

"I hope you can share how other respondents answered these questions. I believe that, for me, reading about these things is easier and also a comfort in some way.

"Thank you very much for doing this survey. Just writing about all this has given me some ease."

MALITSKY: Illness

Carl and Josie Malitsky lost their 18 year old daughter Cynthia Ann on February 2, 1985, to viral pneumonia. Carl writes:

"Our daughter, Cynthia Ann, died on February 2, 1985, of viral pneumonia at the age of eighteen and a half. We feel the doctors could have been more responsive to our concerns about our daughter's feelings and panic as she approached death, which was unexpected. She was aware that she was going to die about five minutes before her death and may have had a Near Death Experience at the moment she died.

"We had a very close family and this is still true. In losing Cindy we lost a daughter who loved everyone and she was loved by them all. Her two surviving brothers were very close to Cindy and they missed her terribly. After she died, they had trouble in school: one in college; one in high school. Eventually they both received their degrees.

"My wife and I had some stress in our marriage and some disagreements about how to handle our grief. Our grief styles are different: I am very active in The Compassionate Friends while Josie is on a more passive path of grief. We now vacation with enjoyment, whereas earlier vacations resulted in 'I cannot run away from what happened . . .'

"It was sad to realize we would not have the pleasure of Cindy's children as our grandchildren and we feel she was cheated out of a full life. We experienced memory loss, inability to concentrate, thoughts of suicide and depression. We didn't seem to care if we lived or died; we just wanted to be with Cindy. But that has now changed and we really appreciate our two sons. We take life a day at a time and have more appreciation of religion than we used to. Our old friends are more or less the same, though we now spend a great amount of our time helping other bereaved parents. I work hard at facilitating a large Compassionate Friends chapter from which I get a lot of rewards. We feel TCF was the only help and really saved our lives at the time of our great need. Professional counseling was fairly helpful; clergy were only marginally helpful.

"If you do write a book about the death of an adult child, tell it just the way it is: it ROTS! There is no right time to die but especially when children die before their parents. There can be nothing worse.

"In many ways, we feel Cindy has communicated with us: through her grandfather (my Dad), one of my sons, my brother and many of her friends.

"The only insight I have to offer is, as I said before, there is no right time to die."

MARSHALL: Accident

Carol Marshall, 44, and her husband lost their son, Larry Allen Marshall II on August 16, 1990, in a car accident. His dates: 11/12/67-8/16/90.

"Our 22-year-old son, Larry Allen Marshall II, was killed in an auto accident on August 16, 1990. He had graduated from college in 1989 and started to work in South Carolina in 1990. Besides his father and me, he is survived by two sisters and a girl friend.

"Our older daughter is 28 now; there was only two years' difference in their ages and they were very close. She has had a very hard time with her brother's death. My youngest was 14 at the time and is now 17. She is doing OK now.

"My husband and I have had very difficult times in our marriage because of our son's death. I always wonder how a child you both loved so much can tear you apart. Other people think you should become closer, but the pain and grief are so great that you are each dealing in your own way and in your own little world. I didn't want anyone else in my world except my son and me, not even my two daughters. I still don't understand that part of my grief. My husband wanted the girls included in everything we did, but I wasn't ready to let anyone into my world of grief: not my girls or anyone in the family. I wanted to be left alone and I did just what my feelings said, no matter who it hurt. I had to handle things my own way so I didn't lose my mind.

"My husband has always hit things head-on, but not me. Of course we were both new at this; it is not something you knew about. It takes you totally by surprise on how you will react. Sometimes you think, 'Is this really me, or someone else in my body?' My husband was always there to take care of me before, and I expected too much of him when our son died. He couldn't take care of me and himself, too. It took me a long time to realize this.

"It has been three and a half years without our son and we have both changed. Our life will never be the way it was before, so we have to start a new life, a life with a part of us missing. But we have to go on with what we have left: two wonderful daughters, a grandson and each other. It takes a lot of hard grief work from both husband and wife to learn to live with the death of your child.

"First of all you have to deal with the things which happen to you as the result of your child's death. I lost my memory, I couldn't concentrate, I couldn't sleep, I thought of suicide, I lost 30 pounds in 3 weeks and had to have my gallbladder removed. I didn't care; they could have taken everything out of me and I didn't care. My daughters cried all the time. My younger one went to the sibling group at The Compassionate Friends but the older one refused.

"When you wrote about the difficulty of shopping after your daughter's death, I was reminded how I have trouble passing the shelf where they display the Snickers Bars; they were Allen's favorites. I also had trouble writing out a check at the check-out counter. Sometimes I felt like signing it 'Bereaved Parent.'

"My son Allen and I used to talk about his having kids some day, and I am sad that I will never have grandchildren from him. It seems so unfair. I am angry that he was cheated out of life. I get upset when people let small problems bother them.

"Although clergy have not been helpful in my bereavement, very good friends have helped and I always try to be there when other people in our town lose a child.

"I talked on the phone one night last week with a woman whose 19-year-old died six months ago of cancer. As I listened to her talk it was like listening to myself for at least three years. She asked me if she would ever feel better and for the first time I could answer 'yes' and feel that I really meant it. I don't know exactly when this happened to me. I think it is such a slow, painful process that we really don't realize that we are starting to heal.

At first I didn't care about anyone or anything. Now I am starting to enjoy life again. I don't think I could tell you if my responses to my loss have come in phases; it would be more appropriate to call it circles, since I was always going in circles. Of course our grief is a scab that will always bleed when we least expect it and the tears will flow, but that's OK. I loved my son Allen with everything that is in me and will always love and miss him. But now I can think of his life instead of always thinking only of his death. I even find myself smiling sometimes when I think of him and what he meant to me. It's like the song: I could have missed the pain, but I would have had to miss the dance.

"My father died recently and I now spend a lot of time helping my mother, who lives about 15 miles from me and doesn't drive. I am very close to my family; Allen's death was so very hard on my parents.

"In the past few months my husband has really had a bad time trying to cope with Allen's death. It's as if he has started grieving all over again. This is the hardest thing in life to understand: one day you can seem fine and the next you are trying to pick yourself up. It happens again and again and again.

"Losing an adult child brings the same pain as losing a small child. But with an adult child, you have so many more memories. Knowing your child inside and out and from a young child to adulthood means you are losing your best friend when that child dies.

"It is a comfort to have had Allen's Boston Terrier 'Pete' until his death recently. We really spoiled him because he loved Allen so much.

"Knowing our son communicated with us after death is where a lot of our strength comes from, just knowing our son is all right.

"I had my son for almost 23 years. I thought he would bury me and I wish he could have had a child."

MERRYMAN: Illness

Olivia Merryman (55), and her husband George, lost their daughter, Rose, on July 14, 1989.

"Our daughter, Rose, was our third child of 6 (3 boys and 3 girls). She lived at home until she married in 1984 at the age of 25. The fellow she married had lost his wife in a car wreck. Rose tried to be a supermom to his three children, ages 14, 7 and 4.

"I think her immune system was compromised. Thirteen months into the marriage, she noticed her hands were swollen. She went to three doctors before she was diagnosed as having scleroderma, a connective tissue disease. It is a terminal illness; no known cause, no known cure. In October of 1986, the doctors indicated she would live about 2 years; she lived 2 years and nine months.

"Rose tried different remedies; nothing really helped, though Prednizone helped for awhile. Her digestive system went haywire, and the last year she existed solely on nightly IV feedings. Each day, as she prepared meals for the family, she would cry because she knew she couldn't eat.

"I grieve because I couldn't do more to help her and because I didn't spend more time with her that last year. She spent her last month in a hospital, taking different drugs.

"One afternoon her husband came to our house; I guessed he wanted to tell us she'd been put on oxygen or something like that. When he said she was dead, I could hardly believe it. We had tried to prepare for her death, but you just can't prepare enough.

"I was surprised at the physical pain I felt in my chest. The Lord helped us through the next few days and the viewing and the funeral.

"I get the Compassionate Friends' newsletter and also a newsletter from Bereaved Parents Share. A book about losing adult children could make me feel I'm not alone. And I am grateful for old friends. I've learned that life is fragile, but I have to go on because Rose would have wanted me to do so. I've tried to accept her absence, even though I will never forget her.

"Although her husband remarried one year and two weeks after Rose died, I see two of her step-sons fairly often. Relations, as you can imagine, are somewhat strained.

"I cherish the gift that she gave me the last Christmas of her life: a beautiful nightgown. When I wear it, I feel especially close to her. Our other children are loving towards us and generous with their hugs. That does help ease the pain of Rose's absence. Now, each year, as many of her siblings who can, join me and we go out to eat and buy a cemetery arrangement, go to the cemetery, have prayer and talk about Rose and what she meant to us. We do this in July or as close as we can to the anniversary of her death.

"I think of her every day and still miss her. After her death I began to have trouble falling asleep; I still have some bad nights. I have also had bad fever blisters.

"Our marriage has been very stressed since Rose's death and my husband and I don't communicate very much. Partly to blame is a serious accident George had in 1981 which paralyzed him for a couple of months.

"I know that one day I'll be reunited with Rose, for I believe in life after death. One of her nephews, on hearing of her death, told his mother, "Mom, now Aunt Rose has a new body." One of George's sisters was asked if Rose was alone when she died. She said she was not alone because the Lord came to meet her. That is so comforting to know He will be with us at the hour of our death, if we know Him as Lord and Savior.

"I wish I could dream that Rose is happy. I am weeping as I write this."

MUSTAPHA: Illness

Gael Mustapha and her husband, Akema, lost their 31-year-old daughter in October 1993.

"My daughter suffered from juvenile diabetes and the doctors thought she had at least another decade to live. She died suddenly in October 1993, while I was traveling in Texas. I had a nightmare time trying to get to Hawaii, our previous home and hers.

"While I was handling arrangements there, I had a heart incident and ended up in the hospital. I was unable to attend her memorial services. Fortunately, a kind friend video-taped it for me.

I have been to a grief group and am currently going through training to become a bereavement counselor. It seems I have come full circle. I still miss her dreadfully.

PATRONE: Illness and Suicide

Marlene Patrone and her husband lost their 33-year-old son, Richard, who committed suicide in 1993.

"My son Richard was a doctor at a hospital he loved. However, he was troubled and needed help. Instead of giving him a chance to receive treatment, his boss dismissed him, although he was a good doctor and beloved by his staff. I find it hard to forgive his boss for letting him go. Richard committed suicide on April 17, 1993. He was 33 and single; I was 57 when he died. We have four surviving children and six grandchildren.

"The holidays are gone now and I can breathe a sigh of relief. The second year was different and worse than the first. The reality of Richard's death and his absence from our family gatherings was so painful. He was always the one we all looked forward to seeing. All this has changed and the holidays will never be the same.

"I have a hard time talking about Richard to my other children. I try to hide my tears and pain from them. I feel comfortable only when I talk with people who have gone through this. Richard's death has had a devastating effect on our marriage, which was very good before he died but now my husband and I don't communicate at all. He goes to church and the cemetery almost every day. I have not been to either yet.

"Being with my two daughters and their children is where I find escape from the terrible memories.

"I am sad and angry about how my son died. It is so unfair; he had so much ahead of him as a doctor and I feel I did not know or do enough to help him. I feel tremendous guilt. To think that he was involved in the medical profession and his colleagues did not try to help him makes me very angry.

"Since Richard died, I have to push myself to do everyday tasks; I have no energy. I haven't had a night of complete sleep since his death. My life is at a standstill. I want a change but don't know what I want. I'm grateful for my surviving kids; they keep me sane.

"As to the differences between the loss of a younger or an adult child, it seems to me that an adult child leaves us with more memories to deal with plus a sense of helplessness that we couldn't do more. We had Richard for thirty-three years and have so many memories: college, graduation from medical school, his first job, his first house, girlfriends, his new Porsche, etc. All these I have to relive when I think of him.

"Since Richard died, I am more accepting of life and the tragedies that can happen to anyone. Although I have not sought professional counseling and clergy have not been helpful, the meetings and the people at The Compassionate Friends have helped me greatly.

"I have not had any communications from my deceased son but I wish I could."

Marlene writes on Christmas Day, 1995:

"I'm sorry it took so long to write to you but now I've been hit with another tragedy. My oldest son, Alfred, 38 years old, married and the father of three children, has been diagnosed with cancer of the stomach. It has been just a month since the diagnosis and he is going through chemotherapy treatments every week, which will go on for two months. They will re-examine him at the end of that time to see if anything has changed. His prognosis is not good but we are all hoping and praying for a miracle.

"I just can't believe this could happen again. I ask WHY? and HOW? a million times with no answer. I don't know how I could go on living if anything happens to him. I have two daughters and a younger son who are helping each other get through this.

"It is Christmas and I've just come home from my daughter's. I'm glad the day is over and can't bear to think of New Years Eve and a new year with this pain in my heart."

A letter dated May 5, 1996.

"Well, here I am writing a letter I never thought I would be writing. My son Alfred died April 17, same day as his brother Richard died just three years ago. His cancer was discovered in November. He had two rounds of chemotherapy, which they thought had worked. A week after his last treatment he started to feel sick. He was in and out of the hospital and finally was admitted March 11. They took tests again and then operated on him. They told us nothing could be done.

"His wife stayed with him in the hospital and never left. I took care of his three children: five-year-old twin girls and a seven-year-old girl.

"I don't know how I'm surviving. I just can't believe this could happen again. It was just three years in April that Richard died. He was 33 and Alfred was 38; both had their whole lives to live!

"Thank you for the article about cancer; wish we had had the chance to pursue another treatment but couldn't. Death came too quickly!

"I hope I have the strength to go on for my 3 children and my grandchildren."

PENNIMAN: Illness

Lavinia B. and Doug Penniman, 62 and 67 respectively: their daughter Leslie died of cancer at age 36.

"Our daughter, Leslie Penniman Hodges, died May 30, 1992, of colon cancer. She was 36 years old, married and the mother of two daughters, age 3 and 9. Besides her husband, her children, her father and me, she is survived by two sisters. I was 62 at the time of her death, her father 67.

"Without my husband, I would be in a state of shambles, although we are probably stronger because of Leslie's death. Yes, we do grieve differently, but realizing this, we try to be supportive of each other. I think we probably communicate as well as other couples. Sometimes there is misunderstanding because we do feel differently. Doug tends to hold things in more than I do, therefore his anger at Leslie's death is still a problem to him. He visits her grave many more times than I do and talks to her, whereas I take flowers and work in the dirt.

"Our relationship with our former son-in-law is extremely difficult. He has remarried and they are expecting a baby. He adored my daughter and I feel he still has a great deal of anger. We see our granddaughters infrequently. It is tragic that my daughter could not live to raise her two little girls, whom she adored.

"Before Leslie died, she had Sara's ears pierced and gave her a permanent. We all knew she wanted to see what Sara would look like as a teenager. A lot like her father in appearance, her ways are all like her mother's. She has the same the dimple in her cheek that Leslie had.

"The girls seem to be doing fairly well, although just recently Sara, who is now 13, had a situation in her school where she shared the story of her mother's death with her class, ending up in tears. The teacher cried and the girls in her class gave her a 'hug-in.' As far as I know, it is the first time Sara has showed her feelings to anyone. I thank the Lord she was able to do it. Perhaps it will help in sharing with more of us in the future. I recently wrote to her, telling her I will always be here for her to share and talk about her mother whenever she feels she would like to do so. I hope she takes me up on it. According to a book I read recently about daughters whose mothers died, Sara was at the most difficult age to lose her mother when Leslie died. Our relations with Sara's father are strained, and it is difficult to establish a more intimate relationship with her.

"Knowing I will not see Leslie again until I, too, go to Heaven, is hard for me because I find loneliness for her to be my biggest hurdle. I feel she was cheated out of being able to watch her little girls grow up. It seems so unfair!

"At a certain point we had to decide whether or not to proceed with a court case because there were medical mistakes. The outcome perhaps would have been different if necessary tests had been done and those mistakes hadn't been made. On the other hand, getting involved with the courts would be very painful and it would not bring Leslie back. We decided against it.

"We realize that this tragedy in our lives is something we will never 'get over.' Rather, we try to weave our lives around it and in many ways we are stronger, deeper and more compassionate people, particularly towards grieving parents. As you know, I have written a book about my bereavement: *A Tribute to Leslie, A Walk Through Grief.* I started it as a journal as therapy after Leslie died and kept it for two years. I was encouraged to publish the book after a friend who lost a daughter at age nineteen read it. She is a creative writing professor at the University of Maryland. I am a piano teacher and had taught her daughter music. I respected her appraisal when she said the book had merit and could be helpful to others in pain. It has become almost a ministry for me and I bless the Lord for helping me write it. As a result of having written the book, I hear from readers from Texas to Connecticut. It always helps to know one is not alone with problems. Having heard from others is beneficial to them and to me.

"Some of my reactions to my grief experience involved lack of concentration and overeating. I have had two cataract operations since Leslie died; nerves in my teeth caused a lot of dental trouble; nerves in my legs put me in a pool for therapy. I never thought of suicide or fell into a real depression, probably because of the support groups we joined.

"The Compassionate Friends have been helpful for the past four years. Before we attended that group, we went to a support group at the hospital called 'Phoenix.' It was more structured, with classes in guilt, anger, etc. I truly believe we were able to handle our grief better because of these groups. We have not needed professional counseling.

"Religion has also been a life-line for us. Our church has surrounded us with their love and support. However, some of our dearest friends were not there for us when Leslie died. I now realize they could not deal with our loss. Therefore they disappeared. This was sad for all of us.

"Since Leslie's death, Doug and I have become involved in the American Cancer Research Center, which has its headquarters in Denver, Colorado. They have chapters all over the United States and we, with others, have started a chapter here in our city. In my opinion, research is the answer and my heart is in that aspect of cancer.

"Although I still miss Leslie terribly, the pain has lessened somewhat. It is not so 'all encompassing' as it once was. I am now able to do things that I never would have done before. I now have nerves of steel! I used to become nervous speaking to a group, playing a recital, etc. But when one has faced the worst, losing a child, fear is dispelled in other areas.

"I don't think there is any difference between the loss of a young or an adult child. Grief is grief, no matter what the age of your child. Perhaps having a lot of history with the person who died could make it more difficult, but maybe not.

"Insofar as having a Near Death Experience, the answer is: yes! absolutely! It is all in my book. However, I have had no after-death communications with Leslie. Sara has had her mother come to her in dreams and she loves it. (That I should be so lucky!) My husband Doug has pleasant dreams about her.

"I want to thank you for providing me yet another healing vehicle by sharing with you. I am sorry you had the accident, breaking your hip, on top of everything else. Isn't that part of it? I realize now how important it is in our own healing to reach out and share with others, whether it is in writing a book, playing music or making a garden. We all want our children REMEMBERED!"

I asked Lavinia a question about the place of music in her life after Leslie's death, as one musician to another. I mentioned that the intimate piano music of Brahms and the symphonies of Rachmaninoff had been comforting to me, but the vocal music I had sung was too painful to hear for a long time.

Her answer:

"After Leslie died I was still able to teach piano but I could not play for myself. It's been only recently that I find myself playing some Mozart. Writing became my way of release; words instead of notes. Night after night I would play Brahms' Fourth Symphony on my Compact Disc player to get to sleep, but nothing else. It's true, the thing you love most slips away for awhile. It is just starting to come back."

PHILLIPS: Accident

John, 59, and Frances, 56, Phillips: Their two sons, John, aged 29, and Peter, 26, and their daughter-in-law, Carol, 24, were killed in an auto accident on April 3, 1987. Each surviving parent answered a separate questionnaire. Frances' report is first:

"Our son Peter had just married Carol on April 3, 1987; his brother John was his best man and Carol's sister was maid of honor. Outside the reception hall the limousine was waiting to turn when it was broadsided by a kid drag racing. Only Carol's sister survived the crash, although she was injured.

"Peter is survived by his parents and four sisters. John was married and he is also survived by his wife and two children. The girls never mention their brothers. If I do, the subject is changed fast. I think it is their inability to deal with our grief. Our daughter-in-law, John's widow, doesn't want to see us. Thus we have not seen our two grandsons for several years. She has since remarried to a friend of our son.

"For the most part, my husband and I are more considerate of each other now. We rarely argue any more. Probably you could say we are closer than ever before.

"It is difficult for us to discuss the three who were killed. I will talk about them to people, but he won't. He opens up the most at The Compassionate Friends meetings. He does not go to sharing sessions at a TCF conference. When he feels bad, he will go off and work by himself. Twice we went to professional counseling, once with our daughter-in-law's parents and once with our daughter-in-law. My husband wouldn't go again. I know one of our daughters went for professional counseling. One of the other daughters used to cry all night for a long time; I found this out from her children. Our youngest daughter was seventeen and very close to her younger brother, Peter. She graduated from High School and went off to college and in three months was back home: flunked out. This all happened during the trial of the young man who killed her brothers. She refused to learn to drive until she was twenty years old.

"The justice system served us only fairly well. There was of course a trial because our sons and daughter-in-law were killed by a drag racer. The second car was never found. According to witnesses, it was a special car. We later found out that only 8 of them were sold in the eastern part of the United States. Amazing that they couldn't find it with such perfect descriptions.

"Being denied grandchildren and the terrible way my sons died seem to be the hardest parts to bear. Just missing them so! After they died, I was unable to read, couldn't concentrate, remembered nothing. I had to take things ten minutes at a time. I slept well. I always had a sleep problem but when this happened I slept all the time. I have gained about 40 pounds and have ailed with various problems. It was recently discovered that I have lupus.

"I don't hurt as much as I did. I still get depressed at times. I'm not angry, but I think I was angry very much. Only one time I remember being angry, thinking I shouldn't have to be in this position. I'm still sad; I'll always be sad. But now I function and can run my business. I think a book about the loss of an adult child might offer comfort, just to know that someone else understands. Because they were adults when they died, people somehow don't think of them as your kids.

"I have little patience for trivial problems that people make a big deal out of. I'm not afraid to die now. My faith helped me survive. The priests in the parish where my kids grew up and were buried from were wonderful. For the past ten years we lived in Pennsylvania and of course had a different priest, who was no help at all. But then again another priest I knew from here found me on Long Island (I'll never know how) and offered to come. He talked to me a long time and really helped.

"Speaking of the differences between the loss of a young and an adult child, I think with an adult child there is not as much chance of feeling guilt. With a younger child you feel that there was something you didn't do, that you should have done, because a younger child is still in your care. It is hard to lose your adult children and it must be very hard to lose a younger child. I lost a baby in the 4th or 5th month of pregnancy and I felt truly bad and had a hard time for awhile. However, losing my adult sons was MUCH, MUCH worse. No comparison. I have spoken to other parents who lost adult children as well as babies and they agree with me.

"My son John always said that he would never live to be 30. He was killed 1 month and 3 days before his 30th birthday. I dream all the time but rarely of the kids. One night they came to me in a dream. I never had a dream like that. They were so clear, vivid. I asked how they were and they said 'fine.' Then I asked if they hurt when they were killed and they said 'no.' They told me it was confusing at first but now everything was great. They were exceedingly happy, so elated that I find it hard to describe. The only problem was, I couldn't figure out who the third person was. After I woke up and thought about it, I realized it wasn't Carol with them but my daughter Mary, who is still alive. She was very close to her brothers. Then I became very upset for days.

"Another time my husband was close to death after a heart attack (he has since improved) and I walked into the room. My sons were standing behind his chair, as if waiting for him. I shooed them away, telling them that I need their father longer. They went. I was sorry I sent them away. This happened long before the dream I mentioned above.

"Another time, before Christmas, I had just finished making a centerpiece and sat down in the next room to do a bit of hand sewing. I looked up and saw Carol come up to the table and look at the centerpiece. I said, 'What are you doing here?' She disappeared.

"It is sad to think that, just when you have your children raised and married and settled down and think everything is OK: whammo! they are dead! I sometimes have a kind of flashback and see them lying on the pavement, after the accident, dead."

John Phillips answers:

"My two sons, Peter and John J., were killed on Peter's wedding day, April 3, 1987, in an accident caused by two young men who were drag racing and hit the limousine which was carrying the wedding party. Carol Ann Zagorski Phillips, the bride, was badly injured and died April 21. Her sister was also injured but survived.

"Peter had lived in his own apartment; Carol with her parents. John was married and had a wife and two sons. My wife and I have four surviving daughters.

"Our son's wife remarried and relations are strained. We are unhappy with the way the surviving children are being raised and we do not see our grandsons.

"My wife and I have no difficulty communicating. She is more open about her grief whereas I tend to keep it more to myself. However, I think we both grieve equally.

"Being denied my sons' companionship and not ever having grandchildren from Peter makes me sad. It is hard to bear the way they died and I feel they were both cheated out of life.

"Justice was not served. Although the man who hit the limo broadside at 90 plus miles per hour was given the maximum jail sentence allowed in the state of New York for killing three people, they never prosecuted the second driver.

"The death of my sons has changed my attitude towards life. I am more aware of my impending death. My wife and I try to get as much as possible out of life.

"I have had help from The Compassionate Friends but when I sought professional counseling it was not helpful. Clergy were not supportive to the extent that I thought they would be.

"Although I think a book on the special problems of parents who lose an adult child would be very helpful to the newly bereaved, it is too late for me.

"My responses to my loss have changed over time. The first year it was disbelief; the second year was the hardest. The third year I realized that it's over for good. From then on, it seems that I decided it was time to move on, but in all these years, the grief does not go away. The fifth year I became involved with TCF. My wife and I became chapter leaders in order to help others as we had been helped.

"Regarding the difference between the loss of a young and an adult child, I feel that parents who lost a young child feel that those whose adult child died did not suffer as great a loss. This is because the adult child has already had life's experience while the young child had very little.

"I suffered severe heart attacks after the death of my sons. Our daughters also suffered but they do not talk to us about that or about their brothers' deaths, which in itself is a problem.

"Our older son, John J., said he would never reach age 30 and he died at 29 just before his 30th birthday. Although I am not aware of any communication with my sons since their deaths, my wife has had such experiences."

PRATT: Murder

Rose Pratt, 50, lost her son Roger (Butch), 22, when he was murdered on June 17, 1988. Rose and her husband were divorced and he died since Roger's death, on September 10, 1994. Roger is survived, in addition to his mother, by a brother Mike, age 30, and a sister Cathy, 29.

"My son's murder was extremely hard to deal with. He was missing for a very long time before his body was found. His murderers were prosecuted and sent to jail. There was no victim bashing and the prosecuting attorney was very compassionate. I took an active part, testifying twice at two separate trials. Three people went to jail; two women lost their teaching license and are on probation. I have continued to do volunteer work for Homicide at the Court House.

"Knowing how my son died is hard to bear, as is being denied his company as I age, and being denied grandchildren. I find myself respecting life more since this happened. I was always religious and God gave me courage to go on. My old friends are still friends. I am a contact for Parents of Murdered Children and have been helped as well by The Compassionate Friends. It lets you know you are not alone in your grief.

"I suffered from insomnia and had to have medical care; I went to a grief counselor as well. I feel that the light of my life is gone. With an adult child, you have many, many more memories and photos to enjoy and love.

"I feel that my son communicated with me after his death: stars, pennies from Heaven, comfort at the cemetery. His dog remembers, too. We visit the cemetery every day; it is close by."

Rose sent a petition to circulate to keep the perpetrators of her son's murder in jail for their full sentence. Along with the petitions, she sent newspaper clippings of the story of Roger's brutal murder, the trials and subsequent efforts of the murderers to get out of prison. Several people whose children were also murdered signed the petition. Her efforts were successful. In January 1997, a movie based on Roger's death was shown on national TV: What Happened to Bobby Earl?

RALPH: Drugs

Rachel Ralph and her husband lost their daughter Eleanor on December 28, 1992, from drug-related sepsis at the age of 31.

"I was 54 when Eleanor died. She was single and did not live at home. In addition to my husband and me, she left a brother and sister. They do not talk about her; if I mention her, they are very uncomfortable. In a lot of ways, her death made my husband and me closer. We rely on each other and he is protective of me. He doesn't like to talk about it, yet I feel the need to. I feel not talking about it is to deny she ever existed.

"I have a lot of anger; I feel Eleanor threw away her life and cheated the whole family. After she died I suffered memory loss, inability to concentrate, difficulty sleeping, overeating, and the need to be busy all the time, which leaves me with no time to think. I have also become compulsive about shopping.

"With a young child, you can't think of her as being away; you have to realize she is dead. Eleanor had been out of the house so it is easier to pretend she is just away.

"The holiday time is hardest, particularly because Eleanor died on December 28. The hustle and bustle and happy family plannings are a little hard to take. I try my best to be happy for the others, but depression has set in bad. It gets harder and harder to sleep.

"I just passed the two year mark. You would think it would be easier. Other people have forgotten and can't understand why you are so sad and they don't like being reminded. My husband and family don't feel comfortable talking about her.

"I now know who my real friends are. This experience also taught me not to waste time with superficial relationships. The only release I have is from my 'Compassionate Friends.'

"I had a charm made with Eleanor's likeness done in a holograph. When I look in a mirror she smiles back at me. That helps. Something I heard on television really gave me a jolt. It said no one is gone until no one remembers them any more. I guess I have to stay alive to keep her alive.

"As for a book on the subject of the death of an adult child, I would welcome any kind of help."

In response to my letter of March 9, 1995, Rachel writes:

"It's really amazing how much we bereaved parents have in common. The loss of memory seems to be one of the effects. No, you did not send me the story you wrote about Eleanor. I would like to see it. She was born January 20, 1961 and is survived by her sister Helen, who has two sons: 6 and 3. They give me the courage to go on. They light up my life! Eleanor also has a brother. He is married and has two step-daughters, 14 and 16. Two teenagers keep him hopping.

"Helen will talk about her sister but her brother will not; he has a lot of anger. My husband doesn't talk about her much; thank God for the Compassionate Friends. I will be going to the regional conference next weekend in Maryland.

"You're right about grieving being a roller coaster experience. I find that I'm doing OK and all of a sudden I'll be crying for no apparent reason. Oh, well, I have to take one day at a time. Now I am starting to do some reading. Up until now I couldn't read any of the books in The Compassionate Friends library. I find that some of them do help.

"I celebrated Eleanor's birthday by going to the cemetery. No one even mentions that it's her birthday. If I say I'm depressed, they ask why. It's so hard to grieve alone. I guess they are grieving in their own way. Every family is different, I guess.

"One of the people in the group has her whole family over for her dead child's birthday. Each member then tells some story about the one who died. Then they have cake together. I wish I could do that. But according to your letter, it didn't work in your family, either, did it?"

RIFKIN: Illness

Jan Rifkin's son Paul died of cancer 9/18/92 at 24.

"I'm going to answer your questions on legal paper but wanted to send you this brief letter as a 'foreword.'

"YES, the grief we older parents feel is very different from those who have lost an infant or pre-adolescent child. We shared an entire lifetime with the child or children we lost. Our children left grown siblings, spouses and even their own children. So to me at least, the loss touches a far greater number of lives than does the loss of a baby and thus the days and months and years following the death seem more complex.

"A bit of background: I was married for 17 years and had 3 children; 2 boys and my daughter. In 1982 my husband and I separated, then divorced and I remarried in 1987. Paul, the son I lost, was 13 when his father and I split up, but the man I married after the divorce had known my family since the children were young and was a close friend of the family. Paul was 8 or 9 when my present husband met him, and a close bond developed between them and stayed strong for the rest of Paul's life. Although Paul's father and I maintain a cordial relationship, as does my husband Stan, with Paul's father, he (Paul's father) could not really accept Paul's illness and became terribly dependent on us throughout the 6 months from diagnosis to death. Paul found it very difficult to have his father with him in the hospital, so Stan and I were his primary caregivers and support during Paul's illness.

"My husband, Stan, adored Paul and gave Paul, my other 2 children and me absolute love and support throughout our ordeal. He was totally devastated as he truly took on the role and responsibilities Paul's Dad should have, had he been able.

"Now on to the answers to your questionnaire.

"My son was 23 years old when he died in September of 1992. I was 51. He was not living at home but was living in New York City, doing what he loved: working on films.

"Paul was single and had a girlfriend at the time he became ill. Our relationship with his girlfriend became very hostile near the end of Paul's life as she was a self-centered, immature girl and caused our family great pain.

"Paul has a brother, now 27 years old, and a 21-year-old sister. Ben, our oldest, has had many of his own problems as a young adult and lives in Albuquerque. We speak regularly on the phone but sometimes our relationship seems strained. My daughter adored Paul, is very close to me and we have grieved together since Paul was diagnosed with cancer. There is no tension between us. She is a senior in college. We speak many times by phone each week and see each other often. I adore her and she is doing very well.

"Paul's father and I have been divorced since 1983. Paul's illness and death brought us closer but he became too dependent on me and my husband. We speak when we need to now and have a cordial relationship.

"Both my husband and I were overwhelmed by Paul's death and for the first year it was a sad and difficult time. We are deeply close and do not have any trouble communicating. I have always been able to let out my grief, whereas Stan has to control it due to constraints of his work schedule. He's felt more anger than I, and he is wonderfully tuned in to my moods and times of great sadness.

"The most difficult aspects of my loss have been the gruesome way Paul died and my ache of missing him. We were so close; he was gifted and sensitive, funny and so loving. I miss him unbearably! Watching what cancer did to his body, helping the hospital staff care for him physically, was horrible and grotesque as we had to be there for him emotionally. His illness was beyond cruel: it was ugly and horrible. Yet strangely, while we were with him, we were so strong.

"It is also very hard, almost unbearable, to watch his friends, or the sons and daughters of some of our friends who are the same age as Paul, do wonderful things with their lives, move on to career successes, marriage, children. When my closest friend tells me of her kids' triumphs, I want to scream 'Shut up!' even though I love her children. The hurt is awful. Often a movie or some event brings back the realization so forcefully: our son is dead, and we feel like we're beginning the grief process all over again. I still find myself thinking other friends are insensitive when they tell me about the joy they have with their child, even though I realize I would do the same if Paul were here. Obviously I am still a bit angry, perhaps always will be. Paul 'validated me.' He thought I was just great, so of course that adds to my missing him. We shared so many good times. As I think of it now, I guess I'm fortunate to have a great family, a very strong life force which permits me to enjoy life. And because there was no 'unfinished business' with Paul and me, there is no guilt. Spending 5 months daily with my son, in spite of the circumstances, was in some perverse way a blessing, and I treasure the times we shared.

"Paul's death in no way changed my attitude towards religion. I was not and am not a believer. His death has changed the way I live in that I realize how precious and fleeting life is so I try hard to enjoy and live each day fully. I am much less tolerant of many people I used to consider close friends. My husband and I protect ourselves, in a sense, from what we perceive might be difficult situations. So we are careful in arranging social activities.

"The Compassionate Friends newsletter has touched me deeply but at the few meetings we've been to, I've felt so sad for all the others there. I feel I've made great progress in working through my grief and I see so many who appear to have barely begun. Elisabeth Kübler-Ross has several books we've read which have been very helpful in giving us the assurance that we did the right things with our son, that the way he finally slipped into a coma and died was normal. We have no guilt.

"It is hard not being over-protective of Paul's sister, not to 'need' the other children too much, not to burden them with my own empty-place. I think I'm doing well and continue to see the wonderful therapist I've been seeing since shortly after Paul's death.

"Over the past year and a half I believe I've come to 'accept' Paul's death. I am so blessed to have had and been loved by such a lovely son who made me so proud and happy. We know that the kind of rare cancer he had is deadly and is not the result of anything he or I did, so there are no thoughts of 'what if?' The unbearably sharp horror of the 6 months from diagnosis to death has quieted and we now just miss him so much. We speak of him all the time and can even laugh as we remember something funny which happened or something he said.

"The loss of an adult child seems to equate with a 'bigger loss' in that we've known and loved our adult children for a lifetime, have been with them as they went from infant to child, from adolescent to adult, have shared the entire process of their becoming independent. That is not so when a very young child dies. Also, adult children have an understanding of what is happening to them, unlike younger children. We've invested so much over the years in our adult children, have so many more memories, and they have touched so many more lives than a young child has.

"I lost a lot of weight during Paul's illness and death and was totally exhausted; cried at everything. But because we knew he was dying, I did a lot of grieving before his actual death. Other than what I think is a rather normal progression through grief, I had no other unusual symptoms or problems. There really is no way to truly describe what I've been through. Losing Paul left me furious, unstable and totally shocked early on. His death resulted in very intense emotional conflicts with my mother and with Paul's father. Therapy has been a tremendous help in working these things out and now I'm very close to my mother. Perhaps it is the absolute love and support of my husband, my sister, my aunt (with whom I lived while Paul was at Memorial-Sloane Kettering in New York City) and a few friends who magically have always said and done the perfect things for me. My daughter and other son are very dear to me so I draw strength from them and love.

"I do not believe in life after death, although I did have—and still do have—a fantasy of Paul holding hands somewhere, with my father and uncle. Paul lives on in me, in his siblings and his friends. Family photos are everywhere in our home. Special ones of Paul as well.

"You asked if I had further insights. I feel we will NEVER get over losing Paul, but we will continue to heal, to love and enjoy our other children and each other, to find our way back to a full life."

Responding to a letter I wrote to Jan on the occasion of her son's death anniversary, she wrote the following:

"It is interesting that I thought of you this past spring when I found myself deeply, profoundly sad. It occurred to me then that I had responded to your questionnaire while I was having an 'up-time' and perhaps left you with the impression that I was 'fine,' that life was back to a relatively normal state.

"The truth is, there have been many 'up-times:' my daughter's college graduation, a visit to my other son in New Mexico, moving my daughter to North Carolina, where she now works, times shared with my wonderful husband or a few very close friends. But every time I've been up for a couple of months, I come crashing down when something triggers the ache and overwhelming sadness over Paul's death. And so it goes, and probably will go, as long as I live. I now understand these ups and downs, particularly on the birthday or death-day of our child, which bring back the feeling of loss and sorrow."

A letter several months later:

"Amazingly, your question about a higher regard for all forms of life after Paul's death struck a deep chord. YES! I now have 5 dogs (2 from the Humane Society who needed homes), 4 bird feeders, 2 bird baths, a squirrel feeder, a new rose garden. I spend every moment I can on our deck or in the yard or with my dogs, walking. I find these all comforting, tranquil, and renewing.

"My son Paul had a great gift for making the smallest thing into something great: a grilled cheese sandwich was caviar; an unheated bedroom was a 'great challenge.' Perhaps I'm trying to put more of him into myself. Perhaps I just need the peace and healing that nature provides.

"An odd thing happened this summer: I went into a two-week period of really feeling low, on the edge of tears, anxious. Never before has that feeling lasted more than a day or two without an 'up-time.' But my husband and I just wallowed in the sadness, embraced it, and agreed it is just plain OK to feel that way. And then, this past week-end, we went to New York City for a long week-end. We were open for any feelings we might have, apprehensive and fearful. To our great surprise, we enjoyed our three full days seeing family and old friends and the city itself with only a few hours of deep sadness. Now we know we can revisit New York City, where Paul died, and not be blown apart.

"Yes, the ups are more frequent but we find the downs to be as strong as ever, despite the generally long periods between them. We miss Paul beyond endurance at times; we still shudder in disbelief at times.

"I stopped therapy last November and I believe I am doing very well. Our lives are different now; we cherish our quiet, alone times. As you well know, we will never be the same, but our lives will hopefully be good, with joys and challenges, but nothing will ever be quite the same as it was before Paul's death."

RODRIGUEZ: Illness

The only child of Rod and Rita Rodriguez, their daughter, Jean Lynn Rodriguez Garant, died on August 16, 1993 at the age of 38.

"Jeanie had been ill for 25 years with lupus. She had her first hip replacement when she was 17. Despite everything, she graduated from high school and Plattsburg State University. Although she taught for a time, problems with hips, knees, back, etc., forced her to stop. She married, had 2 children, and was a source of pride and pleasure for her father and me. I was 63 and her father 67 at the time of her death.

"Besides her parents, spouse and children, her only other survivor is a grandparent. My husband and I have a good relationship, but our ways of grieving differ. We cry together but he does not want to talk about Jeanie.

"I find it distressing that she was alone in the hospital when she died. I really do feel cheated when other mothers talk about their daughters. I'm very angry when I think of the grandchildren without their mother. Jeanie and I were very close companions and I miss that. Her husband had a 'friend' only four months after Jeanie died and we feel uncomfortable about his bringing her home. Our link to Jeanie through her children remains very strong and our relationship with them has always been close.

"I feel that someone should have known she was near death and therefore I don't feel the medical profession served us well.

"Sometimes I feel I can't deal with the loss any longer. I cry a lot; 90% of the time I feel sad. After her death I was unable to concentrate, unable to sleep, ate too much, felt I was going crazy, went into a depression, as did Jeanie's daughter. Her son has nightmares.

"I can't pray; I find myself drawing back from my friends; not very much matters any more, except the grandchildren. I wish I could have traded places with Jeanie so she could live a full life. She is my child and is gone, but I am still here. I feel very guilty about this.

"Neither The Compassionate Friends not the clergy have been helpful to me, but I have had help from a professional counselor. Perhaps a book would help guide bereaved parents; just to know someone else has had the same experience could help.

"After her death, I asked Jeanie many, many times to place a daisy (her favorite flower) where I wouldn't expect to find it, if she were OK. I found an artificial daisy on her grave Christmas Eve afternoon. Also, one night while trying to get to sleep, I suddenly felt as though she were hugging me. Jeanie's husband felt the same thing."

RUDEL: Illness

Loesje (Louise) and Fred Rudel were friends and neighbors of ours when all our children were little. The Rudels had emigrated to the United States from Holland after World War II, in which both husband and wife distinguished themselves as resistance fighters against the Nazis. They raised two children, a beautiful, dark-haired daughter named Patti, and a sunny blond boy named Norbert.

When she became an adult, Patti married and had two children. She was living in the Washington area when she contracted an insect-borne disease which killed her. She was 25. Michele, Patti's daughter, was only 3; the baby boy, Christopher, a year old.

After Patti's death, her husband became quite hostile towards Fred and Loesje, not allowing them to have a warm and close relationship with their only grandchildren. It was a hard thing for them to bear, along with their grief at Patti's death.

In her Christmas letter, 1995, Loesje reported that Michele is now 23, a beautiful woman whom she sees infrequently but speaks with on the phone. Patti's son is almost completely out of touch with his grandmother. Fred died of a heart attack several years ago, so Loesje is now living alone in California. When Michele came to visit a few years ago, her grandmother was hurt to hear her say, "Grandma, if you don't mind, we don't talk about Mommy any more."

The son-in-law, Bill, was a good father to the two surviving children. He never married but had many problems with alcohol, which affected his heart and liver. As a result, Michele had to take time off from college recently to care for her father, who must use a wheelchair to get around. He came near death last year. Loesje feels resentful of Bill's behavior and that of his parents, who turned the children against Loesje and Fred. I often feel that the Rudels had to make Peace Without Justice when they dealt with their son-in-law.

Loesje's son Norby and his wife live in New Zealand; she visited them last year.

I know the strong support of Loesje's sister, who also lives in the United States, and of her mother in Holland, who lived to a very old age and died only a few years ago, were of great importance to her as she dealt with her grief. She also has a host of wonderful friends who love her.

SCOTT: Illness

Winifred Scott lost her 35-year-old son, Donald, on May 26, 1990.

"I lost my beautiful son Donald on May 26, 1990. He was 35 and I was 63 years old when he died. My son died of a heart attack brought on by stress. He was living in Texas at the time, though our home is in Pennsylvania. He had lost his job.

"Donald's father and I were divorced in 1969 and there had been no contact with him; he had been out of our lives for 21 years when Donald died. My former husband died in 1983.

"Besides me, Donald is survived by his sister Dorothy. He had been married twice and is also survived by both wives. He had one son by his first wife and two children by his second, a son and a daughter.

"Shortly before Donald died, he was having family troubles, and financial troubles as well. He had been picked up for drinking and driving and spent 8 months in jail. His wife came back to Pennsylvania from Texas so he was by himself, waiting for his parole to come through so he could come home. The parole had come through at least a month before he died, but they let the papers lie up in Austin, Texas, without notifying him.

"I was trying to help him financially and he stayed with friends for awhile. But they had a small apartment so he tried to go out on his own. He went to a half-way house until he could get home. When he reported for the night at the half-way house, they said he was fine; there was apparently nothing wrong with him. Some time during the night they found him dead in the bathroom.

"The autopsy showed that he had very little alcohol in his system. They were puzzled and said he should not have died. They concluded that his death was caused by a combination of alcohol and stress.

"After Donald's death my relationship with my daughter was very strained at first. Not about anything in particular; just the usual, 'You should have done this,' 'I should have done that'. The guilt and grief are unbearable. Slowly, we are making improvement again in our relationship but I don't know if you ever get over the hurt.

"My relationship with my grandchildren is wonderful. I love them dearly. I don't get a chance to spend as much time with them as I would like to. At first my grief was too deep, so deep that I couldn't even help myself, so I couldn't help them as much as I wanted to. I grieved for all three of them. They idolized their daddy. He spent quality time with his children. There are loads of pictures of him playing with his children. Thank God for those memories!

"When Donald went to Texas with his second wife, his older son was heartbroken. But my son had to find work. He had been employed in the steel mills in Pennsylvania but they closed down and there was no work around here, which is why he relocated to Texas.

"Of course there was conflict about the older boy: who would he stay with? His father wanted him to go to Texas. Donald's first wife wanted him with her. They worked out their differences so that the boy spent the winter with his mother and went to school. As soon as school was out, my son flew John to Texas for the summer. Then he flew John back to his mother in the winter. But they kept in very close contact at all times.

"John is now 18 years old and he graduates this year. I know he grieves deeply for his Dad; my heart breaks for him.

"Donald's little girl, Bonnie, was only a year old when he died, so her memory of him is dim. Bruce was 4 years old, and at 4 his grief was very deep. I believe he has picked up a few behavioral problems because of it.

"So you see I grieve for myself, for my daughter, and I grieve deeply for my grandchildren, and most of all I grieve for my beautiful son: that he was taken so young, and didn't really have a chance to raise his children. It breaks my heart when I see other fathers with their children and I know my son can never be with his children again.

"As far as my two daughters-in-law are concerned, I do have close and good relationships with both of them. I know they both loved my son.

"It seems the death of a loved one is like throwing a pebble in a brook and watching all the ripples. They go in a million different directions. That is the way my mind seems to go. You go back to the time your child was born, all through the years of growing up, to the present and beyond.

"I grieve because my son died alone, all by himself, with no family near him. It seems unfair that he died so young, without being here to live out his life, watching his children grow to adulthood, not being here when they graduate or marry or being able to walk his daughter down the aisle someday; a million other things, taking them to baseball games and football games, which he always did.

"You asked in what way my child's death changed my attitude towards life, religion, old friends. In some ways I have become bitter. In other ways more compassionate. And in other ways angry and depressed. I often wonder just what it all means. I found Rabbi Kushner's book, *When Bad Things Happen to Good People,* very helpful to me.

"When you think you have tried to live right and do right, then this happens and you say 'Why me?' So yes, it has changed my feelings about life drastically.

"As for religion, I was raised in a Christian home, raised by the Bible, sent to church on Sunday, prayer meetings on Wednesday; much church involvement. I wandered away from my religion in my late teens and 20s. I married at 26, had my children, had them baptized, sent them to church every Sunday. They were both involved with the church; I tried to give them good values.

"But I did not go to church with them. Often I worked 5 days a week, sometimes 7 days a week, just to keep a roof over our heads, food in our mouths and clothing on our backs. When I had week-ends off, I spent Saturday and Sunday cleaning and caring for the house.

"I tried to find time for my children. I took them on picnics, to the playground and swimming and for Sunday drives. So I thought I was a good mother. But somewhere along the line I failed.

"Getting back to religion. I always believed in God and I still do. And I know my son is in Heaven; no doubt in my mind. Through the last 5 years since my son's death, I know God has helped me.

"As for old friends, when you lose a child at 63, there aren't that many old friends anymore. You're strictly alone; at least I was. So I carried my grief alone.

"Although my sister came as often as she could, she lives 70 miles from me. But thank God for a wonderful next door neighbor. I couldn't have found a more caring or compassionate friend. I will always love her for being so kind.

"I joined Compassionate Friends when Donald died; it is a wonderful organization. I haven't been to many meetings because they conflicted with my work schedule. Also I became very depressed and tired and all the things that you go through. I usually would just sleep. It seemed that the best thing about living was sleeping, and so I slept. That is the only source of help I had or have.

"My first trip to Compassionate Friends, a young woman came and picked me up because I didn't know how to get to the meeting. It turned out that she had been a friend of my daughter and my son Donald. In fact, we had once lived on the same street and they had gone to school together. She had lost her 4-year-old son. My heart went out to her. I knew our grief was the same yet different. Her small son had still been under her protection and I wondered how she could stand it: an empty bed, all of his toys and clothing. A child turns to his parents for comfort. What a terrible thing to watch a small child die and you can do nothing to help him! And what a lonely house that must be without that little one. It must have been unbearable to stay in her house.

"Yes, we grieve the same and yet differently than the parents of a young child who dies.

"Before my son died, I had no physical or mental problems, but now I have my share. I did not seek help. That could have been because I was alone; I would probably have seen a doctor if someone had suggested it. Instead, I just dragged myself through every day, even though I needed help. I have arthritis all through my body. My mental capacity is not the same; how could it be? I can't concentrate; I almost had three accidents while driving and they would have been my fault.

"And there is the business of going out and buying a car, buying the first one I looked at, wondering how I got myself into that, not knowing how I was going to pay for it. I'm still paying for it. I didn't like the car when I bought it and I still don't like it. The salesman saw me coming and he walked right over the top of me and I let him. I always used to be cautious; never would I have bought that car if I had been in the right frame of mind.

"I could go on and on. I have thoughts of suicide all the time. I really felt I had nothing to live for any more, that no one cared and I wouldn't be missed. I still feel that way.

"I also feel that I have lived my life. I grew up, got married, raised my children, my son died and my daughter has her own life and career. She travels around the country and abroad, so I see very little of her, so she certainly doesn't need me.

"So what is left? All you have to look forward to is aches and pains, and if you're unfortunate enough to live into old age, some kind of nursing home. So yes, lots of thoughts of suicide, lots of depression.

"I feel that my child has communicated with me since his death. My television went off many times when I was watching it, for no apparent reason, and it still does. I interpret it as Donald telling me not to grieve, that everything is all right.

"I know there is a line in the Bible that says to die is to gain. When my mother died, I opened the Bible and the page turned to those words. They were meant for me to see, and I never forgot them: 'To die is to gain'.

"Donald came to me in a dream but not a dream; it took place in three different stages. In the first, he was standing at what looked like a wide, bright intersection. But there were no cars around the intersection. It looked like pearl and beautiful marble. It was a beautiful day and Donald had shorts and a tank top on. He was ready to cross the intersection and walk towards me standing on the other side. Then I woke up.

"The next day, I was sleeping on the couch like the day before. As I said, it was a dream and yet it wasn't a dream. He walked through my front door, wearing the same pair of shorts and the same tank top. I woke up.

"The third step happened the next day. I was again sleeping on the couch and he was sitting beside me. He was still wearing the same outfit. I had awakened as soon as he entered the house but no words were spoken.

"Another experience. I had a rose bush in my front yard which was dying. I was planning to dig it out, but I hadn't gotten around to it. Nearly five months after his May 26th death, Donald's birthday arrived. It was a cold day, October 6th. I looked out my front door and there was a very beautiful peach rose on the bush, just in time for his birthday. After the rose finished blooming, the bush died.

"My daughter also received a message on her answering machine: 'Dorothy, you tell Winifred that God loves her.' There is absolutely no way that she should have received that message. She has no idea where it came from, she did not recognize the voice. The caller did not leave a name or a number. But we both know the message came from beyond.

"In answer to your question as to whether a book would be of any help, I think it is a wonderful idea and I'm sure it would help me. Just writing this down has been of help to me."

SCHLEICHER: Accident

Judy Schleicher, 41, and her husband lost their 20-year-old daughter in an auto accident on March 10, 1989.

"Our 20-year-old daughter, Quintina Marie Schleicher, was killed in an auto accident one mile from our home on March 10, 1989. No one came to inform us even though her death was instantaneous. The hospital called us to come in, telling us it was critical. They were very unsupportive and we had to drive home after hearing this terrible news.

"The loss of the friendship with our daughter, who lived at home, is probably the biggest difference between loss of an older child and a younger.

"All the problems in the questionnaire refer to me: memory loss, inability to concentrate, inability to sleep, eating problems, thoughts of suicide, depression, illness and accidents. They refer to the other survivors also. The relationship with my surviving son was strained at first because I was over-protective of him. Now we have a great relationship and he is our Compassionate Friends group's sibling leader.

"My husband and I are closer now than ever, though our marriage was strained at first after Quintina Marie died. We never considered divorce and have no problem communicating. My husband is not afraid to show his feelings, but he needs to be alone in the woods now and then to 'renew' himself. I respect that and don't go along unless he asks me to.

"Besides my sadness at being denied my child's companionship, I wish she had been able to give me grandchildren. She was really cheated and so was I.

"Our priorities have changed since our daughter died. We don't worry about petty things any more; we try to enjoy today. Our friends are now The Compassionate Friends members. Although we did not seek professional counseling, we credit TCF with saving our relationship as well as our sanity. We are now active in the chapter; my husband is the leader. Now we hope we are helping others whose children have died. Our clergyman was very supportive and recommended TCF to us.

"In answer to the question about how my responses to loss have changed, I would say my grief has slowly eased, but the pain is always with me. It seems the more time goes by, the more I miss my daughter's companionship. We were just beginning to be friends when she died. I don't believe there are phases to grief, only emotions which send us on a roller coaster ride.

"We have had many signs from our daughter and they continue today, five years later."

SETTLE: Accident

Dorothy, 58, and Joe Settle lost their 20-year-old son, Gary, on May 26, 1972, in an auto accident.

"My son Gary was killed in an auto accident on May 26, 1972. He lived at home at the time and had a favorite girl friend. She had a nervous breakdown a few months after his death but subsequently married. Gary's sister Carla was married and living in Colorado at the time of his death. She was very supportive and called us every week.

"Our son's death brought Joe and me much closer. He was a workaholic who suddenly spent less time at work and more with me. He felt sorry that he had not spent more time with his son. I, on the other hand, had spent as much time with him as Gary would allow. He was in the stage of pulling away from family.

"My parents, who lived in Arizona, asked that I find a place near us here, where they could live with some supervision, since my father had Alzheimers Disease. Another change: I lost my job, although I was immediately offered another position teaching emotionally handicapped children. I enrolled in a special course at the University in Albany to prepare for it. At the time, I felt that I was not being allowed an adequate opportunity to grieve. In retrospect it probably was good that I was kept so busy. Friends have told me they felt I came through this difficult time more easily than others they had known.

"I often wonder what Gary would be doing if he were alive today. I'm sure everyone wishes their child would have lived to develop his full potential. When he was killed, Gary was about to go to Reed College in Oregon after working two years out of high school at radio station WMHT.

"Over the years my grief has become less painful, but I think about him each day. There is always some little thing that reminds me of him.

"Private help came from good friends. Two of them called every day for several months. Our daughter called from Colorado; friends offered books on death.

"We did not have a funeral or memorial service. Some of Gary's friends from high school had a get-together in his memory on a Saturday evening afterwards. My husband and I privately scattered his ashes on a mountain in the Adirondacks where we had had many family vacations and happy times together."

SHOBER: Illness

Priscilla Shober, 60, and her husband George lost their 29-year-old son, Gregory, on November 3, 1990, to AIDS.

"My son, Gregory, died of AIDS on November 3, 1990, at the age of 29. He was single and lived at home. Besides his father and me, he is survived by two siblings. We have no problems with them; total acceptance and participation in all things.

"Because I am a registered nurse, the medical personnel in the hospital allowed me to help in my son's case. We were allowed to stay with him all the time in cardiac intensive care.

"My son and I had a very close relationship and were good friends. My husband and Gregory did not have this relationship. It was strained until about a year before his death. Therefore we grieve for different things. My husband grieves openly and shares his grief with others but still has a lot of regrets. He is trying to work them through.

We have both retired since my son's death and have become closer most of the time. We do a lot of things together now.

"The way my child died is difficult to bear, as is being denied his companionship, the unfairness of it all and a feeling that he was cheated out of life. I regret that I have lost a close friend as well as a son. Also I regret having to deal with society's rejection regarding his having AIDS. Because of this I am not able to share my feelings openly.

"My life has changed in many ways. I suffer from memory loss, an inability to concentrate and to sleep. At times I feel that I am losing my mind. I have extreme anxiety and sometimes I have panic attacks. I am more aware of time now and try to make full use of it. I am less hung up on the small troubles in life and try to enjoy it more.

"Religion is still a major part of my life and I continue to have a strong faith. My clergy have been helpful but sometimes I am annoyed with the church for not being as supportive as I felt they could have been. Instead of being as active in our church as I used to be, I try to do more charity work in the community, especially in the AIDS area.

"Friends continue to be a great support and mine have always been there for me when I needed them. The Compassionate Friends, AIDS support group, family, grandchildren, new people I have met in my AIDS work have also been of help.

"If you lose an adult child, there are more personal possessions to deal with; more friends, nieces and nephews, grandchildren and in-laws are involved. You yourself are older. Perhaps a book about the death of an adult child would have been helpful to me at first. But at this point I know most of the books and don't feel I need it. The times of overwhelming grief have lessened in intensity but sometimes overcome me. I call these my 'Gregory days' and I go with the flow for that time. Now I'm able to think of the 'not-so-perfect Greg' instead of the 'perfect Greg.' I may have had some communication from my son but I don't know for sure."

A letter in June, 1995:

"You asked if my Greg Days are better. They are less frequent and now are not as sad and painful. I feel my contact with him through the butterflies I find. Each time a special event occurs or we go someplace new, butterflies appear in some form to comfort me and now I look for them as a sign that my son is with us. For example: at the motel I stayed in in Florida prior to surgery for a ruptured disc, there were butterflies on the tiles in the kitchen area. In the hospital I waited for my sign: one day one of the aides came in with a lap full of butterflies! At the rehabilitation center I became fond of an 89-year-old woman who had had a stroke. We ate lunch together each day and talked a lot. She was moved to a new room one day and when I went to see it, there was a butterfly on the window—a suncatcher. I knew that meant my son had a part in our meeting. I explained this to her and her eyes filled with big tears; mine, too."

In response to my letter to Priscilla telling her of my accident in Italy, where I fell and broke my left hip, she writes:

"It sounds like you had a lovely vacation. That will teach you to stay at home! I hope by now you are well on your way to recovery. I think of you at times and send prayers your way.

"I have some good news to impart. George and I have gotten a home in the retirement center we were going to move to. It became open after only one year of waiting. We are moving into a much smaller house so we have to get all new furniture; ours was too big and bulky. We put our house up for sale and it sold in 2 weeks. We have been frantically throwing, stowing, selling, giving away and packing up 30 years of 'good junk' we have accumulated.

"There have been some bad days during our packing when I discover things belonging to my son Greg and have had to give some of them away. The pain of losing him never really goes away and sometimes hurts just as much as in the beginning. In a way, I hate to leave this house because there was so much of his presence in it. But I hope we will take that with us to our new home. Changes are never easy but we are both hoping that this will be the start of a new adventure for us.

"I was going to have my second eye operation but now I must wait until after we move."

MR. X: Accident

Mr. X, age 61, and his wife, age 60, lost their 34-year-old daughter on December 31, 1984, in an auto accident.

"My wife and I raised three children. We lost our middle child, our daughter Ann, on December 31, 1984, when she was killed in a one-car accident. It has been hard to bear the way my daughter died. Because there was no autopsy, there has always been some doubt as to what caused the accident; it may have been drug or alcohol related. Ann was a professional cellist with a degree in music. She had difficulty surviving in the classical field so she switched to modern: jazz; mostly hard rock. Apparently she got in with the wrong crowd.

"The surviving siblings (29 and 38), particularly one daughter, offended us by her letters to local newspapers, etc., and we did not talk to her for several months. Our marriage was somewhat stressed at first but my wife and I had a good relationship. Unfortunately she died on September 24, 1992, so I am alone now. Prior to her death, the two of us plus two other couples formed our local chapter (1987) of The Compassionate Friends; I am still a co-leader. We had started attending another chapter, my wife in September of 1985 and I in July of 1985. I did my grief work, cried when I knew I had to, talked about Ann, talked about societal problems and family problems. In short, I went through all the phases of grief except anger, which I can NOT seem to express. TCF was what I needed and is a part of my life now, as I try to give back to others what was so freely given to me.

"I gained weight and sank into a depression after Ann's death. The clergy and professional counselors were helpful and some friends were, too. But after six months our best friends told us we should be healed by then, so we did not discuss Ann's death with them.

"I know now that life is fragile and the lives of remaining family have become more important. My faith has deepened, as I know that I shall see Ann and my late wife when I enter the Eternal Kingdom. Friendships have become more important and wider.

"Insofar as a book is concerned, I think reading the actual experiences, with names changed, of course, in a variety of circumstances could be helpful. I really can't believe there is much difference between the loss of a young child and an adult. I have observed that the healing process seems shorter with the loss of a young child. Younger parents seem to heal more quickly.

"As for other insights, I would say that you do not wish to memorialize your deceased child to the exclusion of surviving siblings, but I think it is helpful to have several pictures and mementos of her or his life around the home and to occasionally talk about him or her."

STUART: Suicide

Pearl and Gary Stuart, age 42 and 46, lost their son Joe when he committed suicide at the age of 21 on January 19, 1993.

"Our son Joe committed suicide. It was a shock. We had no prior knowledge of any intentions, depression, or unhappiness in his life. Although he was a little wild and carefree, he was very intelligent and seemed to be heading in the right direction. He had a breakup of a relationship and got in trouble with the law the night it happened. It was his first offense and he would probably have been given probation. I don't know why he thought life was so bad.

"Joe is survived by a brother and sister. His brother holds everything in and is bitter and angry; his sister went through a rough period of hurt, anger and bitterness, but she is strong and has grown a lot through this experience.

"As for my husband and me, there was a distance at first due to different ways that men and women grieve. I couldn't talk about Joe at all, but after awhile when we did and Gary cried, we both felt better. My husband still needs to relieve a lot more, but it will take a long time. I've learned not to bring things up unless he's ready to talk.

"I lost fourteen and a half pounds and was unable to sleep nights for a long time. At first, I didn't even want to live. Not that I would ever resort to suicide, but I wouldn't have cared if I were told I was to die tomorrow. That changed. There are so many people who love and need me and I do love life. I just hope it treats me better. I lost my Dad in May of '92, my son Joe in January of '93, and my Mother-in-law in April of '93. Not to mention a car accident in February, '93, two and a half weeks after Joe's death, and the loss of a job I had had for ten years in April of '93.

"I thought I would feel less responsible for my child once he turned 21, that getting through the teenage years was a relief. Boy, was I wrong! I always had a good outlook on life, religion, and people in general, so I don't think things will change much in this regard. My children and husband, on the other hand, mean more to me now and I realize how much I need and love them.

"I have had some help from The Compassionate Friends as well as Survivors of Suicide. I haven't thought about the adult loss compared to loss of a younger child. Probably it would make you feel worse if a younger person committed suicide.

"Joe bought me an alarm clock for Christmas shortly before he died. It has huge numbers on it, and every time I woke up in the middle of the night there were triple numbers on it. One night 222, another 555, etc. I would hear a song that reminded me of him; when I looked, the license plate number in front of me would have triple numbers on the plate. I felt he was trying to tell me he was OK and he was sorry."

In her response to my letter on her son's death date, Pearl writes:

"Your letter and the essays you sent are very special and greatly appreciated. I don't recall exactly what I answered on your questionnaire so I hope I'm not repeating myself in this letter.

"I can relate to Carol Marshall's statement, 'I always wonder how a child you both loved so much can tear you apart.' I felt that happening immediately, but with outside resources such as Survivors of Suicide, Compassionate Friends, counseling at work and elsewhere, support of friends, co-workers and family, I realized this was normal, since men grieve differently. I think it took the death of my mother-in-law, three months after Joe's death, to help me recognize this. I was so self-centered with my own pain at first, I didn't want to be a wife to my husband or a mother to my other children. I didn't want to deal with problems because I guess I felt that I failed as a parent, since my son decided to leave us. What could I have done differently? This was the question I asked myself so many times. Then I realized that you can't change what happened or go back in time; you can only do something now. Change is a part of everyday life: within less than a year I lost my father, son, mother-in-law and my job of ten years. Also, two and a half weeks after Joe died I was hit from behind while driving my car and my neck was permanently damaged. When that happened, I didn't care if I lived or died. I realize I am not afraid to die, but also realize that I'm not ready to leave this world yet.

"If suffering we must endure, there has to be a reason. I don't think life was meant to be paradise, but if we get through the hell on earth, then we will be eternally happy. It's reassuring to know that almost any problem that I encounter in the future, I can handle, because I've gotten through, hopefully, the worst situation I will ever have to endure. Now the only thing I can do is help others, especially my family, to have the same outlook as I have. I feel sorry for those that do not have faith, who believe that this is it, that there's no eternal life in Heaven, as my husband does. Just the other night I was so happy that he cried, which is so unlike him, that I encouraged him to release it and we hugged and felt closer. I told him I was so worried about him; he has been in so much pain. He assured me he would never take his own life. It was a relief for me.

"A few months ago my other son got in a fight trying to help some friends who were fighting. It happened to be off-duty police officers and the whole situation was like a nightmare! He was arrested; his name was in the paper. The reason it was so frightening to us was that the night Joe killed himself, he had just been released from jail for a minor offense. His brother's arrest was for a far worse offense than Joe's. A friend of ours talked to his brother and made him promise he would not do what Joe did. This taught me one thing: as we say so often at The Compassionate Friends meetings, just because one child does it, it doesn't mean all of your children are going to do it. We're all individuals with our own minds and thoughts. Our parents are not responsible for our actions.

"When Joe became 21 years old I was sort of relieved. He was a mature adult now, responsible for his own actions. I felt, 'Wow, you made it!' I think he felt the same, that he was now on his own and responsible for his own actions. I couldn't punish him like I used to and I felt he punished himself. The guilt feeling is that I felt I didn't do a good job raising him, even though I did the best I knew how. I felt I should have taught him more responsibility.

"We couldn't spoil our children with riches, but we did everything else in our power to make their lives easier: did their laundry, cleaning, paying for school, for books, things they had trouble paying for, getting them out of jams, etc. This I realize was not the right thing to do. Life was not made to be easy. You have to learn by mistakes, not have them taken care of for you, but what did we know as parents?

In a letter many months later, Pearl writes:

"You asked whether my regard for all forms of life was heightened by my bereavement. That regard is not a unique one for me. I have always let flies out of the house instead of killing them. I remember years ago when my kids and I even cried one day when we found out we had a mouse in the basement and had to set a trap to catch it. They wanted it for a pet.

"Although the supervisor who led the monthly meetings of the Survivors of Suicide support group I have been attending lost her job due to cutbacks, she asked if I would coordinate the meetings amongst ourselves. The pastor of our parish called me to his office to ask if I would be interested in being involved in starting a support group for the bereaved. I feel there is nothing that makes me feel better than being able to help others who are in need of support, as I had been and continue to be helped.

"My daughter was in the process of cleaning out a desk where she worked, since the company was relocating, and was surprised to find gold butterfly charms in the desk, actually over 100 of them. As you know, butterflies are cherished by The Compassionate Friends as a sign of hope for the bereaved. She brought them home and suggested that I share them with The Compassionate Friends, who sold them as a fundraiser with a memorial in Joe's name.

"Last summer, TCF had a bench engraved and a tree planted in honor of our children, with the help of our mayor.

"I just want to thank you for letting me express my feelings and thoughts with you because I feel that communicating with others and writing down the way you feel is one of the best forms of therapy. Thank you for listening; it is such a very special feeling to know others genuinely care about you and really understand."

STURCHIO: Accident

Judy Sturchio, 48, and her divorced husband lost their son, Christopher Charles Sturchio, 19, in an auto accident on December 26, 1992.

"My son Christopher was 19 at the time he was killed in an auto accident on December 26, 1992. I am divorced and Christopher lived with his father. My former husband and I have continued a very mutually supportive relationship. He took this loss, as I have, as a devastation. I have a wonderful relationship with our other son as well. I correspond regularly with Kristen, one of Christopher's dearest friends.

"I would underline each of the items in your question about what is most difficult to bear: how my child died; being denied my child's companionship; being denied grandchildren; the unfairness of it all; anger; guilt; a feeling that my child was cheated out of life. I still cannot believe this happened to someone as wonderful as Christopher.

"The State Troopers who told us of Christopher's death were extremely cruel and cold; they practically spit it out in disgust.

"Everything about my life has changed: religion, friends, my attitude about life itself. Not a grain of sand on this earth remains the same as it was before Christopher's death.

"Although friends were often very lacking in support, The Compassionate Friends have been wonderful. They let me know I'm sane. My experience with counseling is great. Books have also been important.

"I can't say what the difference between the loss of a young child and an adult might be; I only really know my own loss. I try to empathize with those who have lost young children but that's just what it is: empathy.

"I experienced many mental and physical symptoms, among them anger, guilt and depression, depression, depression. The other survivors also experienced depression.

"Christopher's 'presence' comes to me sometimes.

"I think my responses were all mixed up and jumbled and they remain so. Nothing is neat about this. Things run together and conflict."

TARBRAKE: Accident

Ann Marie, 53, and Charles Tarbrake lost their daughter Katie, 24, and their granddaughter, Kelly (Katie's sister's child), 6, in an auto-truck accident in July 1993.

"Our daughter Kathleen (Katie) was 24 years old when she died. Besides her father and me, she is survived by 4 brothers and one sister. She had left home 2 years before the accident to teach third grade in Maryland and was about to be engaged.

"Katie and her niece (our oldest grandchild), Kelly, 6, were riding in a car which was hit by a truck hauling 8 thousand pounds of potatoes, which fell on them. Both Katie and Kelly were killed. The truck was in bad shape: no license, no brakes; had been ordered off the road 19 days before the accident. Even though the driver was an independent trucker without a license, we are up against the powerful trucking industry. We are still working on legal ramifications.

"The school where Katie taught had a memorial service and the love she generated moved us greatly. At the same time it angered us because Katie's life was cut short.

"Family relationships are not strained, just difficult. Losing both our daughter and granddaughter has compounded everything. Our other five children, Kelly's parents and siblings in particular, have had lots and lots of rough times. Just the separate grieving, Kelly's family with her primarily; my husband and me primarily with Katie. Just the grief of family to family makes us unable to connect. Our remaining children are 20 and older.

"My husband and I have grown closer since this tragedy. The children are all out of the house and we have only each other to turn to. We have the time to talk and cry together. Patti and her husband (Kelly's parents) do not. As for our own grieving styles, I need to read everything I can; I need pictures, video; my husband cannot look or watch. I'm able to talk freely; he cannot. Now he goes to The Compassionate Friends with me, which does help him. Now, nearly 8 months later, he is able to talk a little and does share more with me. At this time, when there are no words, no answers, we just hold on to each other, to our other children, to our remaining two grandchildren. Of course we are really newly bereaved so cannot comment on whether there are phases of grief. At this point things overlap so much with us; everything kind of runs together.

"I feel very sad about how my child died, being denied her companionship, the unfairness of it all and I feel very angry. Katie was an outstanding teacher and had so much to give. She was a good daughter and sister and gave our family such balance, Of course Kelly never had a chance. But her 6 years brought us only joy.

"We see Patti having as much trouble as we have: her child young, ours an adult; each with its own sense of loss; each trauma heart-wrenching. Maybe time will help us all.

"In some ways our lives have changed for the better: we are more tuned in; we soak up more; we can't get enough of our surviving five and their mates. We try to imprint images so as never to forget. We are much more aware of life's fragility. At the same time we find ourselves less patient with others who complain of their small problems and we find ourselves shying away from them. TCF are a great source of comfort to us. We found no help from the hospital.

"People who have not 'been there' who talk on grief are a real turn-off; understanding this experience cannot be gotten out of a book. Both of the clergy in our lives said little. We appreciated that because they respected us, as there are no words.

"In regard to mental and physical problems, I would have to underline them all: memory loss, inability to concentrate, inability to sleep, overeating, thoughts of suicide, depression, illness, accidents. But the really bad moments have thankfully passed. Each of the other survivors had problems at different times. Some of us had dreams of our deceased children. My husband has; I have not.

"I wish with all my heart I was not answering these questions. Through all this, there are more questions than there are answers."

VAN AKEN: Accident

Jeane Van Aken, 43, and her husband lost their son Richard Paul Van Aken, 22, on February 16, 1989.

"Our son, Richard Paul Van Aken, was 22 years and one month old when he was hit by a bus while walking on the Interstate. He had lived at home and was a senior in college. He left an 18-year-old brother and a girlfriend he had gone with for about five years. Insofar as the justice system is concerned, nothing they could have or would have done would have changed anything or brought my son back, so who cares.

"Richard's surviving brother is now 23 and doing fine, though at first he suffered from most of the things you mentioned on the list of physical and mental problems. I still have a good relationship with Rich's girlfriend. She is married now but still loves and misses him.

"The relationship of my husband and me was strained for awhile. I don't know; I was too involved with my own pain to worry about him. Selfish, I know, but I couldn't help him or myself then. But we never considered separation. Maybe we are closer now.

"Both my husband and I had a very good relationship with Rich so I think this helped us deal with our loss. We didn't have any regrets about the time we had with him.

"In the beginning, I spent a lot of time worrying if he was OK. Now, five years later, I just miss him so much.

"My son's death made me look at the world and life and DEATH differently. Now I am surely not afraid to die. I find some peace from religion. I had one session with a psychiatrist, but The Compassionate Friends, friends and relatives, in that order, have helped the most. In phase one of my grief: severe and constant pain and yearning; phase two: accepting the reality and I had more pain; three: wanting to feel better and working hard at it; four: pain not so constant but just missing him so.

"Perhaps a book might help other people understand that the age doesn't matter: your child is your child, no matter how old. But with an older child, the relationships you build over the years are different. My son was my best friend.

"Both my husband and I experienced everything on the list: memory loss, inability to concentrate, inability to sleep, overeating, thoughts of suicide, depression, illness and accidents.

"In my husband's and in Richard's girlfriend's dreams he communicated with them.

"In all the years of his life, I did for him; we grew up together. All of a sudden, all I can do for him is bring flowers to his grave. I miss doing for him."

In answer to a letter I wrote to Jeane, I received the sad news from her husband that she had died.

VAN SCHAICK: Illness

Sally, 50, and John Van Schaick, 51, lost their daughter Holly, 25, when she died suddenly of apparent heart failure on March 10, 1973.

"When she died, Holly was married, though her marriage was troubled, and she had a two and a half year old son, Eliot. They were living in Berkeley when she died suddenly from a non-diagnosed pre-existing condition: faulty mitral valve, adrenal exhaustion.

"The police always have to check out an unattended death. They were OK. Somehow you don't expect to read your daughter's autopsy report.

"It's been 21 years. How did we cope? Well, for one thing, we were on sabbatical leave in Mexico when Holly died. We were signed up to do a tour of 31 ruins, self-guided, an independent study in Central American anthropology. All our four surviving children were self-sustaining adults and our grandson, Eliot, was in good care. We were superfluous, so after Holly's funeral, we went back to Mexico and did our study. It was very absorbing because we had to do it in Spanish which we weren't that good in. We'd break down from time to time, but the immediate situation we had to cope with would pull us back up.

"When we got back to Schenectady, I did a lot of needlework; I'm sort of a work-as-therapy person. We built a porch on our camp; we

DID things. I changed from high school teaching to elementary school teaching; John got more active in the teachers' union. And we made many trips to California to see our precious Eliot.

"Because we had been on good terms with Holly, I think it helped. If you have 'unfinished business' with the deceased, the death is harder to take. Her husband, David, on the other hand, was very upset and had a lot of guilt. He felt that somehow it was his fault. We have done what we could to help him, at least to not act as if we blame him. His friends helped him make Holly's coffin as sort of interim therapy. A good friend of his picked up all the expenses until we could arrive from Mexico. We then shared expenses with his family. Holly is buried in Berkeley. We would have preferred cremation, but David couldn't stand the thought so we acceded to him.

"We had a bit of cultural flap with the other in-laws. David's mother took to her bed in a darkened room with cold compresses. That was her mode; we respected it. John and I maintained a zombie-like calm which left a lot of people, including David's mother, thinking we were cold and indifferent. Finally John apologized to them for our being late in the morning, saying it took us an hour to pull ourselves together, which was true. I understand that grief takes different forms with different people and I respect them all. We had sleep and eating problems as well as illness: allergies, dermatitis and bronchitis after Holly's death.

"I suppose that our grandson Eliot helped us face things. He was the next generation, needing all the support he could get. David kept him for a year. Then we started a process of many years of shared time. David often sent him to us in the spring and we'd keep him till about November. The schooling was cock-eyed but he survived and did well. We went to California this spring to see him receive a degree from San Mateo Community College.

"Once when Eliot was 9, I was tucking him in and noticed he was crying. When I asked what was wrong he said he'd suddenly had a feeling of all he had lost when his mother died. John and I told him it was all right to grieve; that he'd been too young at two and a half to understand. This happened again a time or two and he has been OK ever since.

"Mostly I have a sorrow that Holly did not live to use her considerable gifts. She was a linguist in Far Eastern languages; she had a major in inter-cultural psychology. She would have been terrific!

"Holly's death occurred long before there were any organizations like Compassionate Friends in existence to help bereaved parents. I had already lost my adult sister. That was when my attitude towards life changed. Also John and I had lost many friends in World War II and we knew that death was part of the equation. John was one of two surviving pilots from his class in the Air Corps. Within six weeks of our wedding our best man was dead. Within 6 years our maid of honor was dead. It was awful but we could see beyond it. We know that at any moment one of our 4 children or 9 grandchildren could be taken; a sort of sword of Damocles that we are constantly aware of.

"When my sister died, she had been away at her new job for only 3 months. My parents were devastated, especially my mother. The empty place at the table; the missing face on holidays.

"With the death of a young child, one has a lot of 'if only I had. . . .' The feeling of not being able to do enough. My heart goes out to the mother and father of the child who darts out into the street and is run over, or the child who falls out of a second-story window. Parents know that there's no such thing as being vigilant enough. The guilt can break up a marriage. When an adult child dies, parents probably know they have done the best they could.

"A book could be helpful just showing us we are not alone.

"The night before she died, Holly was talking on the phone to a friend. She said, 'you know, I really feel that I've finally got it all together.' Her sisters report that she had told them years before that she did not expect to live past the age of 25. I don't feel she has communicated with me since her death but I talk to her occasionally, especially about Eliot. 'Holly, how about that Eliot! Isn't he a wonderful kid?'

"Insofar as religion is concerned, I have always been ambivalent. I want to believe, but I'm a born skeptic.

"Losing a child is like losing a limb: from time to time there is sensation, even though it's gone."

VOUGHT: Accident

Marcy, the daughter of Eleanor and Robert Vought was killed when her car was hit at a toll booth in October, 1988. She was 36.

"My daughter Marcy was waiting in her car at a toll booth when she was struck from behind and killed by an auto driven by a diabetic who passed out. She was 36, married and living in Maine with her husband. She is also survived by a brother and a sister. Our relations with our son-in-law are excellent. From the beginning, he said he wanted to keep in close contact with our family. He participated in our son's wedding party in California and at our large family reunion last summer. We see him two or three times a year and keep in touch by telephone.

"My husband I are even closer now than we were before. We feel sad about the way Marcy died, that we are denied her company, denied HER children. She was cheated out of more than half her life. I regret that she is missing so much. It is so unfair; why should someone who had so much to live for, to contribute, die while people who are a burden and don't want to live continue to live on?

The Justice System did not serve us well. We tried endlessly to get the driver who killed Marcy off the road. We wrote letters to politicians and officials, enlisted our friends in a letter-writing campaign, approached public interest groups to plead our case. There finally was a hearing July 7, 1989, in Concord, New Hampshire. Confronted with information released from the hospital that the driver's blood sugar was extremely low even after being given glucose at the scene of the accident, the man was judged negligent since he had taken his usual insulin but had not eaten. He said he had planned to stop for a soda on the way but had not done so in his haste. His erratic driving and finally his passing out, was due to low blood sugar and 'insulin shock.' Neither he nor his boss had insurance. He was the driver of a privately owned van used to pick up wheelchair passengers. We were commended by people at the New Hampshire DWI Prevention Council for pursuing an indictment as aggressively as we have.

"My attitude towards religion has not changed. I don't believe it was God's will. I think my idea of God is that he cries when a child dies.

"I appreciate old friends all the more since they were so understanding and helpful in our sorrow. The Compassionate Friends were a big help, especially in the first months and years of our bereavement. RID was also very helpful as was Pat Rainboth of NHDWI Prevention Council.

"The anger of the first year has turned to acceptance; the raw wound has healed somewhat but is still there. I think losing an adult child is harder because of all the memories and the years of closeness.

"I feel it is important to keep memories alive. Don't hesitate to talk about your child, especially the happy times. Keep in touch with your child's friends.

"Traveling was helpful, though grief went along. It helps to be in new situations and being busy. I try to do things that would please Marcy if she knew, things like being on the Caring Committee at church, volunteering at an elementary school in a depressed neighborhood. It helps me to be with children.

"Both my husband and I have had health problems since Marcy's death. I was diagnosed as diabetic; the doctors felt it was due to stress. My husband developed colon cancer, also due to stress.

"The morning of Marcy's death I felt very restless for no reason, although she was hundreds of miles away. Sometimes I feel her presence and can almost hear her say, 'Go for it, Mom!' The wind chimes she gave us, stars or the moon through our skylight make me say, 'Hi, Marcy.' "

Bob Vought succumbed to colon cancer in January 1997.

WALLACE: Illness

Peg Wallace, 51, lost her 32-year-old daughter, Winnie, on September 6, 1992.

"In February, 1986, two months after I lost my mother, Winnie and her daughter Valerie went snowmobiling. I was nervous about her going and pleaded with her not to go. I had a strange feeling something was going to go wrong. She backed out of my driveway kind of angry with me and I called to her, 'Please be careful, Winnie; they're dangerous, you know.'

"About 7 that evening her friend Joyce, who had gone along, called from the hospital. 'There's been an accident,' she said. I was terrified and tore off to the hospital. When I walked into Winnie's room I couldn't believe it. She couldn't talk right, they had loaded her up on so much morphine. Her back was broken; 3 vertebrae were crushed. I seems to me now that I must have known things would never be the same. I just prayed that she would live.

"She did live another six years. Through those years I watched with great sorrow a beautiful, healthy girl deteriorate. She took a lot of drugs to kill the pain. Arthritis set in in the broken bones. Sometimes she would fall down. She wore a back brace for a long time.

"She had a breakdown and went into the psychiatric center for treatment. On September 6, 1992, Valerie called and said 'I can't wake Mom up.' Oh my God! I thought. My poor baby girl had overdosed. God help me! Yes, she was dead.

"Winnie was single; her daughter was 14. I am separated from Winnie's father, who was 57 when she died. But we have a good relationship. I see him one or two week-ends a month. He lives in Connecticut.

"It is hard for the survivors to handle my grief. Valerie and I have had a lot of difficulties. At this point, she no longer lives with me but is living with one of her mother's friends.

"I find it hard to bear the unfairness of it all: how my child died, being cheated out of her companionship, the feeling she did not have a full life. I am angry and feel very guilty. Neither the medical nor the legal professions served us well, which adds to the difficulty of her death.

"My life is filled with sadness; I am lonely without Winnie. My feelings towards religion are stronger and I have friends who are supportive. The Compassionate Friends have been, too. Although I have sought professional help from counselors, I really don't know that it has made all that much difference; clergy definitely were not helpful.

"The loss of a young child may produce the same feelings of grief but there are more memories with an adult child. You have had that child longer; that makes it harder.

"I experienced mental and physical problems such as memory loss, inability to concentrate, overeating, depression, thoughts of suicide, extreme fatigue and lack of energy. And I often feel that I am going crazy.

"Winnie's daughter had a very hard time because of the death of her mother. She was hospitalized in a psychiatric hospital because of the loss.

"My daughter has communicated with me since her death. In a dream, she came to me very clearly. She spoke to me to tell me she was OK. Also, one night I awoke to feel her in the house. I called to her; she didn't speak. But I saw her. A shadow moved in the hall and stood by my bedroom door. I spoke to her.

"The life I live now is totally different; I feel changed. What I have experienced is something that not all people will know. There is a depth of sorrow and loss that is an open wound within."

ZOLL: Accident

George and Judith Zoll lost their 27-year-old son in an auto accident.

"Our son Mark was killed on May 15, 1995, the innocent victim of a head-on collision. The woman who struck him was trying to pass a truck and had probably been drinking at the time. We are angry at the authorities because there was no toxology test taken and justice was not done.

"Mark left a wife and young son plus three siblings, grandparents, aunts, uncles, and other close relatives and friends in addition to my husband and me.

"Our four children were always very close and the survivors remain so. Mark was especially close to his brother, who has taken his death very hard. My husband and I have difficulty talking about our son's death and he won't discuss it unless I bring it up. He tends to bury himself in his work, which is very demanding: we run a restaurant.

"Our relations with our daughter-in-law are good; her parents are also thoughtful about making sure we see our grandson frequently. She has remarried since my son's death.

"My faith in God is stronger, for I believe Mark is with the Lord and therefore in a better place. My faith in people has suffered because of the way the authorities handled things. Although some of my friends have been supportive, most of the friends I have now are those who have also lost children; they understand.

"Professional counselors and clergy have been helpful, as have the Compassionate Friends. When others who have lost children share their experiences, it helps the newly bereaved survive, to look beyond their grief and realize they, too, can and will make it. I read the obituaries and empathize with others who have lost a child; at the same time I am thinking of my own son who died.

"The death of a child is horrible, but I feel the longer one has watched this child growing up and into adulthood, helped form this person, then to have this child become a mature friend and confidant, it must surely be harder. You are proud when they make good choices and raise their own children.

"I suffered memory loss, an inability to concentrate, an inability to sleep, and I began to gain weight. Sometimes I have felt I am going crazy; I am depressed and have had thoughts of suicide. Some of Mark's other survivors have had similar difficulties.

"Mark's sister dreams about him; once he told her he was all right. He would be waving goodbye and smiling.

"On his birthday and death anniversary, we meet at the cemetery, sending up balloon messages to him."

BLANK: Illness

Catherine Jane Blank, daughter of Robert H. (71 minus one day) and Jeanne W. Blank (67), died July 12, 1987, of metastasized breast cancer.

"I am Cathy's mother. My husband and I raised three children: two girls and a boy. Our middle child, Catherine Jane Blank, born March 3, 1948, died at a Boston hospital on July 12, 1987, at the age of 39. Catherine did not live at home. She was an accomplished artist who earned her living working for an architectural rendering firm in Boston. At the time of her death, she had been studying at the Boston Museum of Fine Arts to become a book illustrator.

"In May, 1987, she had visited us in our Albany home on Memorial Day week-end and had spent a good share of the time resting on the couch. Fatigued and losing weight, she had been treated for about a month for what the doctor called a food allergy.

"We kept in touch almost daily by phone after her return to Boston. She called early on June 9, 1987, saying she needed us because she was getting too sick to take care of herself. We tossed a few garments into a suitcase and set out for Boston to bring her home, hoping to find care for her in our local hospitals.

"By this time, she was too sick to move. It was a matter of driving her from one specialist to another until she was put into the hospital. We stayed with her through all the tests, which confirmed a diagnosis of breast cancer, metastasized to the liver and bone. The misdiagnosis had cost her precious time and precluded an intervention which might have saved her life. She died less than 3 weeks after the diagnosis. Our other daughter, Laurel, then 42, and Cathy's brother Paul, 37, were with her, as were her father and I, when she died.

"Besides her parents and siblings Laurel and Paul, Cathy was survived by her special friend Arthur and one nephew, then 6. She had never married.

"Her parents had been married 45 years at the time of Catherine's death. Our relationship has become stressful. Our ways of grieving are different. For a long time, we were angry at the world and mildly angry at each other a good share of the time, for no apparent reason except our grief. Things are better now.

"Our relations with Cathy's sister Laurel have also been strained. She has trouble dealing with our pain and her own. Cathy was her best friend. Laurel's son, also named Paul, is a loving child and helps bind us together. They live near us here in Albany. Our son is supportive, though he has always lived far away. Now he and his wife, Annette, who are about to become parents, live in northern California.

"Cathy's friend Arthur came to visit a few times, wrote beautiful letters, sent flowers on Cathy's birthday and date of death for a few years. Then he married Cathy's friend Barbara and we have had no further contact except when we saw him during the trial at the malpractice suit we instituted as a result of Cathy's death. When he married, I felt a certain regret that Cathy had been cheated out of a chance for happiness with a loved one. At the same time, I felt guilty about that regret because of course I wanted Arthur to get on with his life.

"I find it very hard to come to terms with the medical mistakes which led to the inevitability of Cathy's death. This was especially so after we lost our malpractice suit due to what we feel were irregularities in court.

"Because she was single, Cathy was always more dependent on her parents for emotional support than her two siblings were. As a result, I feel she would have been a constant comfort to us as we have grown older. I will always miss that aspect of our relationship. I feel that I am so old that I should have been the one to die, not Cathy. I told her that I wished I could trade places with her as she lay dying.

"I suspect there will always be a certain bitterness as we view the way the legal system was involved. We feel that we were denied justice during the malpractice suit we instituted. The judge exhibited fits of temper if he wasn't addressed properly; allowed a physician to sit on the jury, a physician connected with the same hospital as the defense's expert witness. This was over our lawyer's objection. He had already used up his legal number of jury challenges so couldn't enter an objection to this irregularity. When we lost the case, our lawyer filed an appeal, which we lost. The appeals court accepted that juror's answer to the judge's query thus: 'Yes, I think I can be fair.' With so much riding on the decision . . . a colleague representing the defense; the prospect of an increase in his medical malpractice insurance premiums if we won . . . it is beyond comprehension to think that he would not be biased on the side of the defense.

"The medical system was of course involved. Two doctors failed to follow accepted procedure; even though Cathy went several times to a physician about the lump in her breast, no mammogram was ordered. The first doctor merely measured it as the thickening increased from one visit to another. The specialist did only a cursory examination and the two doctors had not communicated prior to Cathy's visit to the specialist.

"After Cathy's death we hired a lawyer. The Massachusetts state examining board decided we had enough of a complaint to sue the doctors, which has already been described. On a brighter note, the St. Elizabeth's Hospital staff were simply marvelous to us, making all sorts of compassionate accommodations to our family as we awaited Cathy's death. They couldn't have been better.

"My faith in the goodness and fairness of life has been shattered. I am disillusioned and disappointed. Maybe even cynical, but I'm working on that.

"I did not have a traditional religious faith prior to Cathy's death and do not have one now. Some years before she died I had come to believe that there is a life after death. I regard life after death as an aspect of nature that does not necessarily depend on a belief in God. I feel that Cathy still exists somewhere in an altered state.

"Less than a year before Cathy's death, we had moved to Albany from downstate, where we had lived for 40 years and had a host of friends and a very active social and community life. We relocated to Albany to be near our single-parent daughter and our only grandchild; Bob commuted to his office in New York City two days a week until Cathy's illness and death, when he sold his business and retired. Without a network of friends in our new home, we were pretty much on our own as we dealt with our tragedy. A few phone calls from old friends downstate once or twice a month were not of much help.

"In desperation, we initiated a Supper/Symposium at our local Unitarian Church, a copy of a successful program in our former church in Hastings, New York. Limited to the first 30 people who sign up, the group meets once a month at the church for dinner. After our meal, each person addresses a pre-arranged question about some aspect of our lives. It is popular; always oversubscribed; a good way to get to know people. The Supper/Symposium has helped us forge a new network of friends.

"However, we aren't the people we used to be and thus aren't as much fun as we used to be, either. Only a few old friends have shunned us because of the pain we are experiencing, and the addition of some of our new friendships has become very rich and important. We had been told to expect that some people would cut us off, so we don't take it personally. Many who have rallied to our support are those who have lost children, too.

"While we were selecting Cathy's coffin at the funeral home, our son picked up a brochure about The Compassionate Friends. 'Mother,' he said, 'I want you to get in touch with these people right away.' I did. We attended our first meeting less than a week after Catherine's funeral. I was in such a daze that all I could do was look at those bereaved parents assembled around the circle and keep saying over and over to myself, 'If these people can survive the death of their child, then surely I can find a way to do so, too.' The association with this group of bereaved parents and siblings has been a godsend to me.

"In the early days of our bereavement, we were the only parents at The Compassionate Friends meetings who had suffered the death of an adult child; all the others had lost young children or babies. That has changed dramatically in recent years, but in the beginning we felt isolated in our grief. Perhaps it is unkind to say so, but we also felt that our grief was somewhat discounted because we had enjoyed a long and rich association with our deceased child, while the others present had been cheated when their child was cut off in early childhood.

What did we want, anyhow? We should be satisfied with what we had had.

"My husband and I needed some guidance as we confronted our overwhelming grief. The first counselor we saw was not a grief specialist and was not helpful; he actually made things worse. Eileen Leary, a specialist in grief counseling, has been most helpful, both to my husband and me as well as to our surviving daughter.

"We were fortunate to have tremendous support from our clergyman. Our minister, George Williams, propped us up with almost daily visits and phone calls the first couple of years. But he left Albany a few years after Cathy died and has taken a job in Pennsylvania nearer his wife's job.

"I will tell you, somewhat reluctantly because you may be unable to fathom its importance, about another great source of help: our Cathy's parakeet, Denny, who came to live with us after her death. He was, as our counselor said, 'A Rhodes Scholar with Feathers.' He had the freedom of the house and considered himself a person. Tame and affectionate, he kept us laughing with his antics. He shared our meals; had a selective palate (preferred spaghetti; not his mild, unadorned plate in the center of the table, but ours, with sauce). He sat on my shoulder and sang when I played the piano; he loved dinner guests. When I cried, he would jump on my shoulder and peck at my cheek, emitting a loud distress call. When Denny died a few years ago, our grandson said, 'Oh, Grandma, it's just like Cathy died all over again.'

"In my questionnaire, I asked if a book would help bereaved parents of an adult child. My answer is obviously 'yes.' As many of my respondents have said, just knowing you are not alone in your reactions to your grief would be a comfort.

"My responses to grief have changed. As I went through the early stages, there was a kind of barrier, an 'on hold' feeling, as we awaited the malpractice trial, which took place four years after Cathy's death. I became more depressed after the trial, which knocked down another of the pillars of my belief structure: my faith in the justice system. Since then I have taken an antidepressant off and on, which I didn't seem to need before the trial. At the same time, the immediacy of my grief has become less painful. I decided some time ago against suicide. I no longer cry on the way to the supermarket or flee before I have made my purchase. I am able to comfort others; before, I didn't have the emotional energy. Trying to break grief down into phases becomes murky, however. I realize that I am now in the Reality phase most of the time. I know that the end of the grieving process is supposed to arrive when a reinvestment in life occurs. Sometimes I think that has happened in my case; sometimes I revert to pure sadness so I know I am still grieving. This only verifies my understanding of the roller-coaster aspect of parental grief.

"I experienced mental and physical problems/changes after the death of my child. Memory loss; inability to concentrate; sleep problems (I tend to handle stress by going to sleep, so my problem is too much sleep. Getting up in the morning to face yet another day is a monumental task). I have eating/weight problems. Food is a comfort and I gained 15 pounds. I considered suicide and have been depressed periodically. I have taken medication for depression. I developed cancer (now in remission), had digestive problems, irritable bowel syndrome, bad back, slight stroke, kidney stone, major surgery.

"Accidents have plagued me. I fell and broke my foot/sprained ankle (my left leg was in a cast up to my knee for 6 weeks). I slipped and fell again while visiting the cemetery and was once more on crutches. I fell while on vacation in Italy during the 1995 Christmas holiday and broke my hip, with subsequent hip replacement in a foreign hospital, a nightmare experience.

"Like many bereaved parents, I have felt many times that I was going crazy. I suffer from extreme fatigue and lack of energy.

"The other survivors of my adult child suffered some physical, mental and job-related problems as a result of her death. Both her siblings have needed counseling. Our daughter recently had a biopsy to determine the cause of a positive mammogram. Fortunately, it was benign. She also had a hysterectomy.

"While Cathy lay dying, she said to me, 'Have Arthur tell you about my dream.' In the stress of those days I completely forgot, but after her funeral, Arthur said, 'Let me tell you about Cathy's dream.' It seems she was dreaming that she was in a forest among many women, dressed in white gowns, as she was. She retired to a quiet place and began to write a letter to her parents to tell them about her new life. But she had to stop writing because she knew it was going to make us very sad. Arthur said he met her the next day, a Sunday, and they went to the shore and she cried and cried.

"Besides that prescient dream, Cathy had a Near death experience. About two or three days prior to her death she described what she called a 'religious experience' of being in a wonderful place, being restored to health, dancing. As she told me about it, there was a kind of glow in her eyes which seemed to transform her. At the moment of her death, she called out to her grandmother, my mother, who had died 8 months before, as though Cathy saw her coming to greet her. There was a note of surprise and disbelief in her voice, and I like to think, joy.

"I feel my child communicated with me after death. There is a long list of events which I feel were communications from Cathy after her death. These range from a sense of her presence, her perfume, objects moving in an unexplainable way, several 'signs,' the appearance of a fresh-picked bouquet of flowers in the middle of the pathway as I walked alone in the woods, an exotic butterfly which appeared at the end of a ceremony when we planted a garden in her memory.

"One early Thanksgiving morning, Bob and I drove into the cemetery to visit her grave. Out of the mist came a beautiful deer; it stood still and watched us for several minutes. On Cathy's birthday, March 3, 1994, we tried to visit her grave but even the stone was completely buried in snow. We couldn't get to the gravesite to leave flowers. I felt very sad. I said, silently, 'Oh, Cathy, give me a sign, some sign that you're OK.' I had never done that before, but it was a low point. After leaving the cemetery, we stopped a few minutes later in the parking lot of a supermarket. I stepped down into the slushy snow and there, at my feet, was a whole pile of pennies: 20 or more. I saved those pennies for the Halloween visitors.

"I have come to understand that the world of the bereaved parent is a different, unfamiliar place, uncharted and threatening. It is not the world ordinary people exist in, people who have not suffered the death of a child. In order to find my way in this forbidding territory, in this dark wood, I realize how important it is to rely on the wisdom of others who have walked the same rough, painful road. I have learned that I must seek direction not only from professional counselors when I need them, but also from other bereaved parents through correspondence, group meetings and conferences (either regional or national) of The Compassionate Friends. They are the only ones who really know and understand. Each one of these contacts, I know from experience, will give me one more bit of advice, one more suggestion, towards healing. Besides guidance and hope, they also give me comfort.

"I wonder if I can ever again make an affirmation about life. That is what I am striving for. I miss and love my daughter so. The longing for her never goes away."

Index